THE FABER BOOK OF PARODIES

THE FABER BOOK OF
P·A·R·O·D·I·E·S

EDITED BY
Simon Brett

faber and faber
LONDON·BOSTON

First published in 1984
by Faber and Faber Limited
3 Queen Square London WC1N 3AU
Reprinted 1984, 1985
Printed in Great Britain by
Redwood Burn Limited, Trowbridge, Wiltshire
All rights reserved

British Library Cataloguing in Publication Data

The Faber book of parodies.
1. Parodies   2. English prose literature
I. Brett, Simon, 1945–
828'.08   PN6110.P3

ISBN 0–571–13125–5
ISBN 0–571–13254–5 Pbk

CONTENTS

7

10

11

INTRODUCTION

The first duty of parody is to entertain. It may incidentally perform other functions, but if it does not entertain the reader, these become irrelevant.

Since entertainment value is a matter of personal opinion, this is inevitably a personal selection. It is not a definitive anthology of all the great parodies; it is an anthology of parodies which entertain me and which, I hope, will entertain others.

There is no dearth of material to choose from. Parody, at its various levels, has always been one of the most popular of literary exercises. Any verbal formula that becomes familiar—be it poem, song, hymn, or advertising jingle— quickly inspires its own mocking echoes, but few of these survive the cold stare of retrospect.

The worst reaction that a parody can inspire is "So what?" There are many works whose study requires a dutiful recognition that they are parodies, but whose entertainment value is not enhanced by the fact. Chaucer's "Tale of Sir Thopas" is, as every schoolboy knows, a parody of medieval romance. So what? That doesn't automatically make it entertaining. Isaac Hawkins Browne's verses from "A Pipe of Tobacco" are interesting historically because there weren't too many books of parodies around in 1736. So what? They make pretty dull reading today, so neither they nor "Sir Thopas" figure in this anthology. For me they lack that spark of mischief that makes a parody appealing.

In taking entertainment value as my guiding principle, I am following that excellent anthologist, Carolyn Wells, who wrote in 1904: "The main intent of the vast majority of parodies is simply to amuse; but to amuse intelligently and cleverly. This aim is quite high enough, and is in no way strengthened or improved by the bolstering up qualities of avowed virtuous influences."

My approach probably means that I have used a wider definition of parody than some authorities would admit. Certainly this selection contains items which work on different levels of subtlety. Though I support the principle enunciated by Dwight Macdonald in his scholarly selection, that in parody "the broader the worser", there are exceptions where the use of the axe can be quite as telling as that of the scalpel. A broad effect is not automatically a cheap effect. For example, I would not make great claims for the subtlety of J. B. Morton's:

> Hush, hush,
> Nobody cares!
> Christopher Robin
> Has
> Fallen
> Down-
> Stairs

and yet it is a wonderfully apposite comment on A. A. Milne at his most twee.

There are two main types of parody: those that imitate the style of an original and those that imitate only its form.

Stylistic parody is the more powerful. It is here, if anywhere, that "the bolstering up qualities of avowed virtuous influences" can be felt. Literary excesses can be identified and ridiculed in this sort of parody. As Sir Arthur Quiller-Couch wrote, "no neater or swifter vehicle of criticism has ever been invented". And parody can be a valuable weapon in the armoury of a professional critic, as Kenneth Tynan demonstrated with devastating effect.

Properly used, it can go straight to a writer's weakness. The first two lines of Hugh Kingsmill's Housman poem immediately expose the vein of sentimental pessimism in "A Shropshire Lad".

> What, still alive at twenty-two,
> A clean upstanding chap like you?

One cannot approach T. S. Eliot with quite the same awe after reading the following lines by Henry Reed:

> As we get older we do not get any younger.
> Seasons return and today I am fifty-five,
> And this time last year I was fifty-four,
> And this time next year I shall be sixty-two.

And Iris Murdoch's novels don't retain quite the same mystery after one has read the opening line of Malcolm Bradbury's "A Jaundiced View": "Flavia says that Hugo tells her that Augustina is in love with Fred."

These examples immediately raise one of the criticisms that has always been levelled against parody—that it is purely destructive. This was Goethe's view: "I have never made a secret of my enmity to parodies and travesties. My only reason for hating them is because they lower the beautiful, the noble, the great." This criticism was amplified by H. A. Page in 1881: "If we enjoy the parody a little is taken from the poem. A new association has inwoven itself with its metre, its movement, its rhythm and something is lost."

I feel that what is lost is the bit that doesn't need replacing. Great art can survive the grapeshot of parody, but lesser art may sink under the attack. At its best parody sharpens the judgement. Henry Reed's lines do not challenge the authority of T. S. Eliot's best work, but they do alert their reader to the poet's occasional lapses, the moments when simplicity descends to banality or obscurity becomes an end in itself.

Despite parody's power as a weapon of criticism, there seem to have been few occasions when it has caused major offence. One famous exception was the feud that sprang up between the Sitwells and the young Noël Coward after his characterization of them as "The Swiss Family Whittlebot" in the revue "London Calling". In retrospect the outrage seems excessive, because the parody in question, though amusing, is neither particularly close nor particularly vicious. Perhaps the disproportionate reaction arose from one of the failings the sketch satirized—the tendency of some artists to take themselves too seriously. It was typical of Coward's humour that he should have continued the joke by creating a Hernia Whittlebot poem which virulently attacked him.

The Sitwells' response was unusual. Parody is frequently welcomed by its victims, who recognize it as a compliment, however backhanded. And the form seems to incorporate its own controls. The success of a parody is often in inverse ratio to its violence. Like all good writing, the form requires great care and a sense of morality.

When a parody is good and the subject deserves censure, then its effect is justified. When a parody is too broad, or takes on a subject which does not merit ridicule, it is usually the parody that suffers in the encounter by falling flat on its face. In the words of a *Saturday Review* article of 1885: "There is nothing in the world as pitiful as poor fun, and a bad parody is perhaps the poorest kind of fun."

The best stylistic parody, like the best criticism, recognizes the virtues as well as the defects of its subject. There can, for example, be few fairer assessments of Wordsworth's poetry than J. K. Stephen's sonnet, whose tone is as much of sorrow as of anger.

> Two voices are there: one is of the deep;
> It learns the storm-cloud's thunderous melody,
> Now roars, now murmurs with the changing sea,
> Now bird-like pipes, now closes soft in sleep:
> And one is of an old half-witted sheep
> Which bleats articulate monotony,

And indicates that two and one are three,
That grass is green, lakes damp, and mountains steep:
And, Wordsworth, both are thine: at certain times
Forth from the heart of thy melodious rhymes,
The form and pressure of high thoughts will burst:
At other times—good Lord! I'd rather be
Quite unacquainted with the ABC
Than write such hopeless rubbish as thy worst.

Though its first line is a direct quotation, that sonnet is a "stylistic" rather than a "form" parody—in other words, it does not model itself closely on any single poem by Wordsworth. But the two types are not mutually exclusive. Sometimes a form parody is also stylistically critical, as in Hartley Coleridge's "He lived amidst th' Untrodden ways", but more often it simply uses the shape of the original for unrelated—and usually bathetic—subject-matter.

Form parodies are no less entertaining than stylistic parodies but they are usually more playful. Innocent of literary criticism, they are ideal for topical squibs or intellectual games. Frequently they are based on nothing more than similarity of sounds and many originate in the playground.

Some of these are remarkably pertinacious. How many people can sing the carol "While Shepherds Watched their Flocks by Night" without hearing an echo of sock-washing?

Occasionally the form is transcended and something new emerges. Noël Coward's "The Stately Homes of England" has its origin in a parody of Felicia Hemans, but as a song it takes on a completely new identity. Roger Woddis's "The Hero", about the Birmingham pub bombings, is more than a parody; it uses the form of Yeats's work to create a new poem. Gavin Ewart does the same with Betjeman.

In this anthology I have mixed the different types of parody, gathering them under the names of their subjects and ordering those names alphabetically. This reflects my beliefs that anthologies are to be dipped into, not read straight

21

through, and that anthologies that begin with Anon., followed by Chaucer, have a depressing predictability about them. So a reader searching for a parody *by victim's name* should work through alphabetically; the *names of parodists* will be found in the index at the end of the book.

Parody must always rise above mere imitation. In this it can be compared to the art of the television impressionist. His first laugh comes from the audience's identification of the victim, but impersonation is not enough; he needs a script that adds another element of humour. Parody also needs that extra element. Anyone can write in the style of an author; the skill of the parodist is to be entertaining in that style.

Frequently the extra element he adds is topicality, and this raises the major problem of all parodies—their short shelf-life. By their nature they are fixed in time, their fortunes rising and falling with those of their subjects. And the more apposite and detailed the parody, the more perishable it becomes. Some of the most effective of the genre are *jeux d'esprit* written for specific occasions—retirement parties or after-dinner speeches—works full of the names of individuals, in-jokes and local allusions. Transplanted from their context, these quickly shrivel and die.

The same is true of topical and political parody. An issue or a name that is in the news can give birth to a verse or an article whose impact at a given moment is devastating. But politicians and causes enjoy even briefer fame than poets and most of the parodies they inspire perish with that fame. No matter how skilled the parodists, their work loses impact when the reader does not understand the subject-matter. Much of the brilliant "Rejected Addresses" suffers in this way, and very little of Canning and Frere's skilful work in "The Anti-Jacobin" stands up without a disproportionate scaffolding of introductions and footnotes.

I have tried to avoid such scaffolding in this anthology, leaving the items to stand or fall on their own merits. Too academic or analytical an approach to any sort of humour will always kill it stone-dead. And I have not identified the originals of form parodies. Individual items will have more or less significance according to the literary tastes of the individual reader, and knowing that something is a parody of a work with which you are not familiar adds little to its entertainment value.

But it is remarkable how many parodies stand up without their originals and how some stand up even for readers who have never encountered the original. One would be hard put to it now to find a reader of Jean Ingelow's poetry, and yet many know C. S. Calverley's version of it. The parodist has removed the necessity of reading her work; "Lovers, And A Reflection" says all one needs to know about it.

In the same way, one does not need to have read Arnold Bennett to appreciate Max Beerbohm's "Scruts". Indeed, this is an example of a parody whose subject has diversified and spread since it was written. There have been plenty more writers in the school of gritty but soft-centred Northern realism since 1912, and on them too "Scruts" makes its prescient comment. It is a supreme example of a parody in which, even if we don't know the parodist's specific original, we know *exactly the sort of thing he means*, and are entertained accordingly.

What makes a writer ripe for parody?

The two essentials are success and excess.

The success is necessary so that the reader understands the terms of reference, knows—if not the specific author—at least the genre that is being sent up.

The excess is the writer's weakness, his tendency from time to time "to go over the top", to allow a point of style or subject-matter to become an idiosyncrasy. Or perhaps the writer has become, as many do with increasing age and success, too self-regarding. An eminent author who has begun to believe his own publicity is a sitting target for the sharp-shooting parodist.

23

The excess that invites parody frequently arises when an author aims for an effect of extreme simplicity or extreme elaboration. Wordsworth, Hemingway and Housman have all suffered for the first reason; Browning, Swinburne and Joyce for the second.

What appears to be stylistic excess is not always the writer's fault. Time and changing fashions can render ridiculous what was written with honesty and humility.

Familiarity can have the same effect. The massive number of parodies of Gray's "Elegy" or Wolfe's "The Burial of Sir John Moore at Corunna" do not reflect weaknesses in the original poems, merely the fact that they had become over-anthologized, over-recited and, as a result, hackneyed. Parodies of such classics almost always work by retaining the lofty style of the original and substituting a trivial theme.

Parody is the scourge of self-indulgence in writing, and the best parodies are those that first detect such signs. Jane Austen's *Northanger Abbey* did the job for the gothic novel and Stella Gibbons's *Cold Comfort Farm* for the Rural Primitive school. Both are great parodies, but since they need to be read in full, they are unfortunately beyond the scope of this anthology.

The mention of Jane Austen raises another point. Though it is possible—even easy—to parody a humorous work that has ceased to be funny, this cannot be done to a work whose humour endures. Anyone can write in the style of Jane Austen, but no one can add that extra ingredient which makes such writing a parody.

Some authors set themselves up for parody simply by their originality. A truly innovative style which alters the existing preconceptions of literature will in time become ripe for attack. And again this may not be the originator's fault. His impact may be diluted by imitation, and familiarity with what was once exciting will breed its customary contempt. Nothing is so despised as yesterday's sensation. And if a writer continues, as Wordsworth did, in the same style, however innovative, for too long, parody is inevitable.

Some writers endear themselves to parodists just by being easy. The mannerisms of Longfellow, Kipling or Dylan Thomas are so distinctive as to be positive invitations.

But one must never forget the dependent role of parody. It is a parasitic art and, though it can hold the eminent up to ridicule, without them it could not exist.

Parody, like revue writing, has been said to be a young man's game, and there is some truth in this. Form parody, which is more of an intellectual recreation for lovers of literature, is produced by writers of all ages. Roger Woddis and many of the regular *New Statesman* competition winners, with their intriguing pseudonyms, have produced a consistently high standard of form parodies over some decades. But the very best example of critical stylistic parody have been the products of young minds.

There are many reasons for this. Young writers are often more sensitive to the onset of self-indulgence and less tolerant of pomposity than their seniors. They may also have less patience with the literary establishment and be more prepared to challenge its values. Those who are learning their craft may, like painters, study technique by copying the acknowledged masters. This is what Alexander Pope did as a young man, and from copying it is not such a great step to parody. Most important of all, taking on the styles of other writers is a valuable exercise for those who have yet to evolve their own. Michael Frayn and Alan Bennett, for instance, both produced parodies before finding their individual voices as playwrights.

The consistently great parodists have been young. C. S. Calverley and J. K. Stephen were removed prematurely from the literary scene and Max Beerbohm, though he survived to old age, wrote his best parodies before he was forty. It will be interesting to see whether today's most skilled exponents of the medium, Russell Davies, Clive James (both under their own names and under the much-shared pseudonym 'Edward

Pygge') and Wendy Cope, will continue to produce parodies into middle age.

In the preparation of this book I owe a great deal to the long tradition of parody anthologists, particularly Carolyn Wells, W. Jerrold and R. M. Leonard, J. A. S. Adam and B. C. White, and of course Dwight Macdonald. I am also indebted to that inexhaustible source of everything, *Notes and Queries*, and to the *New Statesman*, whose Weekend Competitions have done so much to keep the art of parody fresh and alive.

For their help with the book I would like to thank the staff of the British Library and the London Library, and Rosamund Botting, who helped organize the mountains of paper I accumulated.

But I owe most to the parodists represented in the book, writers who all share, in Carolyn Wells's phrase, "an intense sense of the humorous and a humorous sense of the intense".

S. B.

June 1983

DOUGLAS ADAMS
1952–

THE SCRIPTWRITER'S GUIDE TO THE GALAXY

One of the most interesting things about the six-headed Omni-Quarrgs of the planet Cygo-Swarreldong in the star system of Grudni-Vogar-actinax, in the constellation of "Go-and-upset-another-scrabble-board-Les-I-need-a-new-name", is that they have only one word to stand for all 400 million nouns, adjectives, prepositions, verbs and adverbs. This is both a good thing and bad thing. Bad for *them*, because since the word is obscene, no one's allowed to use it anyway, but good for science-fiction scriptwriters, because it enables *me* to go on and on and on about it for sixteen pages before we even start the story. . . .

ANDREW MARSHALL AND DAVID RENWICK

WOODY ALLEN
1935–

WOODY ALIEN

In space, no one can hear you laugh.

Space. Black, empty space. Thousands of silent, motionless stars. There is only one moving object, a tiny dot—it is the spacecargo Anhedonia.

Close-up of the prow of the spaceship, with the inscription

EARTH CARGO 56/A738 ANHEDONIA. *Underneath someone has chalked, "If found, please return to Brooklyn."*

Cut to the crew leisure centre, where three astronauts are sitting. They are BRAD, SCOTT *and* OTIS. BRAD *and* SCOTT *are tall and white.* OTIS *is white, but short, freckled and bespectacled.*

OTIS: Of course, we only *think* the stars are silent and motionless. I mean they're all moving at incredible speeds, and probably making a lot of noise, if earth is anything to go by. The only motionless body round here is the Anhedonia. Pretty quiet, too. What do you think, fellows?
(Total silence.)
Do you think we'll ever find signs of life on this apparently dead spacecruiser? On Friday evenings, maybe?
(Silence.)
Well, just a thought.
BRAD: Why don't you read a magazine and shut up?
SCOTT: When did reading a magazine ever shut him up?
OTIS: OK, OK. I can take a hint. I'll go see if the new *New Yorker* is on the streets yet.

(He crosses to a console marked Earth Publications *and presses a knob. On a huge screen appears a page of the* New Yorker, *with a cartoon showing several people at a party. The caption reads: "This is Mort. Mort's into ecology. He thinks ecology is ruining the environment."* OTIS *stares at it, silenced for a short while.)*

OTIS: Amazing, isn't it? Science can now beam visual images through millions of miles, but it can't explain *New Yorker* cartoons. I never met anyone yet who laughed at a *New Yorker* cartoon. Or do you think it's some kind of scientific experiment? I mean, if we beam out incomprehensible messages into space, do you think there's a

28

chance that some alien civilization will find it easy meat? Do you think five-legged mutants are roaring with laughter at the *New Yorker*? Do you think the *New Yorker* is *produced* by five-legged mutants? Do you—

SCOTT: Look, Otis—

OTIS: OK, OK. I can take a hint. Actually, I could take a capsule. Anyone feel like a capsule? Just a quick one, before supper?

(He crosses to an automat marked CAPSULES *and hesitates in front of knobs marked variously Bourbon Flavour, Rye Flavour, Southern Comfort Flavour, etc. He presses one marked Gin Flavour. A capsule drops out. He presses another marked Tonic Water Flavour. A sign flashes up: "Sorry— Fresh Out.")*

OTIS: Well, send out for some, for God's sake!

SCOTT: Otis, will you *please*—

OTIS: We have a crisis on our hands, Scott. A million miles from earth and we're fresh out of tonic water capsules, and all you can do is tell me to shut up! What kind of leadership is that? And have you got a lemon on you?

BRAD: Shut up, Otis.

OTIS: Yes, sir.

(He switches to the next page of the New Yorker. *It has a cartoon showing several people at a party, one of them black with a huge Afro. The caption reads: "This is Coleman. Coleman thinks Token Black is Beautiful."* OTIS *stares at it for a while.)*

Did it ever strike you as odd that we don't have a token black on this ship? I mean, I'm Jewish and Joe is Italian and you two are WASP—

BRAD: I'm not WASP. I'm Italian.

OTIS: With a name like Brad?

29

BRAD: That's not my real name. Real name is Joe, but the Space Rules forbid two guys on the same ship with the same name. So I chose Brad.

OTIS: I'd prefer Scott any day. Brad is kinda limiting. Brad of the Antarctic. Brad's Waverley Novels. Doesn't sound right.

BRAD: How come you're called Otis, anyway? That's not Jewish. Did they give you a token black name?

OTIS: My father worked for an elevator company. Named me after it. I'm just very happy he wasn't an employee of Hydromatic. I guess in a way my father was an early space traveller, too; he would get in his capsule at street level, press a button and shoot off towards the stars. Course, then they didn't have the technology to get an elevator into space and he'd generally get out at the 18th floor.

BRAD: So you joined the Space Force to do better than your father?

OTIS: Yes. That, and my warts.

BRAD: *Warts?*

OTIS: I heard they had this really terrific laser treatment in the Space Force for warts, so I applied to join when I was 18.

BRAD: And what happened?

OTIS: I failed the medical because of my warts. Next year I reapplied, and lied about my warts. Now, here I am, warts and all. A space Cromwell.

BRAD: How's that?

OTIS: Know what I think, every time I look out of that window and see us surrounded by 10,000 burnt-out stars? I think, it's no different from the Oscar Presentation Ceremony. Except we haven't got Bob Hope up in space.

SCOTT: Sometimes I wonder.

(OTIS *is about to wax indignant when a huge shock shakes the spaceship.*)

Jesus, what was that?

OTIS: I think we ran over a dog.

SCOTT: Turn on the scanner.

(OTIS obeys. On the screen flashes the message: "Passing through debris of dead planet. No damage incurred. Minute electronic particles.")

BRAD: Well, thank God for that. OK, fellows, time to relieve the other three.

(They cross to the small personnel lift.)

OTIS: Going up, going up. Third floor, hardware, computers, lingerie. . . .

(Two weeks later. In the Anhedonia's *control room.* BRAD, SCOTT, *and* OTIS *are on duty.)*

OTIS: Of course, that's only two weeks later in space time. How long have we been up here in real time, Brad?

BRAD: 20,000 years.

OTIS: Makes you think, doesn't it? It's 20,000 years since I last kissed a girl. Even with my luck, that's pushing it. Not that I rate girls that highly. In fact, I've gone right off them in the last, oh I don't know, 5000 years.

BRAD: Knock it off, Otis.

OTIS: Oh, don't get me wrong. I'm not a misogynist. I can't stand men either.

SCOTT: Brad, take a look at this, would you? We've got some kind of malfunction in the read-out.

BRAD: How do you mean?

SCOTT: I'm not getting any response from the internal security system.

BRAD: Try the communications computer for an up-to-date.

(SCOTT *throws a switch. The screen fills out with a repeated message: "There is an alien intelligence on board. There is an alien intelligence on board. . . ."*)

SCOTT: What in hell does that mean?

OTIS: Maybe it's found out I'm Jewish. Maybe it's an anti-Semitic computer.

SCOTT: That's ridiculous.

OTIS: I hope so. The computer and I have got on terrifically so far. Hey, maybe there's a woman on board! That would fit alien intelligence, wouldn't it?

SCOTT: The read-out dates the interference to two weeks ago.

BRAD: That's when we hit that debris.

SCOTT: Do you think it came aboard then?

OTIS: Well, *that's* ridiculous. We'd have noticed the signs by now—the smell of scent, dirty tights, hairpins—

SCOTT: The computer's getting a contact on the alien force. Nothing definite; just very heavy messages of hate, and hostility and aggression.

OTIS: My God! It's my first wife.

BRAD: You mean, it's communicating with us?

SCOTT: No. No attempt to communicate.

OTIS: It *is* my first wife!

BRAD: This is frightening. Somewhere on this ship . . . an alien force . . . watching us . . . Scott, you take over while I tell the others.

(BRAD *leaves via the lift.*)

OTIS: Something tells me that Brad is going to come back with awfully bad news, like one of the crew is missing.

SCOTT: How do you reckon that?

OTIS: I've seen the movie before. See, there's this dark force lurking and one by one we become the victims, and then in the final scene, the ultimate in horror . . .!

SCOTT: What's that?

32

OTIS: Bob Hope, handing out medals to the survivors.

SCOTT: Wait a moment, we're getting signals . . . I think I've got the wavelength of the alien.

OTIS: Ask him if he's got any tonic water.

SCOTT: Think we can communicate with it?

OTIS: It's worth trying.

SCOTT: OK, I'll try a short signal. I'll identify us as earth people, bringing peace and friendliness.

OTIS: And loads of gin capsules. Don't forget that. He may be fresh out of gin. We could ask it up for a party.

SCOTT: Jesus! I'm getting incredible electronic reactions of hate and fury. The circuits are overheating.

(The lift door opens and BRAD *comes back, looking shaken.)*

BRAD: They're nowhere to be seen! The whole goddamned crew has vanished. I've checked every which where.

OTIS: That's incredible.

BRAD: I know.

OTIS: I mean, we're meant to disappear one by one. Not in batches! Know what I think?

SCOTT: What?

OTIS: I think the alien is overacting. Scott, you tell him—tell him he'll never get an Oscar for Best Performance by Any Monster if he goes on the rampage. Tell him to stick to the damn script!

BRAD: Scott, you and I go for another look. Otis, you stay and handle the controls.

OTIS: Fellows, haven't *you* seen the movie? Splitting up for a search is the best way for one of you to disappear. Only one of you will come back! *(They leave.)* Well, so long, whichever of you it is. *(He grabs the internal systems mike.)* And as for you, knock it off, will you? What's your mother going to think when she learns that a nice alien like you is going around consuming earthlings? Three at a time! Know what I call that? I call it discrimination. *(He*

33

studies the read-out.) Well, I'm sorry, but I do. And by the way, if you have to take one of them, make it Scott, would you? I couldn't stand another season of baseball results. 20,000 already, would you believe? *(He studies a fresh read-out.)* No, he's the one with the moustache. Check. *(A thought strikes him.)* By the way, alien, can I try something on you? Just testing for size. There's this party and a woman saying, This is Mort, Mort's into ecology, he thinks ecology is ruining the environment. *(A short pause.)* Sure, I think it's pretty snappy too. Over and out.

(The lift door opens and BRAD *stumbles out.)*

BRAD: It's Scott . . . he . . . suddenly he was taken by this . . . thing!

OTIS: Sure, sure. Now, listen—

BRAD: But what are we going to do?

OTIS: Well, not grow a moustache, for one. Now listen, I've been in touch with the alien, and guess what?

BRAD: What?

OTIS: It's into *New Yorker* humour!

BRAD: What?

OTIS: I know. Terrifying, isn't it? A million-plus technology and an IQ of nil. Here's what we've got to do. Humour the thing and feed it all the cartoons we can get. And let *me* talk to it. I don't want to boast but I think it's got a Jewish mentality. It's got all the classic symptoms— feeling threatened by its environment, eating up well, and pretending to enjoy the smart magazines. It's just a shame that it's *us* he's eating up. But I think if we play our cards right . . .

(Fade and dissolve to two weeks later. OTIS *is at the commands alone.)*

Well, welcome back to two weeks later everyone, that's 20,000 years for those of you listening in real time, and I'm only sorry that Brad couldn't be here on the show tonight. Talking of which, I have a bone to pick with our programme supervisor. *(He switches on the internal systems mike.)* Alien, what was the big idea of eating Brad? I thought we'd agreed you were going to lay off him. *(He studies the read-out.)* What do you mean, *you've* seen the movie too? God, I hate wise guys. Hey, look, let's not argue, because have I got good news for you! You remember that idea we cooked up the other night? That's right. Well, they've taken it! No, no kidding. Take a look.

(OTIS *switches on the screen and a cartoon from the* New Yorker *lights up. It shows people at a party, of whom one is an extra-galactic being. The caption reads:* "This is Zvolg. Zvolg is an alien. He's here to make a horror movie about humans.")

Isn't that great? And they want more like it!
Yes, I know I said I didn't like it, and I'm sorry. I was wrong. OK? I said I'm sorry! Jesus, you creative aliens . . . So, OK, I'll be in touch tomorrow . . . You what? You feel like . . . a date? But that's crazy. I'm a good earth boy and you're a good alien boy . . . You're a good alien girl. I didn't know that. I'm sorry. This is one movie I've never seen. Oh, my God. Look, I have this terrible headache and I'm awfully tired and I never hold antennae on the first date and . . . You'll be along in a moment. OK. Yes, ma'am. Yes, I'll break out the crackers. Over and out . . . Oh, mother, I'm sorry I haven't written for 40,000 years! I've got good news for you, though. Yes, I'm dating a nice alien girl. Please try and understand. She's called Zvolg. I'll tell you more about her as soon as I've met her.

(The cabin door starts to open very slowly.)

Diane? Is that you, Diane? It is you, isn't it, Diane?
Diane . . .?

MILES KINGTON

KINGSLEY AMIS
1922–

WHAT ABOUT YOU?

When Mrs Taflan Gruffyd Lewis left Dai's flat
She gave her coiffe a pat
Having straightened carefully those nylon seams
Adopted to fulfil Dai's wicked dreams.
Evans didn't like tights.
He liked plump white thighs pulsing under thin skirts in
   packed pubs on warm nights

That's that, then, thought Evans, hearing her Jag start,
And test-flew a fart.
Stuffing the wives of these industrial shags may be all
Very well, and *this* one was an embassy bar-room brawl
With Madame Nhu.
Grade A. But give them that fatal twelfth inch and they'll
   soon take their cue

To grab a yard of your large intestine or include your glans
Penis in their plans
For that Rich, Full Emotional Life you'd thus far ducked
So successfully.
Yes, Evans was feeling . . . Mucked

-up sheets recalled their scrap.
Thinking barbed thoughts in stanza form
    after shafting's a right sweat. Time for a nap.

ANON

MURIE SING

Plumber is icumen in;
Bludie big tu-du.
Bloweth lampe, and showeth dampe,
And dripth the wud thru.
Bludie hel, boo-hoo!

Thawth drain, and runneth bath;
Saw sawth, and scruth scru;
Bull-kuk squirteth, leakë spurteth;
Wurry springeth up anew,
Boo-hoo, boo-hoo.

Tom Pugh, Tom Pugh, well plumbës thu, Tom Pugh;
Better job I naver nu.
Therefore will I cease boo-hoo,
Woorie not, but cry pooh-pooh,
Murie sing pooh-pooh, pooh-pooh,
Pooh-pooh!

A. Y. CAMPBELL

ANCIENT MUSIC

Winter is icummen in,
Lhude sing Goddamm,
Raineth drop and staineth slop,
And how the wind doth ramm!
           Sing: Goddamm.
Skiddeth bus and sloppeth us,
An ague hath my ham.
Freezeth river, turneth liver,
           Damn you, sing: Goddamm.
Goddamm, Goddamm, 'tis why I am, Goddamm.
           So 'gainst the winter's balm.
Sing goddamm, damm, sing Goddamm,
Sing goddamm, sing goddamm, DAMM.

EZRA POUND

JOHN AUBREY
1626–97

MISCELLANEA CURIOSA

*Selected from the "Miscellanies" of J. Aubrey, Esq.,
contained in the Ashmolean Museum, at Oxford*

Shoes came into Englande with Henry the Fourth his wife,
Joan of Navarre. Before that time the nobles did wear dried
flat fish, cunningly tied on with thongs of hide. And hence
the name of *soles* as used to this day, and by alle men.

In 1580, a shower of potatoes did fall in Lancashire, at

which the husbandmen were sorelie afraid. They were sayde to have been brought from America in a whirlwind, and, being hitherto unknown, became directly common.

The Polka is a measure danced by salvage men and women in Hongrie. *Item.*—Sir Francis Drake assures me he hath seen it kept up for twenty minutes and more, until the salvages were like to drop; the reason whereof is difficult to tell; but he takes it to be a religious ceremony, as the whirling dervishes in the Indies doe practise.

Tobacco is a plant growing in China on inaccessible mountains, whence it is plucked by people in balloons made of fish-skin, and preserved in red leather bottles underground. Sir Walter Raleigh did use it first. Its vapour inhaled is an admirable narcotic; and one Master Aytoun, deprived of it, did, in its stead, smoke strips of *Blackwood's Magazine*; but this well nigh coste him his life.

The first drinking glasse used in Englande had no foote whereon to stand (to encourage drinking), but fell away; and was hence called a tumbler.

A Bristow man, living in Castile, did learn the art of making soap, which he set up here: and straightway upon this it became common to wash one's self twice and thrice in the week. Nay, Mrs Gregoire, the commissioner his wife, did cleanse her hands, and eke her face each daie. Soe that it was soon the rage; and people before they went to stay with such and such a one would saie to him, "How are you off for soape?" meaning therebye that if he had not good store, they would none of him; and soe went on their way betymes.

I do remember when they did call cats *Tomassins*, which, being corrupted to Tom, is still in use with the vulgar; but the etymologie thereof I could never learn, save that the word came from Flanders. *Item.*—My good friend, Mr Marmy, assures me that he heard them shriek and cry like infants, beneath his chambers; such as could only be frighted by tossing the fire-irons and fender about their ears. But he verilie believes they were devils' imps and familiars.

Item.—Mr Glanville gave him a charm to exorcise them, which is as follows, writ on fayre parchment:—

> Tomassin, tomassine, alabra
> Parlak vak abracadabra.

The which being pronounced, they would frantically take to their heels and scuffle off like mad, to return no more.

To preserve beer from being soured by thunder:—*Summa,* it is best to drinke it all off before the storm. They doe practise this in Kent with certainty, and other parts of England. This also on the authority of Mr Glanville.

Men in liquor have droll conceites. I knew such a one, being a justice of the peace, who, when tipsie, would take off his peruke to salute the company with obeisance, and then, putting it on a bottle, would sing a song that had neither beginning nor end, but went merrilie on over again: the which he wold never stop until carried awaie to bed. And yet he was well to doe, and a clever man, but lacked prudence.

My Lord Saye his gardener tells me that during the late storm he did track a flash of lightning through a gooseberrie bush, which marvel he had often heard of, but never saw before.

ANON
from *Cruikshank's Comic Almanac*

W. H. AUDEN
1907–73

SELF-CONGRATULATORY ODE ON MR AUDEN'S ELECTION TO THE PROFESSORSHIP OF POETRY AT OXFORD

He has come back at last, the boy with the inky fingers,
Who scrawled on the lavatory walls and frightened his
   granny
By roaring his inexplicable
Songs in the bathroom, grubby, embarrassing visitors,

Ran off to sea without warning or explanation,
Wrote long letters home in a mixture of languages,
Acquired an undoubtedly foreign
Accent, was given up for lost but can now cock a snook

At the smooth FO type and the bard-intoxicated professor
By sanction of his granny who taught him his tables,
Cuffed him and feared him and lost him, and now will be
   taught in her
Turn to suck eggs.

RONALD MASON

TO HIS COY MISTRESS

A mistress allows an average lover.
working slowly,
to roll her over in an afternoon.

41

Such physical compassion
may not guarantee a marriage
but it helps.

Time watches from the shadow
and coughs when I would show
my faithless hand.

Let's yoke our bodies at your liquid centre
in the tiny world of lovers' arms and
challenge time.

JOHN FLOOD

DEAR FATHER CHRISTMAS

I

Dear Father Christmas. What are you bringing
Over the rooftops of Oxford winging?

Crackers for the mad, boaters for the Seine,
A drop of the hard stuff, a choo-choo train.

Zipping past Balliol, a shower of sparks
The porter's collie-dog, Prurient, barks

Past coffee-bars and ancient tuckshops
Peeping through windows of red-lit brothels

"Look at Merton," Santa hollers,
"Silent miles of toil-bent scholars."

Statues awaken as on he races,
Peep from niches at his Day-Glo braces.

A startled owl stops dead in its tracks
And gets knocked cold by the flying sacks.

In the Ashmolean, never a word
But on to the roof slops a reindeer turd.

II

Dawn threatens. Is Santa done?
Down towards Reading he inclines
Towards the Third Division of the Football League
Towards the feel of Lux-lene curtains, the new settees
Set on the foam-back like reclining hippos.
All Berkshire waits for him:
In Suburb, settee of the plain,
Men long for socks.

III

Stockings of green, stockings obscene,
Stockings that smell and swell as well,
Abysmal stripe and ghastly tartan
Hairy calf-length, anklet spartan,
"Product of Italy", "Made in Dumbarton",
Wrapped in a tissue, sealed in a carton,
" 'Never without 'em,' says E. Lustgarten."
Hose enjoyable, hose unemployable,
Tights giving too much room for the kneecaps
Tights kitted out with rude-looking pee-flaps
Tights for the winter, ballet and sex,
Tights where the spot is marked with an X,
Thick tights for journeyers, thicker for hernias,
Knitted in nylon of every shade
The puce, the indigo, orange and jade,
The knotty, the spotty, the been-to-the-menders,
The very hard-wearing from Marks and Suspenders,

43

See-through, stay-fresh, tweed or twee,
The limp and the lumpy and the just–not–me.

IV

Millions are still abed
Dreaming of mollifying taxmen
Or a friendly feel behind the shelves in stock–room or
   store–room:
Abed in working Reading, working in well–read
   Oxford,
Reading in Welwyn Garden City,
They continue their snooze,
But shall wake soon and nudge their neighbour
And none will play at postman's knock
Without a heartening of the quick.
For who can bear to feel himself
At Christmas?
   Yours documentarily,
   W. H. AUDEN (master)

P.S. I hope you agree with me that this is worth an extra bottle
of Elizabeth Arden Crow's–Foot Creme this Xmas, you old
stinge.

RUSSELL DAVIES

SAMUEL BECKETT
1906–

from SLAMM'S LAST KNOCK

The den of Slamm, the critic. Very late yesterday. Large desk with throne behind it. Two waste-paper baskets, one black, one white, filled with crumpled pieces of paper, on either side of the stage. Shambling between them—i.e., from one to the other and back again—an old man SLAMM. *Bent gait. Thin, barking voice. Motionless, watching* SLAMM, *is* SECK. *Bright grey face, holding pad and pencil. One crutch.* SLAMM *goes to back basket, takes out piece of white paper, uncrumples it, reads. Short laugh.*

SLAMM: *(Reading)* " . . . the validity of an authentic tragic vision, at once personal and by implication cosmic . . ."

(Short laugh. He recrumples the paper, replaces it in basket, and crosses to other—i.e., white—basket. He takes out piece of black paper, uncrumples it, reads. Short laugh.)

(Reading) " . . . Just another dose of nightmare gibberish from the so-called author of* Waiting for Godot. *. . ."*

(Short laugh. He recrumples the paper, replaces it in basket, and sits on throne. Pause. Anguished, he extends fingers of right hand and stares at them. Extends fingers of left hand. Same business. Then brings fingers of right hand towards fingers of left hand, and vice versa, so that fingertips of right hand touch fingertips of left hand. Same business. Breaks wind pensively. SECK *writes feverishly on pad.)*

We're getting on. *(He sighs.)* Read that back.

SECK: *(Produces pince-nez with thick black lenses, places them on bridge of nose, reads)* "A tragic dose of authentic gibberish from the so-called implication of *Waiting for Godot*." Shall I go on?

SLAMM: (*Nodding head*) No. (*Pause.*) A bit of both, then.

SECK: (*Shaking head*) Or a little of neither.

SLAMM: There's the hell of it. (*Pause. Urgently*) Is it time for my Roget?

SECK: There are no more Rogets. Use your loaf.

SLAMM: Then wind me up, stink-louse! Stir your stump!

(SECK *hobbles to* SLAMM, *holding rusty key depending from piece of string round his [*SECK's*] neck, and inserts it into back of* SLAMM's *head. Loud noise of winding.*)

Easy now. Can't you see it's hell in there?

SECK: I haven't looked. (*Pause.*) It's hell out here, too. The ceiling is zero and there's grit in my crotch. Roget and over. (*He stops winding and watches. Pause.*)

SLAMM: (*Glazed stare*) Nothing is always starting to happen.

SECK: It's better than something. You're well out of that.

SLAMM: I'm badly into this. (*He tries to yawn but fails.*) It would be better if I could yawn. Or if you could yawn.

SECK: I don't feel excited enough. (*Pause.*) Anything coming?

SLAMM: Nothing, in spades. (*Pause.*) Perhaps I haven't been kissed enough. Or perhaps they put the wrong ash in my gruel. One or the other.

SECK: Nothing will come of nothing. Come again.

SLAMM: (*With violence*) Purulent drudge! *You* try, if you've got so much grit in your crotch! Just one pitiless, pathetic creatively critical phrase!

SECK: I heard you the first time.

SLAMM: You can't have been listening.

SECK: Your word's good enough for me.

SLAMM: I haven't got a word. There's just the light, going. (*Pause.*) Are you trying?

46

SECK: Less and less.

SLAMM: Try blowing down it.

SECK: It's coming! (*Screws up his face. Tonelessly*) Sometimes I wonder why I spend the lonely night.

SLAMM: To many f's. We're bitched. (*Half a pause.*)

SECK: Hold your pauses. It's coming again. (*In a raconteur's voice, dictates to himself*) Tuesday night, seven-thirty by the paranoid barometer, curtain up at the Court, Sam Beckett unrivalled master of the unravelled revels. Item: *Krapp's Last Tape*, Krapp being a myopic not to say deaf not to say eremitical eater of one and one-half bananas listening and cackling as he listens to a tape-recording of twenty years' antiquity made on a day, the one far gone day, when he laid his hand on a girl in a boat and it worked, as it worked for Molly Bloom in Gibraltar in the long ago. Actor: Patrick Magee, bereaved and aghast-looking grunting into his Grundig, probably perfect performance, fine throughout and highly affecting at third curtain-call though not formerly. Unique, oblique, bleak experience, in other words, and would have had same effect if half the words *were* other words. Or any words. (*Pause.*)

SLAMM: Don't stop. You're boring me.

SECK: (*Normal voice*) Not enough. You're smiling.

SLAMM: Well, I'm still in the land of the dying.

SECK: Somehow, in spite of everything, death goes on.

SLAMM: Or because of everything. (*Pause.*) Go on.

SECK: (*Raconteur's voice*) Tuesday night, eight-twenty by the Fahrenheit anonymeter. *End-Game*, translated from the French with loss by excision of the vernacular word for urination and of certain doubts blasphemously cast on the legitimacy of the Deity. Themes, madam? Nay, it *is*, I know not themes. Foreground figure a blind and lordly cripple with superficial mannerisms of Churchill, W., Connolly, C., and Devine, G., director and in this case impersonator. Sawn-off parents in bins, stage right, and

47

shuffling servant, all over the stage, played by Jack MacGowran, binster of this parish. Purpose: to analyse or rather to dissect or rather to define the nature or rather the quality or rather the intensity of the boredom inherent or rather embedded in the twentieth or rather every other century. I am bored, therefore I am. Comment, as above, except it would have the same effect if a quarter of the words were other words and another quarter omitted. Critique ended. Thesaurus and out.

SLAMM: Heavy going. I can't see.

SECK: That's because of the light going.

SLAMM: Is that all the review he's getting?

SECK: That's all the play he's written.

(Pause.)

SLAMM: But a genius. Could you do as much?

SECK: Not as much. But as little.

(Tableau. Pause. Curtain.)

KENNETH TYNAN

ARNOLD BENNETT
1867–1931

SCRUTS

I

Emily Wrackgarth stirred the Christmas pudding till her right arm began to ache. But she did not cease for that. She stirred on till her right arm grew so numb that it might have been the right arm of some girl at the other end of Bursley. And yet something deep down in her whispered "It is *your* right arm! And you can do what you like with it!"

She did what she liked with it. Relentlessly she kept it moving till it reasserted itself as the arm of Emily Wrackgarth, prickling and tingling as with red-hot needles in every tendon from wrist to elbow. And still Emily Wrackgarth hardened her heart.

Presently she saw the spoon no longer revolving, but wavering aimlessly in the midst of the basin. Ridiculous! This must be seen to! In the down of the dark hairs that connected her eyebrows there was a marked deepening of that vertical cleft which, visible at all times, warned you that here was a young woman not to be trifled with. Her brain despatched to her hand a peremptory message—which miscarried. The spoon wabbled as though held by a baby. Emily knew that she herself as a baby had been carried into this very kitchen to stir the Christmas pudding. Year after year, as she grew up, she had been allowed to stir it "for luck". And those, she reflected, were the only cookery lessons she ever got. How like Mother!

Mrs Wrackgarth had died in the past year, of a complication of ailments.[1] Emily still wore on her left shoulder that small tag of crape which is as far as the Five Towns go in the way of mourning. Her father had died in the year previous to that, of a still more curious and enthralling complication of ailments.[2] Jos, his son, carried on the Wrackgarth Works, and Emily kept house for Jos. She with her own hand had made this pudding. But for her this pudding would not have been. Fantastic! Utterly incredible! And yet so it was. She was grown-up. She was mistress of the house. She could make or unmake puddings at will. And yet she was Emily Wrackgarth. Which was absurd.

---

[1] See *The History of Sarah Wrackgarth*, pp. 345–482.
[2] See *The History of Sarah Wrackgarth*, pp. 231–344.

She would not try to explain, to reconcile. She abandoned herself to the exquisite mysteries of existence. And yet in her abandonment she kept a sharp look-out on herself, trying fiercely to make head or tail of her nature. She thought herself a fool. But the fact that she thought so was for her a proof of adult sapience. Odd! She gave herself up. And yet it was just by giving herself up that she seemed to glimpse sometimes her own inwardness. And these bleak revelations saddened her. But she savoured her sadness. It was the wine of life to her. And for her sadness she scorned herself, and in her conscious scorn she recovered her self-respect.

It is doubtful whether the people of southern England have even yet realized how much introspection there is going on all the time in the Five Towns.

Visible from the window of the Wrackgarths' parlour was that colossal statue of Commerce which rears itself aloft at the point where Oodge Lane is intersected by Blackstead Street. Commerce, executed in glossy Doultonware by some sculptor or sculptors unknown, stands pointing her thumb over her shoulder towards the chimneys of far Hanbridge. When I tell you that the circumference of that thumb is six inches, and the rest to scale, you will understand that the statue is one of the prime glories of Bursley. There were times when Emily Wrackgarth seemed to herself as vast and as lustrously impressive as it. There were other times when she seemed to herself as trivial and slavish as one of those performing fleas she had seen at the Annual Ladies' Evening Fête organized by the Bursley Mutual Burial Club. Extremist!

She was now stirring the pudding with her left hand. The ingredients had already been mingled indistinguishably in that rich, undulating mass of tawniness which proclaims perfection. But Emily was determined to give her left hand, not less than her right, what she called "a doing". Emily was like that.

At mid-day, when her brother came home from the Works, she was still at it.

"Brought those scruts with you?" she asked, without looking up.

"That's a fact," he said, dipping his hand into the sagging pocket of his coat.

It is perhaps necessary to explain what scruts are. In the daily output of every potbank there are a certain proportion of flawed vessels. These are cast aside by the foreman, with a lordly gesture, and in due course are hammered into fragments. These fragments, which are put to various uses, are called scruts; and one of the uses they are put to is a sentimental one. The dainty and luxurious Southerner looks to find in his Christmas pudding a wedding-ring, a gold thimble, a threepenny-bit, or the like. To such fal-lals the Five Towns would say fie. A Christmas pudding in the Five Towns contains nothing but suet, flour, lemon-peel, cinnamon, brandy, almonds, raisins—and two or three scruts. There is a world of poetry, beauty, romance, in scruts—though you have to have been brought up on them to appreciate it. Scruts have passed into the proverbial philosophy of the district. "Him's a pudden with more scruts than raisins to 'm," is a criticism not infrequently heard. It implies respect, even admiration. Of Emily Wrackgarth herself people often said, in reference to her likeness to her father, "Her's a scrut o' th' owd basin."

Jos had emptied out from his pocket on to the table a good three dozen of scruts. Emily laid aside her spoon, rubbed the palms of her hands on the bib of her apron, and proceeded to finger these scruts with the air of a connoisseur, rejecting one after another. The pudding was a small one, designed merely for herself and Jos, with remainder to "the girl"; so that it could hardly accommodate more than two or three scruts. Emily knew well that one scrut is as good as another. Yet she did not want her brother to feel that anything selected by him would necessarily pass muster with her. For his benefit she ostentatiously wrinkled her nose.

"By the by," said Jos, "you remember Albert Grapp? I've

asked him to step over from Hanbridge and help eat our snack on Christmas Day."

Emily gave Jos one of her looks. "You've asked that Mr Grapp?"

"No objection, I hope? He's not a bad sort. And he's considered a bit of a ladies' man, you know."

She gathered up all the scruts and let them fall in a rattling shower on the exiguous pudding. Two of three fell wide of the basin. These she added.

"Steady on!" cried Jos. "What's that for?"

"That's for your guest," replied his sister. And if you think you're going to palm me off on to him, or on to any other young fellow, you're a fool, Jos Wrackgarth."

The young man protested weakly, but she cut him short.

"Don't think," she said, "I don't know what you've been after, just of late. Cracking up one young sawny and then another on the chance of me marrying him! I never heard of such goings on. But here I am, and here I'll stay, as sure as my name's Emily Wrackgarth, Jos Wrackgarth!"

She was the incarnation of the adorably feminine. She was exquisitely vital. She exuded at every pore the pathos of her young undirected force. It is difficult to write calmly about her. For her, in another age, ships would have been launched and cities besieged. But brothers are a race apart, and blind. It is a fact that Jos would have been glad to see his sister "settled"—preferably in one of the other four Towns.

She took up the spoon and stirred vigorously. The scruts grated and squeaked together around the basin, while the pudding feebly wormed its way up among them.

II

Albert Grapp, ladies' man though he was, was humble of heart. Nobody knew this but himself. Not one of his fellow clerks in Clither's Bank knew it. The general theory in Hanbridge was "Him's got a stiff opinion o' hisself." But this arose from what was really a sign of humility in him. He made the most of himself. He had, for instance, a way of his own in the matter of dressing. He always wore a voluminous frock-coat, with a pair of neatly striped vicuna trousers, which he placed every night under his mattress, thus preserving in perfection the crease down the centre of each. His collar was of the highest, secured in front with an aluminium stud, to which was attached by a patent loop a natty bow of dove-coloured sateen. He had two caps, one of blue serge, the other of shepherd's plaid. These he wore on alternate days. He wore them in a way of his own—well back from his forehead, so as not to hide his hair, and with the peak behind. The peak made a sort of half-moon over the back of his collar. Through a fault of his tailor, there was a yawning gap between the back of his collar and the collar of his coat. Whenever he shook his head, the peak of his cap had the look of a live thing trying to investigate this abyss. Dimly aware of the effect, Albert Grapp shook his head as seldom as possible.

On wet days he wore a mackintosh. This, as he did not yet possess a great-coat, he wore also, but with less glory, on cold days. He had hoped there might be rain on Christmas morning. But there was no rain. "Like my luck," he said as he came out of his lodgings and turned his steps to that corner of Jubilee Avenue from which the Hanbridge–Bursley trams start every half-hour.

Since Jos Wrackgarth had introduced him to his sister at the Hanbridge Oddfellows' Biennial Hop, when he danced two quadrilles with her, he had seen her but once. He had nodded to her, Five Towns fashion, and she had nodded back at him, but with a look that seemed to say, "You needn't nod next time you see me. I can get along well enough without your nods." A frightening girl! And yet her brother had since told him she seemed "a bit gone, like" on him. Impossible! He, Albert Grapp, make an impression on the brilliant Miss Wrackgarth! Yet she had sent him a verbal invite to spend Christmas in her own home. And the time had come. He was

53

on his way. Incredible that he should arrive! The tram must surely overturn, or be struck by lightning. And yet no! He arrived safely.

The small servant who opened the door gave him another verbal message from Miss Wrackgarth. It was that he must wipe his feet "well" on the mat. In obeying this order he experienced a thrill of satisfaction he could not account for. He must have stood shuffling his boots vigorously for a full minute. This, he told himself, was life. He, Albert Grapp, was alive. And the world was full of other men, all alive; and yet, because they were not doing Miss Wrackgarth's bidding, none of them really lived. He was filled with a vague melancholy. But his melancholy pleased him.

In the parlour he found Jos awaiting him. The table was laid for three.

"So you're here, are you?" said the host, using the Five Towns formula. "Emily's in the kitchen," he added. "Happen she'll be here directly."

"I hope she's tol-lol-ish?" asked Albert.

"She is," said Jos. "But don't you go saying that to her. She doesn't care about society airs and graces. You'll make no headway if you aren't blunt."

"Oh, right you are," said Albert, with the air of a man who knew his way about.

A moment later Emily joined them, still wearing her kitchen apron. "So you're here, are you?" she said, but did not shake hands. The servant had followed her in with the tray, and the next few seconds were occupied in the disposal of the beef and trimmings.

The meal began, Emily carving. The main thought of a man less infatuated than Albert Grapp would have been "This girl can't cook. And she'll never learn to." The beef, instead of being red and brown, was pink and white. Uneatable beef! And yet he relished it more than anything he had ever tasted. This beef was her own handiwork. Thus it was because she had made it so. . . . He warily refrained from complimenting

54

her, but the idea of a second helping obsessed him.

"Happen I could do with a bit more, like," he said.

Emily hacked off the bit more and jerked it on to the plate he had held out to her.

"Thanks," he said; and then, as Emily's lip curled, and Jos gave him a warning kick under the table, he tried to look as if he had said nothing.

Only when the second course came on did he suspect that the meal was a calculated protest against his presence. This a Christmas pudding? The litter of fractured earthenware was hardly held together by the suet and raisins. All his pride of manhood—and there was plenty of pride mixed up with Albert Grapp's humility—dictated a refusal to touch that pudding. Yet he soon found himself touching it, though gingerly, with his spoon and fork.

In the matter of dealing with scruts there are two schools—the old and the new. The old school pushes its head well over its plate and drops the scrut straight from its mouth. The new school emits the scrut into the fingers of its left hand and therewith deposits it on the rim of the plate. Albert noticed that Emily was of the new school. But might she not despise as affectation in him what came natural to herself? On the other hand, if he showed himself as a prop of the old school, might she not set her face the more stringently against him? The chances were that whichever course he took would be the wrong one.

It was then that he had an inspiration—an idea of the sort that comes to a man once in his life and finds him, likely as not, unable to put it into practice. Albert was not sure he could consummate this idea of his. He had indisputably fine teeth—"a proper mouthful of grinders" in local phrase. But would they stand the strain he was going to impose on them? He could but try them. Without a sign of nervousness he raised his spoon, with one scrut in it, to his mouth. This scrut he put between two of his left-side molars, bit hard on it, and—eternity of that moment!—felt it and heard it snap in two. Emily also heard it. He was conscious that at sound of the percussion she started forward and stared at him. But he did not look at her. Calmly, systematically, with gradually diminishing crackles, he reduced that scrut to powder, and washed the powder down with a sip of beer. While he dealt with the second scrut he talked to Jos about the Borough Council's proposals to erect an electric power-station on the site of the old gas-works down Hillport way. He was aware of a slight abrasion inside his left cheek. No matter. He must be more careful. There were six scruts still to be negotiated. He knew that what he was doing was a thing grandiose, unique, epical; a history-making thing; a thing that would outlive marble and the gilded monuments of princes. Yet he kept his head. He did not hurry, nor did he dawdle. Scrut by scrut, he ground slowly but he ground exceeding small. And while he did so he talked wisely and well. He passed from the power-station to a first edition of Leconte de Lisle's *Parnasse Contemporain* that he had picked up for sixpence in Liverpool, and thence to the Midland's proposal to drive a tunnel under the Knype Canal so as to link up the main-line with the Critchworth and Suddleford loop-line. Jos was too amazed to put in a word. Jos sat merely gaping—a gape that merged by imperceptible degrees into a grin. Presently he ceased to watch his guest. He sat watching his sister.

Not once did Albert himself glance in her direction. She was just a dim silhouette on the outskirts of his vision. But there she was, unmoving, and he could feel the fixture of her unseen eyes. The time was at hand when he would have to meet those eyes. Would he flinch? Was he master of himself?

The last scrut was powder. No temporizing! He jerked his glass to his mouth. A moment later, holding out his plate to her, he looked Emily full in the eyes. They were Emily's eyes, but not hers alone. They were collective eyes—that was it! They were the eyes of stark, staring womanhood. Her face had been dead white, but now suddenly up from her throat, over her cheeks, through the down between her eyebrows,

56

went a rush of colour, up over her temples, through the very parting of her hair.

"Happen," he said without a quaver in his voice, "I'll have a bit more, like."

She flung her arms forward on the table and buried her face in them. It was a gesture wild and meek. It was the gesture foreseen and yet incredible. It was recondite, inexplicable, and yet obvious. It was the only thing to be done—and yet, by gum, she had done it.

Her brother had risen from his seat and was now at the door. "Think I'll step round to the Works," he said, "and see if they banked up that furnace aright."

NOTE. The author has in preparation a series of volumes dealing with the life of Albert and Emily Grapp.

MAX BEERBOHM

SIR JOHN BETJEMAN
1906–

BETJEMAN AT THE POST OFFICE

Fridays, when I draw my pension,
Thoughts I hardly dare to mention
Deep inside of me uncoil;
Through the grille I gaze so sweetly
At Miss Fanshawe, who—how neatly!—
Rubber-stamps my counterfoil.

Brisk the business, bright the glancing,
Slow the lengthy queue advancing
In our High Street GPO;

No room here for doubt or failure,
"What's the airmail to Australia?"
Trust my blue-eyed girl to know.

Senior citizen I may be
But my Civil Service baby
Telescopes the years between;
As she hands the money to me
Half-forgotten lust runs through me—
Senex becomes seventeen.

STANLEY J. SHARPLESS

PLACE-NAMES OF CHINA

Bolding Vedas! Shanks New Nisa!
Trusty Lichfield swirls it down
To filter beds on Ruislip Marshes
From my loo in Kentish Town.

The Burlington! the Rochester!
Oh those names of childhood loos—
Nursie knocking at the door
"Have you done your Number Twos?"

Lady typist—office party—
Golly! All that gassy beer!
Tripping home down Hendon Parkway
To her Improved Windemere.

Chelsea buns and Lounge Bar pasties
All swilled down with Benskin's Pale,
Purified and cleansed by charcoal,
Fill the taps in Colindale.

Here I sit, alone and sixty,
Bald, and fat, and full of sin,
Cold the seat and loud the cistern,
As I read the Harpic tin.
ALAN BENNETT

JOHN BETJEMAN'S BRIGHTON

for Charles Rycroft

Lovely in the winter sunshine lies the Haslemere
   Hotel,
Near the Homeleigh and the Sussex, home of
   ex-King Manoel.
Lager in the West Pier Tavern, cocktails in the
   Metropole,
Who can spot Lord Alfred Douglas—not the gross
   and coarse of soul!

Stained our hands, our lips polluted, with a sinful
   cigarette,
We who saw "The Dance of Love"—we are not
   likely to forget
Those moustaches and those knickers, seen through
   that machine of shame.
Palace Pier, beloved of wavelets, hushed the breath
   that bears thy name!

We remember shouting breakfasts, old men who
   forgot their teeth,
Exchanging photographs of nurses, symptoms,
   means to gain relief.

We remember that Pavilion, Moorish, with
 chinoiserie,
And the Ice Rink and the High Street, Fuller's layer-
 cake for tea!

Still we see those sugar-daddies flashing by in
 terraplanes,
On the Hove Lawns lonely colonels fight again their
 last campaigns;
Wickedly we drank our coffee in Sherry's where the
 bad girls go,
From the balcony we watched them bathed in purple
 light below.

O Finlandia, heavenly music, played by massed
 bands on the pier,
O those automatic palmists, how I wish that I were
 there!
O pin tables, Russian billiards, where the ball
 melodious clicks,
And the languid coloured postcards, bathing-girls of
 1906!

O voluptuous! O ecstatic! O the convalescent air!
In the sun those terraced houses, wonderful
 wonderful Regency Square!
There among the winds of winter we were gay in
 spite of gales,
Still a memory we cherish though the recollection
 pales.

GAVIN EWART

BELLE DE JOUR

for J. B.

Strolling vaguely after luncheon through the streets
    of Amsterdam
Plants and lace in every window, dodging motorbike
    and tram,
John and I in some confusion, turning left instead of
    right
Crossed a bridge and round a corner glimpsed, above
    a door, a light.
Near extinguished by the sunbeams yet it bravely
    glimmered red.
In a window sat a lady and behind her stretched a
    bed
In the next room sat another, yet another 'cross the
    way
No detective needs to ponder where we'd wandered
    yesterday.
Bars and porno-shows and sex-shops lined both
    banks of a canal
(I'd been here an earlier summer, drinking with
    another pal).
Paid for lust in many cities—had to as my girth
    increased,—
But I'd never knocked and entered at the portals of
    the East.
Said to John I'd like a woman. Didn't say what I'd
    espied,
Standing in a sunlit doorway, raven-haired and
    almond-eyed.
White skirt split to show a lemon slice of thigh above
    the knee,

61

Brought back thoughts of adolescence. In the
    nursery after tea,
Scorning halma, snap or ludo, how my little willy
    grew,
As I, pressed against the lino, read *The Bride of Fu
    Manchu.*
John announced that he'd be going, strode away
    without a glance.
Minutes later found me paying fifty guilders in
    advance.
Curtain drawn and rubber ready, gazing into slanted
    eyes
Ask her name to aid tumescence, "It is Linda," she
    replies.
Jolly nearly my undoing. "Linda" is a name that
    should
Grace a typist in the rush hour swaying home to
    Cricklewood.
Not that I'm averse to typists. Lusted after quite a
    few,
Pressed against them in the tube trains bound for
    Hendon, Neasden, Kew.
"Pam" or "Christine", "Pat" or "Maureen"; names
    to stir me in the dark,
Dreaming of them playing tennis on the courts of
    Finsbury Park.
I could love a girl called Linda. I could yield my
    ageing heart,
But it's not a name to conjure up a Dutch East-Asian
    tart.
Still although she says I'm heavy and asks me if I'm
    drunk,
In the end I find I'm standing with a letter full of
    spunk.
She is busy at the bidet, my 7-minute bride,
But she indicates a "tidibin", a pedal by its side.

Stockinged foot upon the pedal, in the bin my rubber
   drop
Quite surprised to see that others almost fill it to the
   top.
She apologizes nicely but explains it all away,
By pointing out my visit comes toward the end of
   day.
"Ten to three!" I murmur crossly "There's no need to
   shoot that line!"
But my Linda (we are dressing) says she always starts
   at nine,
Much prefers to take the day shift, though the
   district's less alive,
Men more sober and less bother when you finish
   work at five.
Nine till five she works, my Linda, and then climbs
   aboard a tram!
As she speaks a fresh desire stokes my loins in
   Amsterdam.
Not for soppy Lotus blossom, not for teeth of orient
   pearl
But for nine-till-fiver Linda, a thrifty working girl.

GEORGE MELLY

CHARLOTTE BRONTË
1816–55

from MISS MIX

CHAPTER I

My earliest impressions are of a huge, mis-shapen rock, against which the hoarse waves beat unceasingly. On this rock three pelicans are standing in a defiant attitude. A dark sky lowers in the background, while two sea-gulls and a gigantic cormorant eye with extreme disfavour the floating corpse of a drowned woman in the foreground. A few bracelets, coral necklaces, and other articles of jewelry, scattered around loosely, complete this remarkable picture.

It is one which, in some vague, unconscious way, symbolizes, to my fancy, the character of a man. I have never been able to explain exactly why. I think I must have seen the picture in some illustrated volume, when a baby, or my mother may have dreamed it before I was born.

As a child I was not handsome. When I consulted the triangular bit of looking-glass which I always carried with me, it showed a pale, sandy and freckled face, shaded by locks like the colour of sea-weed when the sun strikes in it deep water. My eyes were said to be indistinctive; they were a faint ashen grey; but above them rose—my only beauty—a high, massive, domelike forehead, with polished temples, like door-knobs of the purest porcelain.

Our family was a family of governesses. My mother had been one, and my sisters had the same occupation. Consequently, when, at the age of thirteen, my eldest sister handed me the advertisement of Mr Rawjester, clipped from that day's *Times*, I accepted it as my destiny. Nevertheless, a mysterious presentiment of an indefinite future haunted me in my dreams that night, as I lay upon my little snow-white bed. The next morning, with two band-boxes tied up in silk handkerchiefs, and a hair trunk, I turned by back upon Minerva Cottage for ever.

CHAPTER II

Blunderbore Hall, the seat of James Rawjester, Esq., was encompassed by dark pines and funereal hemlocks on all sides. The wind sang weirdly in the turrets and moaned through the long-drawn avenues of the park. As I approached the house I saw several mysterious figures flit before the windows, and a yell of demoniac laughter answered my summons at the bell. While I strove to repress my gloomy forebodings, the housekeeper, a timid, scared-looking old woman, showed me into the library.

I entered, overcome with conflicting emotions. I was dressed in a narrow gown of dark serge, trimmed with black bugles. A thick green shawl was pinned across my breast. My hands were encased with black half-mittens worked with steel beads; on my feet were large pattens, originally the property of my deceased grandmother. I carried a blue cotton umbrella. As I passed before a mirror, I could not help glancing at it, nor could I disguise from myself the fact that I was not handsome.

Drawing a chair into a recess, I sat down with folded hands, calmly awaiting the arrival of my master. Once or twice a fearful yell rang through the house, or the rattling of chains, and curses uttered in a deep, manly voice broke upon the oppressive stillness. I began to feel my soul rising with the emergency of the moment.

"You look alarmed, miss. You don't hear anything, my dear, do you?" asked the housekeeper nervously.

"Nothing whatever," I remarked calmly, as a terrible scream, followed by the dragging of chairs and tables in the room above, drowned for a moment my reply. "It is the silence, on the contrary, which has made me foolishly nervous."

The housekeeper looked at me approvingly, and instantly made some tea for me.

I drank seven cups; as I was beginning the eighth, I heard a crash, and the next moment a man leaped into the room through the broken window.

CHAPTER III

The crash startled me from my self-control. The housekeeper bent toward me and whispered:

"Don't be excited. It's Mr Rawjester—he prefers to come in sometimes in this way. It's his playfulness, ha! ha! ha!"

"I perceive," I said calmly. "It's the unfettered impulse of a lofty soul breaking the tyrannizing bonds of custom," and I turned toward him.

He had never once looked at me. He stood with his back to the fire, which set off the Herculean breadth of his shoulders. His face was dark and expressive; his under-jaw squarely formed, and remarkably heavy. I was struck with his remarkable likeness to a Gorilla.

As he absently tied the poker into hard knots with his nervous fingers, I watched him with some interest. Suddenly he turned toward me:

"Do you think I'm handsome, young woman?"

"Not classically beautiful," I returned calmly; "but you have, if I may so express myself, an abstract manliness—a sincere and wholesome barbarity which, involving as it does the naturalness"—but I stopped, for he yawned at that moment—an action which singularly developed the immense breadth of his lower jaw—and I saw he had forgotten me. Presently he turned to the housekeeper:

"Leave us."

The old woman withdrew with a courtesy.

Mr Rawjester deliberately turned his back upon me and remained silent for twenty minutes. I drew my shawl the more closely around my shoulders and closed my eyes.

66

"You are the governess?" at length he said.

"I am, sir."

"A creature who teaches geography, arithmetic, and the use of the globes—ha!—a wretched remnant of femininity—a skimp pattern of girlhood with a premature flavour of tea-leaves and morality. Ugh!"

I bowed my head silently.

"Listen to me, girl!" he said sternly; "this child you have come to teach—my ward—is not legitimate. She is the offspring of my mistress—a common harlot. Ah! Miss Mix, what do you think of me now?"

"I admire," I replied, calmly, "your sincerity. A mawkish regard for delicacy might have kept this disclosure to yourself. I only recognize in your frankness that perfect community of thought and sentiment which should exist between original natures."

I looked up; he had already forgotten my presence, and was engaged in pulling off his boots and coat. This done, he sank down in an armchair before the fire, and ran the poker wearily through his hair. I could not help pitying him.

The wind howled fearfully without, and the rain beat furiously against the windows. I crept toward him and seated myself on a low stool beside his chair.

Presently he turned, without seeing me, and placed his foot absently in my lap. I affected not to notice it. But he started and looked down.

"You here yet, Carrothead? Ah, I forgot. Do you speak French?"

"*Oui, Monsieur.*"

"*Taisez-vous!*" he said sharply, with singular purity of accent. I complied. The wind moaned fearfully in the chimney, and the light burned dim. I shuddered in spite of myself. "Ah, you tremble, girl!"

"It is a fearful night."

"Fearful! Call you this fearful—ha! ha! ha! Look! you wretched little atom, look!" and he dashed forward, and, leaping out of the window, stood like a statue in the pelting storm, with folded arms. He did not stay long, but in a few minutes he returned by way of the hall chimney. I saw from the way that he wiped his feet on my dress that he had again forgotten my presence.

"You are a governess. What can you teach?" he asked, suddenly and fiercely thrusting his face in mine.

"Manners!" I replied calmly.

"Ha! teach *me*!"

"You mistake yourself," I said adjusting my mittens. "Your manners require not the artificial restraint of society. You are radically polite; this impetuosity and ferociousness is simply the sincerity which is the basis of a proper deportment. Your instincts are moral; your better nature, I see is religious. As St Paul justly remarks—see chap. 6, 8, 9 and 10—"

He seized a heavy candlestick, and threw it at me. I dodged it submissively, but firmly.

"Excuse me," he remarked, as his under-jaw slowly relaxed. "Excuse me, Miss Mix—but I can't stand St Paul. Enough—you are engaged."

BRET HARTE

SIR THOMAS BROWNE
1605–82

SIR THOMAS BROWN ON WELSH RABBITS

Being a Continuation of his "Inquiries into Vulgar and Common Errors"

The common opinion of the Welsh Rabbit conceits that it is a species of *Cuniculus* indigenous to Wales; of which assertion, if Prescription of time and Numerosity of assertors were a sufficient Demonstration, we might sit down herein as an orthodoxical Truth, nor should there need ulterior Disquisition. *Pliny* discourseth of it under the Head of *De Animalibus Walliæ*. *Seneca* describeth it as an exosseous Animal, or one of the invertebrated or boneless kind. *Claudian* saith that it delighteth to burrow underground in Coal Holes and Cyder Cellars. *Scaliger* affirmeth it to be like to the Hyena, incapable of Domitation or taming, for the cause that he never heard of one being domesticated in a Hutch. *Sarenus Sammonicus* determineth it to be like unto the Salamander, moist in the third degree, and to have a mucous Humidity above and under the Epidermis, or outer skin, by virtue whereof it endureth the Fire for a time. Nor are such conceits held by Humane authors only, for the holy Fathers of the Church have likewise similarly opinioned. *St Augustine* declareth it to be an unclean Animal; insomuch that like to the Polecat it is Graveolent, emitting a strong Murine, or Micy Effluvium. *The Venerable Bede* averreth that it is Noctiparent, as the Bat or Owl, and seldom quitteth its Warrenne until Midnight, for food; for the reason being that being Cœcigenous, or possessing no organs of Vision, it loveth Tenebrosity.

All which notwithstanding, upon strict inquiry, we find the Matter controvertible. *Diodorus*, in his Eleventh Book, affirmeth the Welsh Rabbit to be a creature of Figment, like unto the Sphinx and Snap-Dragon. *Mathiolus*, in his Comment on *Dioscorides*, treateth it not as an Animal, but as a Lark. *Sextius*, a Physitian, saith that having well digested the matter, he was compulsed to reject it; whilest *Salmuth*, the Commentator of *Pancirollus*, averreth that one *Podocaterus*, a Cyprian, kept one for Months in a Cage, without ever having attained the sight of the remotest Manifestation of Vitality.

Now, besides Authority against it, Experience doth in no way confirm the existence of the Welsh Rabbit as an Animant Entity. But, contrariwise, the principles of Sense and Reason conspire to asseverate it to be, like unto the Myths of Paganism, an Inanimant Body, vivificated by the Ignoration and Superstitiosity of men. For had they but inquired into the Etymon, or true meaning of the name of the Entity in question, they would have experienced that it was originally merely the Synonyme for a British Dainty, or Cymric Scitamentum; insomuch as it was primitively appellated, "The Welsh Tid, or Rare-Bit;" which, by elision, becoming Metamorphosed into Ra'bit, was, from its Homophony, vulgarly supposed to have respect to the *Cuniculus* rather than to the *Scitamentum* of Wales.

Again, the Doctrine of the Existence of the Welsh Rabbit as a Vivous Entity, doth in nowise accord with the three definitive Confirmators and Tests of things dubious: to wit, Experiment, Analysis, and Synthesis. And first by Experiment. For if we send to Wales for one of the Rabbits, vernacular to the Principality, we shall discriminate on the attainment of it, no Difformity in its Organism from that of the Cuniculi vulgar to other Countries. And if we then proceed to discoriate and exossate the Animal thus attained, or to deprive it of both its Skin and Bones, and after to macerate the residuary Muscular Fibre into a papparious Pulp, we shall experience, upon diffusing the same on an *Offula tosta*, or a thin slice of toast, that so far from the concoction partaking in the least of the delectable Sapor of the

70

Welsh *Scitamentum*, it will in no way titillate the lingual Papillæ, but, contrariwise, offer inordinate Offence to the Gust.

And, secondly, by Analysis. If, in the stead of sending to Wales, we betake ourselves to any Hostelrie or place of Cenatory Resort, vicine to Covent Garden (whereanent they be celebrious for the concoction of such like Comestibles, for the Deipnophagi or eater of Suppers), and thence provide ourselves with one of the Welsh Rarebits or Scitamenta, whereof we are treating, we shall discriminate upon the Dissolution or Discerption of its part, that it consisteth not of any Carnal Substance, but simply of a Superstratum of some flavous and adipose Edible, which, to the Sense of Vision, seemeth like unto the Unguent, denominated Basilicon, or, the Emplastrum appellated Diachylon; whilest to the Sense of Olfaction it beareth an Odour that hath an inviting Caseous or Cheesy Fragror, and fulfilleth all the conditions and Predicaments of caseous matter or Cheese, which hath undergone the process of Torrefaction; whereof, indeed, if we submit a portion to the Test of the Gust, we shall, from the peculiar Sapor appertinent thereto, without Dubitation determine it to consist.

And, thirdly and lastly, by Synthesis. If we provide ourselves with about a Selibra or half pound of the Cheese, entitulated *Duplex Glocestrius*, or Double Gloucester; and then go on to cut the intrinsic caseous Matter into tenuous Segments or Laminæ; and, positing such Segments within the coquinary commodity distinguished by Culinarians as the *Furnus Bataviæ* or Dutch Oven, submit the same to the Fire, until by the action of the Caloric they become mollified unto Semiliquidity: whereupon, if we diffuse the caseous fluid on an Offula of Bread, the Superfices whereof hath been previously torrified, and then Season the same with a slight aspersion of the Sinapine, Piperine, and Saline Condiments, or with Mustard, Pepper, and Salt, we shall find that the Sapor and Fragror thereof differ in no wise from the Gust and

71

Odour of the Edible we had præ-attained from the Covent Garden Cœnatorium; and, consequentially, that the Welsh Rabbit is not, as the Vulgar Pseudodox conceiteth, a species of Cuniculus vernacular to Wales, but as was before predicated, simply a Savoury and Redolent Scitamentum or Rarebit, which is much existimated by the *Cymri* or Welsh people, who, from time prætermemorial, have been cognized as a Philocaseous, or Cheese-loving, Nation.

ANON

from *Cruikshank's Comic Almanack, 1847*

ROBERT BROWNING
1812–89

THE COCK AND THE BULL

You see this pebble-stone? It's a thing I bought
Of a bit of a chit of a boy i' the mid o' the day—
I like to dock the smaller parts-o'-speech,
As we curtail the already cur-tail'd cur
(You catch the paronomasia, play 'po' words?)
Did, rather, i' the pre-Landseerian days.
Well, to my muttons. I purchased the concern,
And clapt it i' my poke, having given for same
By way o' chop, swop, barter or exchange—
"Chop" was my snickering dandiprat's own
    term—
One shilling and fourpence, current coin o' the
    realm.
O-n-e one and f-o-u-r four
Pence, one and fourpence—you are with me,
    sir?—

What hour it skills not: ten or eleven o' the clock,
One day (and what a roaring day it was
Go shop or sight-see—bar a spit o' rain!)
In February, eighteen sixty nine,
Alexandria Victoria, Fidei
Hm—hm—how runs the jargon? being on throne.

   Such, sir, are all the facts, succinctly put,
The basis or substratum—what you will—
Of the impending eighty thousand lines.
"Not much in 'em either," quoth perhaps simple
   Hodge.
But there's a superstructure. Wait a bit.

Mark first the rationale of the thing;
Hear logic rival and levigate the deed.
That shilling—and for matter o' that, the pence—
I had o' course upo' me—wi' me say—
(*Mecum*'s the Latin, make a note o' that)
When I popp'd pen i' stand, scratch'd ear, wiped
   snout,
(Let everybody wipe his own himself)
Sniff'd—tech!—at snuffbox; tumbled up, he-
   heed,
Haw-haw'd (not hee-haw'd, that's another guess
   thing:)
Then fumbled at, and stumbled out of, door,
I shoved the timber ope wi' my omoplat;
and *in vestibulo*, i' the lobby to-wit,
(Iacobi Facciolati's rendering, sir,)
Donn'd galligaskins, antigropeloes,
And so forth; and, complete with hat and gloves,
One on and one a-dangle i' my hand,
And ombrifuge (Lord love you!), case o' rain,
I flopp'd forth, 'sbuddikins! on my own ten toes,
(I do assure you there be ten of them),

And went clump–clumping up hill and down dale
To find myself o' the sudden i' front o' the boy.
Put case I hadn't 'em on me, could I ha' bought
This sort–o'–kind–o'–what–you–might–call toy,
This pebble–thing, o' the boy–thing? Q.E.D.
That's proven without aid from mumping Pope,
Sleek porporate or bloated Cardinal.
(Isn't it, old Fatchaps? You're in Euclid now.)
So, having the shilling—having i' fact a lot—
And pence and halfpence, ever so many o' them,
I purchased, as I think I said before,
The pebble (*lapis, lapidis, -di, -dem, -de*—
What nouns 'crease short i' the genitive, Fatchaps,
    eh?)
O' the boy, a bare–legg'd beggarly son of a gun,
For one–and–fourpence. Here we are again.

   Now Law steps in, bigwigg'd, voluminous–jaw'd;
Investigates and re–investigates.
Was the transaction illegal? Law shakes head
Perpend, sir, all the bearings of the case.

   At first the coin was mine, the chattel his.
But now (by virtue of the said exchange
And barter) *vice versa* all the coin,
Per juris operationem, vests
I' the boy and his assigns till ding o' doom;
(*In sæcula sæculo-o-o-orum*;
I think I hear the Abate mouth out that.)
To have and hold the same to him and them.
Confer some idiot on Conveyancing.
Whereas the pebble and every part thereof,
And all that appertaineth thereunto,
Quodcunque pertinet ad eam rem,
(I fancy, sir, my Latin's rather pat)
Or shall, will, may, might, can, could, would or

should,
(*Subaudi cætera*—clap we to the close—
For what's the good of law in a case o' the kind)
Is mine to all intents and purposes.
This settled, I resume the thread o' the tale.

    Now for a touch o' the vendor's quality.
He says a gen'lman bought a pebble of him,
(This pebble i' sooth, sir, which I hold i' my hand)—
And paid for't *like* a gen'lman, on the nail.
"Did I o'ercharge him a ha'penny? Devil a bit.
Fiddlepin's end! Get out, you blazing ass!
Gabble o' the goose. Don't bugaboo-baby *me*!
Go double or quits? Yah! tittup! what's the odds?"
—There's the transaction view'd i' the vendor's light.

    Next ask that dumpled hag, stood snuffling by,
With her three frowsy blowsy brats o' babes,
The scum o' the kennel, cream o' the filth-heap—
    Faugh!
Aie, aie, aie, aie! ὀτοτοτοτοτοῖ,
('Stead which we blurt out Hoighty toighty now)—
And the baker and candlestickmaker, and Jack and Gill,
Blear'd Goody this and queasy Gaffer that.
Ask the schoolmaster. Take schoolmaster first.

    He saw a gentleman purchase of a lad
A stone, and pay for it *rite*, on the square,
And carry it off *per saltum*, jauntily,
Propria quæ maribus, gentleman's property now
(Agreeably to the law explain'd above),
In proprium usum, for his private ends.
The boy he chuck'd a brown i' the air, and bit
I' the face the shilling: heaved a thumping stone
At a lean hen that ran cluck clucking by,
(And hit her, dead as nail i' post o' door,)

Then *abiit*—what's the Ciceronian phrase?—
Excessit, evasit, erupit—off slogs boy;
Off like bird, *avi similis*—(you observed
The dative? Pretty i' the Mantuan!)—*Anglice*
Off in three flea skips. *Hactenus*, so far,
So good, *tam bene. Bene, satis, male*—,
Where was I with my trope 'bout one in a quag?
I did once hitch the syntax into verse:
Verbum personale, a verb personal,
Concordat—ay, "agrees," old Fatchaps—*cum*
Nominativo, with its nominative,
Genere, i' point o' gender, *numero*,
O' number, *et persona*, and person. *Ut*,
Instance: *Sol ruit*, down flops sun, *et* and,
Montes umbrantur, out flounce mountains. Pah!
Excuse me, sir, I think I'm going mad.
You see the trick on't though, and can yourself
Continue the discourse *ad libitum*.
It takes up about eighty thousand lines,
A thing imagination boggles at:
And might, odds-bobs, sir! in judicious hands,
Extend from here to Mesopotamy.

C. S. CALVERLEY

SINCERE FLATTERY OF R. B.

Birthdays? yes, in a general way;
For the most if not for the best of men:
You were born (I suppose) on a certain day:
So was I: or perhaps in the night: what then?

Only this: or at least, if more,
You must know, not think it, and learn, not speak:

There is truth to be found on the unknown shore,
And many will find where few will seek.

For many are called and few are chosen,
And the few grow many as ages lapse:
But when will the many grow few: what dozen
Is fused into one by Time's hammer-taps?

A bare brown stone in a babbling brook:—
It was wanton to hurl it there, you say:
And the moss, which clung in the sheltered nook
(Yet the stream runs cooler), is washed away.

That begs the question: many a prater
Thinks such a suggestion a sound "stop thief"
Which, may I ask, do you think the greater,
Sergeant-at-arms or a Robber Chief?

And if it were not so? still you doubt?
Ah! yours is a birthday indeed if so.
That were something to write a poem about,
If one thought a little. I only know.

    P.S.

There's a Me Society down at Cambridge,
Where my works, *cum notis variorum*,
Are talked about; well, I require the same bridge
That Euclid took toll at as *Asinorum*:

And, as they have got through several ditties
I thought were as stiff as a brick-built wall,
I've composed the above, and a stiff one *it* is,
A bridge to stop asses at, once for all.

J. K. STEPHEN

HOW I BROUGHT THE GOOD NEWS
FROM AIX TO GHENT OR VICE VERSA

I sprang to the rollocks and Jorrocks and me,
And I galloped, you galloped, we galloped all three.
Not a word to each other: we kept changing place,
Neck to neck, back to front, ear to ear, face to face:
And we yelled once or twice, when we heard a clock
  chime,
"Would you kindly oblige us, *is that the right time?*"
As I galloped, you galloped, he galloped, we galloped, ye
  galloped, they two shall have galloped: *let us trot.*

I unsaddled the saddle, unbuckled the bit,
Unshackled the bridle (the thing didn't fit)
And ungalloped, ungalloped, ungalloped, ungalloped a
  bit.
Then I cast off my buff coat, let my bowler hat fall,
Took off both my boots and my trousers and all—
Drank off my stirrup-cup, felt a bit tight,
And unbridled the saddle: it still wasn't right.

Then all I remember is, things reeling round,
As I sat with my head 'twixt my ears on the ground—
For imagine my shame when they asked what I meant
And I had to confess that I'd been, gone and went
And *forgotten* the news I was bringing to Ghent,
Though I'd galloped and galloped and galloped and
  galloped and galloped
And galloped and galloped and galloped. (Had I not would
  have been galloped?)

ENVOI

So I sprang to a taxi and shouted "To Aix!"
And he blew on his horn and he threw off his brakes,

78

And all the way back till my money was spent
We rattled and rattled and rattled and rattled and rattled
And rattled and rattled—
And eventually sent a telegram.

WALTER CARRUTHERS SELLAR
AND ROBERT JULIAN YEATMAN

JOHN BUCHAN
(1875–1940)

THE QUEEN OF MINIKOI

We were talking of coincidences. It had been a hard day. For
eleven hours we had stalked a shootable sixteen-pointer over
the Runnoch screes and up and down the corries of Sgurr
Beoch, until Old Mac, who had been with me in the Bourlon
Wood show, groaned: "Yon beastie's a deil." Finally Lord
Trasker had flung himself down and fired up-wind into the
eddies of mist; a chance shot, the outcome of overwrought
nerves. But as he fired, the stag came loping from behind a
knoll, and took the shot full in the mazzard.

"Deid," cried old Mac, "a straucht shot for a braw cantlin. I
wull no' ha' seen mony better shots at all."

"It was a fluke, you know," said Trasker, "I just had an
instinct. . . ."

We dragged our quarry down Glenlivet and across Rui-
seach Side to the Tollig, and arrived back at Sir Robert
Manningham's shooting lodge, weary but well pleased with
ourselves. And then, after an admirable dinner, prepared by
Marston, who had been with Sir Robert in the Festubert
show, somebody had remarked that Lord Trasker's shot
had been a coincidence. And General the Hon. Derrick

McQuantock had said, in that voice which always brought Eton back to me:

"Yes, but what is coincidence? There are forces outside the world of which we know next to nothing. Why did I meet Eric—" he pointed his pipe-stem at Sir Eric Chalmers Troope—"Why did I meet Eric in Zerka when we were both supposed to be in Bigadich? Or what made Philip" (indicating Admiral Sir Philip Delmode) "suspect our Dutch friend Joos Vuyterswaelt?"

We all laughed at the memory of the neat way in which the Admiral had outwitted the Roumanian Secret Service. And while we were still laughing, the squat little figure of Sandy Argyll, that astounding baker from Forfar, who had become a merchant adventurer and had helped to save the Queen of Holland from the Red Hand Society—that squat figure moved in a chair by the fire. "Coincidence," he said. "Hm! Ask Graham to tell you about the hat that didn't fit."

We all turned to the Earl of Moorswater, and in a silence deeper than that of the night-shrouded Whang Scaur outside the windows, he told this story.

"Any of you fellows ever hear of Minikoi? No, it's not the name of a girl. It's an island in the Arabian Sea, and I myself had only heard of it vaguely, when, on a certain spring day after the war, I came out of the Premier, and turned down Pall Mall. I had dined well, and old Fossett, who was with me in the St Quentin show, had brought up a bottle of the club port—'58. I was feeling pretty pleased with life. As I passed through the door into the street I noticed that Carson, the head hall-porter—"

"Sorry to butt in," said the General, "but wasn't he given the DCM after the Cambrai stunt? I thought so. A white man."

"—Old Carson," continued the Earl, "stared at me curiously. At the same time I felt a pressure on my head. Now as you all know, I get my hats from Challoner, and no man in town makes a better hat. And yet my hat was too

80

tight. I took it off, and to my amazement found a thick piece of paper stuffed inside the lining. There was writing on it, and I stood under a lamp-post to read it. Now, I'm considered pretty good at languages, as you all know, but I must confess this screed puzzled me. It was written in faded red ink, and it seemed to be no modern tongue. Well—it wasn't any modern tongue. After puzzling over it for some minutes, I noticed a certain syllable which recurred very frequently, and at once I knew what the writing was. It was the language of the old Icelandic sagas of Snorre Sturlason—the Heimskringla— stories of the Norsemen just before they were Christianized by the Anglo-Saxons. I recognized it thanks to a job of work I had done for the Foreign Office towards the end of the war. I took the paper home with me, intending to get to work on it, but my man Truslove—you remember him, Derrick, at Le Cateau"—the General nodded—"Truslove informed me that there was a gentleman waiting for me in the library. It turned out to be Sir Ronald Waukinshaw, my old chief at the FO. You should have seen his face when I said: 'Ronnie, ever heard of Minikoi?' The old boy glanced round nervously. Then he said: 'In heaven's name, Graham, what on earth do you know about it?' I produced the bit of paper, and he whistled softly.

'This is a pretty big thing,' he said. 'It's old Icelandic, of course. But how did you come by it?' I told him that I had found it in my hat. 'Then somebody,' said he, 'must have mistaken your hat for someone else's.' 'But what does it mean?' I asked. 'Read it yourself,' he replied dryly. I read slowly: 'The sword of the giant-queen of the rock and snow, the ring-bearer, shall be dyed in the gore of Geysa's sons on May 4th at Minikoi.' 'Isn't it clear?' asked Ronnie. 'Not particularly,' I said. 'We must go back to your club at once,' he rejoined. And in the taxi he told me the most incredible story I have ever listened to.

"It appeared that for some time past the Foreign Office had been worried by signs of unrest in the Laccadive and Maldive islands. There was talk of an ancient Arabian Queen who had returned to earth to lead the islanders against the English in India, and to re-establish a vast heathen Empire from the Malabar coast to the Himalayas. As a sign that she was the expected monarch she was to show a heavy ring of beaten gold to her followers, chief among whom was a certain Afghan, at present in England to raise money for the rising, which, it was hoped, would quickly spread to the islands in the Bay of Bengal and the South China Sea. 'This message,' he said, 'must have been intended for that Afghan's hat, for it gives the date of the rising.' 'But what has the Icelandic business to do with it?' 'They thought they'd be safe if they used that language. As it is, you and I are probably about the only people who understand it.' 'And why are we going back to the club?' 'To hunt for that Afghan—unless—' We met each other's eyes, as men do at such moments, and I read his purpose. 'You want me to be that Afghan, and put a stopper on the whole affair.' 'It's almost certain death,' he said. 'That's one's job,' I answered. 'Good man,' he said. 'Today's May 1st. Not much time.'

"Ronnie came back to my flat and watched while my man made me up as an Afghan. Then we rang up Donald Ritchie, who had been with my mob in the first Somme push. To my delight he was just starting off on one of his mad flights round the world, for though he had left an ear at Loos and a thumb at Suvla, he was the same old Donald who had trekked across Greenland to cure his insomnia. He said he could have his 'plane ready in an hour. At that moment Truslove informed me that a message had come from the garage to the effect that my car was out of action. 'It was all right this morning,' I said. 'That Afghan works quickly,' said Ronnie. 'Luckily there is still mine.'

"So under cover of darkness he drove me down to Donald's private aerodrome, and a fine shock the dear old fellow got when he saw me in my outlandish togs, and with my face stained and my hair darkened. That flight was a perfect nightmare. We took charge in turn, and lived on coffee and sandwiches. And we were actually flying over the Arabian Sea, and almost in sight of the island of Minikoi, when the trouble began. Throughout the journey I had kept my eyes open for signs of pursuit. I was just congratulating myself that we had won the race, and the first battle in the campaign, when the engine began to flutter and spit and jerk. 'Damn,' said Donald. As we dropped like a plummet seawards I had just time to note a blob on the horizon which I knew must be Minikoi. The impact with which we struck the water temporarily stunned us. Then, disentangling ourselves from the wreckage, we struck out in the direction of the island. Now I'm considered a fairly strong swimmer, but the long flight and the crash had knocked it out of me a bit. And as night fell, and the sea roughened, I began to wish I had not left my comfortable flat. However, after perhaps three hours, Donald, who had not turned a hair, said: 'There's your comic island, old man.' Exhausted, we plugged away, and were soon stumbling over the wet rocks of a small creek. And there, still intact, on a little spit of sand, was an aeroplane. 'Dilcott monoplane,' said Donald. 'That landing was a miracle, whoever made it.' I had my own ideas about that, and my blood boiled when I remembered that this was May 3rd and that within twelve hours the British Empire would be tottering. Ronnie had trusted me, and I had let him down. Despair lent me new strength. I half crawled, half stumbled over rocks and through swamps, now hauling myself up crumbling cliffs by slimy tree-branches that threatened to snap at any moment, now staggering into bottomless ravines, where, in the impenetrable darkness, swollen torrents roared over stony beds. Once a huge bird slashed my cheek with its wing and buffeted me sideways into a quagmire, and once some swiftly moving animal snapped at my legs, and was kicked back into its cavern by Donald. The poisonous roots of nauseating plants twined round our feet and tripped us, and moment by moment boulders, loosened by the damp,

83

tumbled into the abysses all about us. Cascades of wet earth blinded us, and blood poured from a square cut over Donald's left eye. And all the while a pulse in my brain kept on beating out: 'You may be in time yet. You *must* be in time.' And then, just as my heart seemed to be bursting through my chest, and a moment after Donald had said: 'This is probably the wrong island,' I heard voices. We crept nearer. Somebody said, in the Laccadive dialect: 'If thou art the Great Queen who is to lead us to victory, show us the ring.' A roar as of a thousand voices cried: 'Yes. The ring. The ring.' The first voice went on: 'How can we know that thine order to start the rising tomorrow at dawn is not a device of the enemy?' Then a very beautiful voice—the voice of a young girl, answered: 'I am indeed the Great Queen, and at the appointed time I will show the ring.' Menacing shouts replied to her, and in a flash I forgot that the Empire was in danger, and thought only of a girl in deadly peril. Followed by Donald, I dashed forward and found myself on an uneven plateau of light coral sand covered with pulse and coarse grain. We were only just in time to pull ourselves up on the brink of a precipice of sand and rock. Flinging ourselves down we gazed at a kind of rugged amphitheatre, fringed by banana trees, fifty feet beneath us. And then we saw the strangest sight that white men ever looked upon—a sight that froze our blood. I saw Donald clutch his revolver, but I checked him. One doesn't shoot sitting birds in the back, and the crowd below us was unaware of our presence.

"The amphitheatre, lit by a hundred banana-root torches, was packed with Moplas, wild, half-Arabian Malabars and lithe Hindus. The light shone on their dusky bodies and the steel of their long hunting-spears. They crouched pell-mell, with their backs to us, and in their forefront was a big fellow in a scarlet sari. He was evidently their leader. Facing them, and not a hundred yards from us, was the most beautiful girl I had ever seen. She was tall and slim, and the carriage of her head as she confronted the mob made me want to cheer. She was dressed in a long white robe, which was fastened at the waist with a golden girdle. Her long auburn hair flowed loose to her waist. She looked every inch a queen. As we watched, the leader took a menacing step forward.

" 'Where is the ring?' he demanded, 'and where is Humbullah?' 'That's you,' whispered Donald. The leader's question was answered by a roar from all those savages. But the girl did not flinch. She was staring up at us, and I put my finger to my lips. She nodded imperceptibly. Before she could speak again to the leader, a drum began to beat, one of the devil-drums of the Yalabalim, and immediately the mob was on its feet. Spears were brandished and a weird death-dance began. The leader held up his hand, and the noise died down. 'For the third and last time,' he said, 'where is the ring, and where is Humbullah? Answer, or you die at dawn.' And even as he spoke the sky seemed to brighten in the east. 'She's forgotten the ring,' said Donald. And upon my soul, I could not follow her game. But I had seen enough. The blood-intoxicated horde was slowly closing in on her. By good fortune I always wear a heavy gold ring which a minor Balkan royalty had given me for a job of work I had done in Cettinje. 'Come on,' I said to Donald, and we skirted the amphitheatre very stealthily, keeping on the lip of the precipice, until we were behind the girl. As we leapt, two men were moving forward to secure her with ropes. While Donald placed himself before her, I knelt at her side and kissed her hand, taking care to slip the ring into it. She seemed amazed, but she held the ring up, and said: 'It is here.' 'And here,' I shouted, 'is Humbullah.' The effect was magical. The leader prostrated himself, and the mob, frantic with joy, followed suit. 'We strike at dawn,' said the Queen. 'And now I must withdraw to consult with Humbullah.' She then took my hand, and led me behind a little screen of coco-nut trees, and I nearly jumped out of my skin when she said, in perfect English: 'That was a near thing.' 'Who on earth are you?' I asked. 'Sylvia Farquharson,' she answered. 'Perhaps

85

you've heard of General Farquharson?' I should say I had. Every man who was in the Thiepval show had cause to bless 'Tiger' Farquharson. 'Please explain,' I said. And there, behind the coco-nut trees, she told me how Sir Ronald Waukinshaw had let her into the secret of his plan to scotch the rising, and had asked her to take the place of the expected queen; how she had arrived by 'plane, made a difficult landing, and announced her return to the natives; how they were to be made to rise at dawn on this very day, so that troops landed from a cruiser could deal with them, and put an end to the business before it had time to spread. I was about to congratulate her when a low-caste Hindu approached us, and said to me in a dialect of the Dushkandhila hill-country: 'If you are Humbullah, how is it that your skin is white?' I had forgotten that my long hours in the water had washed the stain off my face and body and hair! But I had to bluff it out. I replied in Afghan: 'Alas, my brother, it is my shame. A white trader dishonoured my mother, and that is why I have sworn vengeance.' This appeared to satisfy him, and I was about to ask Miss Farquharson what I was to do next when we heard three blasts of a siren. 'The signal!' she said. A moment later there was the whistle of a shell, and an explosion in the very middle of the amphitheatre. I caught her arm and ran with her towards the shore. Behind us came the maddened natives, aware at last that they had been betrayed. Sylvia was as lithe as a young deer, and I am considered a pretty good long-distance runner. Never had we greater need of speed and endurance. Once a well-aimed spear struck a tree four feet ahead of us, and hung quivering there, and once a serpent sprang at us, and missed by a hair's-breadth. 'All right?' I breathed. 'You bet,' she panted back, and I swore to get her to safety. Our most dangerous man was the big leader, and I saw that he was gaining on us, I could have done with that fellow, I told myself, as my second-string in the three miles at Queen's in 1913. He had the long stride and the natural poise of the born runner, and even as I cursed him, I admired the confounded chap. Sylvia, I could see, knew that he was gaining. I kept on wondering why he didn't chuck his spear at us. He got to within twenty feet of us . . . fifteen, ten, five feet. I turned and prepared to dot him one, for big as he was, I'm considered a fairly useful man with the gloves on. To my amazement he grinned, and said: 'This is my revenge for the beating you gave me in '12.' And there I was, looking into the artificially darkened eyes of dear old Leamington-Furze, my opposite number in the 'Varsity sports before the war. 'Keep on going,' he said, 'and I'll follow. Don't give the game away.' 'Wonders never cease,' said Sylvia, as we plunged through a swamp, and came in sight of the shore. And there, ahead of us, were English infantrymen disembarking from several boats, and preparing to scatter across the island, and to round up the rebels. We sat down on a rock, and Leamington-Furze explained that Sir Ronald Waukinshaw had sent him out to work up the mob, but had kept the idea secret, so that Sylvia would act her part better. 'You knew who I was, then?' asked Sylvia. 'Oh, yes. Ronnie told me to expect you. I knew your father. We were in the Dickebusch affair together.'

"Well, to cut a long story short, we were put on board the cruiser, where Sylvia's father took one look at me, and said: 'Who's this wallah?' Donald was on board, too. Not liking the look of things when the mob closed in on Sylvia, he had rushed for her monoplane, but couldn't start it. So he had swum out to sea for help, had bumped into the cruiser, and had told them to hurry up and do something about it.

"That night, as we walked about the deck, Sylvia said to me: 'By the way, remind me to give you back your ring. It's in my cabin.' 'Is our engagement broken off, then?' I whispered. Down came her lovely lashes over her eyes. 'I couldn't possibly wear a great hulking thing like that,' she said. . . .

"Now it seems to me," concluded the Earl, "that the long arm of chance played a pretty big part in that little adventure.

Not many men have met their wives under such conditions.

"But why Icelandic?" asked Trasker.

"Oh, Ronnie saw to that," said the Earl. "He knew I'd fall for it."

"One more question," asked the General, "who put the paper in your hat?"

"That," said the Earl, "I never discovered. One of Ronnie's men, I suppose."

"Did you not notice any queer people in the club that night?" asked Sandy Argyll.

"Why, no. I don't think so."

"The man that gave you your hat, for instance?"

"Now I come to think of it, I didn't recognize him. He was a new fellow—bright red hair, I remember. Looked like a wig."

"It was a wig," said Sandy. "And it was me."

J. B. MORTON

ROBERT BURNS
1759–96

RIGID BODY SINGS

Gin a body meet a body
  Flyin' through the air,
Gin a body hit a body,
  Will it fly? and where?

Ilka impact has its measure,
  Ne'er a' ane hae I,
Yet a' the lads they measure me,
  Or, at least, they try.

Gin a body meet a body
 Altogether free,
How they travel afterwards
 We do not always see.

Ilka problem has its method
 By analytics high;
For me, I ken na ane o' them,
 But what the waur am I?
JAMES CLERK MAXWELL

GEORGE GORDON, LORD BYRON
1788–1824

A GRIEVANCE

Dear Mr Editor: I wish to say—
 If you will not be angry at my writing it—
But I've been used, since childhood's happy day,
 When I have thought of something, to inditing it;
I seldom think of things; and, by the way,
 Although this metre may not be exciting, it
Enables one to be extremely terse,
Which is not what one always is in verse.

I used to know a man, such things befall
 The observant wayfarer through Fate's domain
He was a man, take him for all in all,
 We shall not look upon his like again;
I know that statement's not original;
 What statement is, since Shakespere? or, since Cain,
What murder? I believe 'twas Shakespere said it, or
Perhaps it may have been your Fighting Editor.

89

Though why an Editor should fight, or why
 A Fighter should abase himself to edit,
Are problems far too difficult and high
 For me to solve with any sort of credit.
Some greatly more accomplished man than I
 Must tackle them: let's say then Shakespere said it;
And, if he did not, Lewis Morris may
(Or even if he did). Some other day,

When I have nothing pressing to impart,
 I should not mind dilating on this matter.
I feel its import both in head and heart,
 And always did,—especially the latter.
I could discuss it in the busy mart
 Or on the lonely housetop; hold! this chatter
Diverts me from my purpose. To the point:
The time, as Hamlet said, is out of joint,

And perhaps I was born to set it right,—
 A fact I greet with perfect equanimity.
I do not put it down to "cursed spite",
 I don't see any cause for cursing in it. I
Have always taken very great delight
 In such pursuits since first I read divinity.
Whoever will may write a nation's songs
As long as I'm allowed to right its wrongs.

What's Eton but a nursery of wrong-righters,
 A mighty mother of effective men;
A training ground for amateur reciters,
 A sharpener of the sword as of the pen;
A factory of orators and fighters,
 A forcing-house of genius? Now and then
The world at large shrinks back, abashed and beaten,
Unable to endure the glare of Eton.

I think I said I knew a man: what then?
    I don't suppose such knowledge is forbid.
We nearly all do, more or less, know men,—
    Or think we do; nor will a man get rid
Of that delusion, while he wields a pen.
    But who this man was, what, if aught, he did,
Nor why I mentioned him, I do not know;
Nor what I "wished to say" a while ago.

J. K. STEPHEN

GEOFFREY CHAUCER
1340?–1400

IMITATION OF CHAUCER

Women ben full of Ragerie,
Yet swinken not sans secresie
Thilke Moral shall ye understand,
From Schoole-boy's Tale of fayre Ireland:
Which to the Fennes hath him betake,
To filch the gray Ducke fro the Lake.
Right then, there passen by the Way
His Aunt, and eke her Daughters tway.
Ducke in his Trowses hath he hent,
Not to be spied of Ladies gent.
"But ho! our Nephew," (crieth one);
"Ho," quoth another, "Cozen John";
And stoppen, and laugh, and callen out,—
This sely Clerk full doth lout:
They asken that, and talken this,
"Lo here is Coz, and here is Miss."
But, as he glozeth with Speeches soote,

The Ducke sore tickleth his Erse-root:
Fore-piece and buttons all-to-brest,
Forth thrust a white neck, and red crest.
"Te-he," cry'd Ladies: Clerke nought spake:
Miss star'd; and gray Ducke crieth Quake.
"O Moder, Moder" (quoth the daughter)
"Be thilke same thing Maids longen a'ter?
"Bette is to pyne on coals and chalke,
"Then trust on Mon, whose yerde can talke."

ALEXANDER POPE

THE SUMMONEE'S TALE

A MAYDE ther was, y-clept Joan Hunter Dunn,
In all of Surrie, comelier wench was none,
Yet wondrous greet of strength was she withalle,
Ful lustily she smote the tenis-balle,
And whether lord or lady she wolde pleye,
With thirtie, fortie-love wolde winne the day.
A SQUYER eke ther was, in horseless cariage,
And he wolde fayn have sought her hand in marriage,
Though he coulde songes make, with mery rime,
At tennis she out-pleyed him every time;
To make her wyfe he saw but little chaunce,
But then be-thought to take her to a daunce
In gentil Camberlee, where after dark
They held long daliaunce in the cariage park;
Eftsoons Cupide had the twain in thralle,
And this they found the beste game of alle.

STANLEY J. SHARPLESS

AGATHA CHRISTIE
1891–1976

from THE REAL INSPECTOR HOUND

The phone rings. MRS DRUDGE *seems to have been waiting for it to
do so and for the last few seconds has been dusting it with an intense
concentration. She snatches it up.*

MRS DRUDGE: (*Into phone*) Hello: the drawing-room of Lady
  Muldoon's country residence one morning in early
  spring? . . . He*llo*!—the draw——Who? Who did you
  wish to speak to? I'm afraid there is no one of that name
  here, this is all very mysterious and I'm sure it's leading
  up to something, I hope nothing is amiss for we, that
  is Lady Muldoon and her houseguests, are here cut
  off from the world, including Magnus, the wheel-chair-
  ridden half-brother of her ladyship's husband Lord
  Albert Muldoon who ten years ago went out for a walk
  on the cliffs and was never seen again—and all alone,
  for they had no children.

  Should a stranger enter our midst, which I very much
  doubt, I will tell him you called. Goodbye.
  (*She puts down the phone and catches sight of the previously
  seen suspicious character who has now entered again, more
  suspiciously than ever, through the french windows. He senses
  her stare, freezes, and straightens up.*)

SIMON: Ah!—hello there! I'm Simon Gascoyne, I hope you
  don't mind, the door was open so I wandered in. I'm a
  friend of Lady Muldoon, the lady of the house, having
  made her acquaintance through a mutual friend, Felicity
  Cunningham, shortly after moving into this neighbourhood just the other day.

MRS DRUDGE: I'm Mrs Drudge. I don't live in but I pop in on
  my bicycle when the weather allows to help in the
  running of charming though somewhat isolated Muldoon

Manor. Judging by the time (*glances at the clock*) you did well to get here before high water cut us off for all practical purposes from the outside world.

SIMON: I took the short cut over the cliffs and followed one of the old smugglers' paths through the treacherous swamps that surround this strangely inaccessible house.

MRS DRUDGE: Yes, many visitors have remarked on the topographical quirk in the local strata whereby there are no roads leading from the Manor, though there *are* ways of getting *to* it, weather allowing.

SIMON: Yes, well I must say it's a lovely day so far.

MRS DRUDGE: Ah, but now that the cuckoo-beard is in bud there'll be fog before the sun hits Foster's Ridge.

SIMON: I say, it's wonderful how you country people really know weather.

MRS DRUDGE: (*Suspiciously*) Know whether what?

SIMON: (*Glancing out of the window*) Yes, it does seem to be coming on a bit foggy.

MRS DRUDGE: The fog is very treacherous around here—it rolls off the sea without warning, shrouding the cliffs in a deadly mantle of blind man's buff.

SIMON: Yes, I've heard it said.

MRS DRUDGE: I've known whole weekends when Muldoon Manor, as this lovely old Queen Anne House is called, might as well have been floating on the pack ice for all the good it would have done phoning the police. It was on such a weekend as this that Lord Muldoon who had lately brought his beautiful bride back to the home of his ancestors, walked out of this house ten years ago, and his body was never found.

SIMON: Yes, indeed, poor Cynthia.

MRS DRUDGE: His name was Albert.

SIMON: Yes indeed, poor Albert. But tell me, is Lady Muldoon about?

MRS DRUDGE: I believe she is playing tennis on the lawn with Felicity Cunningham.

SIMON: (*Startled*) Felicity Cunningham?

MRS DRUDGE: A mutual friend, I believe you said. A happy chance. I will tell them you are here.

SIMON: Well, I can't really stay as a matter of fact— please don't disturb them—I really should be off.

MRS DRUDGE: They would be very disappointed. It is some time since we have had a four for pontoon bridge at the Manor, and I don't play cards myself.

SIMON: There is another guest, then?

MRS DRUDGE: Major Magnus, the crippled half-brother of Lord Muldoon who turned up out of the blue from Canada just the other day, completes the house-party.

TOM STOPPARD

SAMUEL TAYLOR COLERIDGE
1772–1834

ON A RUINED HOUSE IN A ROMANTIC COUNTRY

And this reft house is that the which he built
Lamented Jack! And here his malt he pil'd,
Cautious in vain! These rats that squeak so wild,
Squeak, not unconscious of their father's guilt.
Did ye not see her gleaming thro' the glade?
Belike, 'twas she, the maiden all forlorn.
What though she milk no cow with crumpled horn,
Yet *aye* she haunts the dale where *erst* she stray'd;
And *aye* beside her stalks her amorous knight!
Still on his thighs their wonted brogues are worn,
And thro' those brogues, still tatter'd and betorn,

95

His hindward charms gleam an unearthly white;
As when thro' broken clouds at night's high noon
Peeps in fair fragments forth the full-orb'd harvest-moon!

SAMUEL TAYLOR COLERIDGE

THE ANCIENT MARINER

The Wedding Guest's Version of the Affair from His Point of View

It is an ancient Mariner,
    And he stoppeth one of three—
In fact he coolly took my arm—
    "There was a ship," quoth he.

"Bother your ships!" said I, "is this
    The time a yarn to spin?
This is a wedding, don't you see,
    And I am next of kin.

"The wedding breakfast has begun,
    We're hungry as can be—
Hold off! Unhand me, longshore man!"
    With that his hand dropt he.

But there was something in his eye,
    That made me sick and ill,
Yet forced to listen to his yarn—
    The Mariner'd had his will.

While Tom and Harry went their way
    I sat upon a stone—
So queer on Fanny's wedding day
    Me sitting there alone!

Then he began, that Mariner,
  To rove from pole to pole,
In one long-winded, lengthened-out,
  Eternal rigmarole,

About a ship in which he'd sailed,
  Though whither, goodness knows,
Where "ice will split with a thunder-fit",
  And every day it snows.

And then about a precious bird
  Of some sort or another,
That—was such nonsense ever heard?—
  Used to control the weather!

Now, at this bird the Mariner
  Resolved to have a shy,
And laid it low with his cross-bow—
  And then the larks! My eye!

For loss of that uncommon fowl,
  They couldn't get a breeze;
And there they stuck, all out of luck,
  And rotted on the seas.

The crew all died, or seemed to die,
  And he was left alone
With that queer bird. You never heard
  What games were carried on!

At last one day he stood and watched
  The fishes in the sea,
And said, "I'm blest!" and so the ship
  Was from the spell set free.

And it began to rain and blow,
  And as it rained and blew,
The dead got up and worked the ship—
  That was a likely crew!

However, somehow he escaped,
  And got again to land,
But mad as any hatter, say,
  From Cornhill to the Strand.

For he believes that certain folks
  Are singled out by fate,
To whom this cock-and-bull affair
  Of his he must relate.

Describing all the incidents,
  And painting all the scenes,
As sailors will do in the tales
  They tell to the Marines.

Confound the Ancient Mariner!
  I knew I should be late;
And so it was; the wedding guests
  Had all declined to wait.

Another had my place, and gave
  My toast; and sister Fan
Said "'Twas a shame. What could you want
  'With that seafaring man?'

I felt like one that had been stunned
  Through all this wrong and scorn;
A sadder and later man
  I rose the morrow morn.

ANON

WILLIAM CONGREVE
1670–1729

RESTORATION PIECE

The COMPERE *comes out in front of the tabs.*

COMPERE: Ladies and gentlemen . . . if distinguished revue artists like Mr Cyril Ritchards and Miss Madge Elliot can get away with Restoration Comedy, we see no reason why we shouldn't do the same: and we are presenting now one of the lesser-known works of Mr Congreve entitled *Virtue in Labour* or *'Tis Pity He's a Coxcomb.*

This is the first time that this company has played Restoration Comedy, and there is one thing which we feel ought to be explained. The company rehearsed from the original eighteenth-century copies of the play, in which—as you know—the letter "s" very often appears looking rather like the letter "f". There has been a certain amount of confusion over this . . . however:

The characters are: Sir Militant Malpractice, a sop—I beg your pardon, a *fop*: Sir Solemnity Sourpuss, a cuckold: Lady Wanton Malpractice, wife to Sir Militant: and Simple, a maid.

(He exits. The tabs open on a Restoration boudoir. LADY WANTON MALPRACTICE *is restoring herself in front of a Restoration mirror. She calls off R.)*

LADY MALPRACTICE: Fimple! . . . Fimple! . . .

(There is no reply.)

A pox on all fervants! . . . *(She calls again.)* Fimple! . . .

(SIMPLE *enters R.*)

SIMPLE: My Lady fummoned me?

LADY MALPRACTICE: Fummoned thee, i' faith? I ha' fummoned thee, wench, fince a quarter past fix.

SIMPLE: La, ma'am, you flander me!

LADY MALPRACTICE: Flander thee, by my troth! Here I fit—fad and forlorn—while you, perfidious jade, are gone to a cockfight with that tatterdemalion of a foldier! (*Aside, she comes right down to the footlights.*) Flap my vitals if the bawd is not in labour wi' the fauciest foldier that ever ferved as a fentry! . . .
(*She goes back to her seat.*)

SIMPLE: He is not a foldier, ma'am. He is a failor.

LADY MALPRACTICE: Foldier or failor, what matter? And I left here, fitting on the fofa like a midwife wi' the vapours! (*Accusingly*) I faw you, Fimple—behind the fummerhoufe. *Kiffing.*

SIMPLE: La, ma'am, 'tis not a fin to kiff.

LADY MALPRACTICE: Nay, good Fimple, 'tis a most fatisfying fenfation.

(SIMPLE *and* MALPRACTICE *come right downstage to hold a carefully posed picture and sing:*)

BOTH: Passion's a teafing, fickle jade
    Coming to mifftress as to maid.
    Love is a trollop, fo, 'tis faid,
    Fex is a whore that lies abed.
        Fa–la–la–la–la–la! . . .
        La–la–la! . . .
        Fa–la–la–la–la–la–la! . . .
        La! . . .

(*They scuttle back to their former positions.*)

LADY MALPRACTICE: What's his name, this coxcomb of yours?

SIMPLE: Fam.

LADY MALPRACTICE: Fam? (*Aside*) Vouchsafe my virtue, I'll warrant they'll be married and bedded by fummer.

SIMPLE: Before fummer, ma'am. 'Tis fixed for the fecond Funday after Feptuagefima.

LADY MALPRACTICE: La, my fine flut! . . . 'tis plain what is the matter with you. Thou'rt over-fexed! . . .

(They run down again to hold another attractive picture and sing gaily:)

BOTH: If a bawd wi' the vapours
    Starts cutting her capers,
    A fig for the fate of the strumpet
    She'll take tea with a cuckold
    And very soon look old
    Demanding a helping of crumpet!
    Fol-de-rol-lol-de-lol-lol-de-lol-lay!
    The Lord help a bawd i' the family way!

(They scamper back to their former positions. There is a knock off.)

LADY MALPRACTICE: But foft! . . . fomeone comef! Fee who it is, Fimple.

(SIMPLE *looks off L.*)

SIMPLE: 'Tis Fir Folemnity Fourpuff, my Lady.

LADY MALPRACTICE: (*Rising and over-acting a good deal*) Folemnity! . . . oh, a fleek, flimy, flippery fellow if ever I knew one! A beperiwigged cuckold wi' the face of a faint and the foul of a finner!

101

(Aside, she goes right downstage.)

Flap my fide-faddle, 'tis a forry fituation! He lies on my stomach as heavy as a fuet dumpling! And yet I'll warrant that this very night—and on that very fofa—he'll feduce me!
(She goes upstage.)
Fimple, my ratafia! . . . *(She looks in the mirror.)* La, my face is a fight! . . . *(She powders herself.)* Bid him enter, Fimple.

(SIMPLE goes to the door L., and then announces:)

SIMPLE: Fir Folemnity Fourpuff! . . .

(SIR SOLEMNITY enters, beperiwigged and bedizened.)

LADY MALPRACTICE: Folemnity! . . .
SIR SOLEMNITY: Lady Fufan! . . .
(Aside, going down to the footlights:) Burst my britches, I ha' feldom feen her looking more fancy! These filks and fatins become her well, methinks, and yet I'll warrant if I do not have them off by fundown my name is not Fourpuff!
LADY MALPRACTICE: Leave us, Fimple.
SIMPLE: *(Curtseying)* Your fervice, ma'am.

(SIMPLE exits, banging the door.)

LADY MALPRACTICE: *(Calling after her)* Fimple! . . .
SIMPLE: *(reappearing):* Yef? . . .
LADY MALPRACTICE: Don't flam the door.
SIMPLE: Forry.

(She exits.)

102

LADY MALPRACTICE: Folemnity! . . .
SIR SOLEMNITY: Fufan! . . .

(*They embrace, then tear downstage to sing:*)

SIR SOLEMNITY: When a man meets a bawd who is willing,
                Who is flighty and flender and flim,
                Then i' faith, you can wager a shilling
                That the flut will be fleeping with him.
LADY MALPRACTICE: When a maid meets a cuckold who's
                eager,
                Who adores her and presses his fuit,
                Her virginity may have been meagre:
                'Tis now, stap my vitals, caput!
SIR SOLEMNITY: He may say many things to incense her,
                Make improper suggestions all day—
LADY MALPRACTICE: But you get all the lines past the censor
                Because it's a classical play.
BOTH: *Sing la! for the trollop*
        Who likes a good dollop
        Of Congreve and similar chaps!
        Sing folderol-dirral!
        For Madge and for Cyril
        When romping around in *Relapse!*

(*She goes upstage.*)

SIR SOLEMNITY: (*Aside*) And now—to feduce her!
        (*He joins her.*)
        Fufan—
LADY MALPRACTICE: Not fo fast! Fomeone might fee.
SIR SOLEMNITY: 'Tis perfectly fafe.
LADY MALPRACTICE: Then pray be feated.
SIR SOLEMNITY: (*sitting*): I come to your clofet as a humble
        fuitor.
LADY MALPRACTICE: I beg your pardon?

SIR SOLEMNITY: A fuitor. Fomeone who fain would folace you.

LADY MALPRACTICE: Folace me? Fie, are you fuggesting—?

SIR SOLEMNITY: Come, don't be filly—fubmit! . . .

LADY MALPRACTICE: Oh, this is fo fudden! My falts! . . . my falts! . . .

SIR SOLEMNITY: I know all about them.

LADY MALPRACTICE: No, no.
(*She points to some smelling salts.*)
My *falts*! . . .

SIR SOLEMNITY: (*Handing them to her.*) Oh. Forry.

LADY MALPRACTICE: Oh, I feel fick.

SIR SOLEMNITY: My Lady should fee a furgeon.

LADY MALPRACTICE: Nay, fir—'tis not a fickness that can be cured by a furgeon. By my troth, 'tis not my body that is fick. 'Tis my foul. Fick and fad with forrow.
(*She sees him bringing out a snuff-box.*) What's that?

SIR SOLEMNITY: Fnuff. (*Aside*) If I can but lure the bawd to yonder inner fanctum, i' faith, I shall make her mine more quickly than an apothecary mixes a potion for the gall-bladder—powder my periwig! . . .

LADY MALPRACTICE: (*Aside*) Ods my life, 'tis a ferious fituation to be faddled with a coxcomb with one eye on a maiden's virtue and the other on her purfe-strings—bedizen my bloomers! . . .

SIR SOLEMNITY: (*Aside*) Marry, if I could but fample her kiffes I warrant I should belch with content—freeze my assets! . . .

LADY MALPRACTICE: (*Aside*) I' faith, I would as soon to bed with the philanderer as take coach to Colchester for the cock-fighting—rot my ratafia! . . .

(*After these four asides, they turn to face each other again on the sofa and shake hands solemnly.*)

LADY MALPRACTICE: How d'you do?

SIR SOLEMNITY: How d'you do?

(*There is a knock off.*)

LADY MALPRACTICE: Lift! . . .
SIR SOLEMNITY: Lift what?
LADY MALPRACTICE: No, no. Methought I heard a found.

(SIR MILITANT MALPRACTICE *is heard off.*)

SIR MILITANT: Fufan! . . .
LADY MALPRACTICE: My hufband! He must not fee us!
   Quick—fecrete yourfelf!
SIR SOLEMNITY: In the fitting-room?
LADY MALPRACTICE: No, no—behind the fettee! . . .

(*But it is too late,* SIR MILITANT *enters.*)

SIR MILITANT: Fo! . . . thif if a forry fight I fee! . . .
LADY MALPRACTICE: Oh, that I should fuffer so! . . .
SIR MILITANT: Out of my houfe, you finful flut! . . .

(SIMPLE *makes a dramatic entrance.*)

SIMPLE: Ftop! . . .I have fomething to fay. 'Twas not Lady
   Fufan that Fir Folemnity came to fee. 'Twas I—
   Fimple! . . .
SIR SOLEMNITY: Fimple! . . .
SIMPLE: Folemnity! . . .

(SIMPLE *and* SOLEMNITY *embrace.*)

SIR MILITANT: Fufan! . . .
LADY MALPRACTICE: Fefil—damn! *Cecil!* . . .

(SIR MILITANT *and* LADY MALPRACTICE *embrace.*)

LADY MALPRACTICE: (*Coming down to address audience*)
> Fo ends our flight and flender faga, and—thank God!—
> Fo alfo ends my hufband's foul fufpicions—filly
> fod! . . .

(*The* QUARTET *takes positions for the final song and dance*:)

ALL: Virtue's a vessel that easily cracks:
> La! for a lecherous life!
> Lust is a fatal diceace which attacks
> Husband and mistress and wife!
> Passion can pierce through virginity's crust:
> La! for a life that is gaudy!
> Plays you might think would be drier than dust
> Run for a year if they're bawdy!
> Fol-de-rol-lol-de-rol-lol-de-lol-lay!
> La! for the Restoration Play!
> Fol-de-rol-lol-de-rol-lol-de-lol-lay!
> With plenty of smut
> And not a line cut
> And no Entertainment Tax to pay!

(*They curtsey and bow to each other. Black out.*)

ALAN MELVILLE

JAMES M. CONNELL
1852–1929

THE BLUE FLAG

The Tories' flag is deepest blue,
Blue blood has stained it through and through.
But Tories now aren't chinless fools,

They're sharp young men from grammar schools.
So let us have a new flag that's
Appropriate for technocrats.
Let's sing and dance down Brighton Pier
And fly the skull and crossbones here.

CHRIS MILLER

JOSEPH CONRAD
(1857–1924)

THE FEAST

The hut in which slept the white man was on a clearing between the forest and the river. Silence, the silence murmurous and unquiet of a tropical night, brooded over the hut that, baked through by the sun, sweated a vapour beneath the cynical light of the stars. Mahamo lay rigid and watchful at the hut's mouth. In his upturned eyes, and along the polished surface of his lean body black and immobile, the stars were reflected, creating an illusion of themselves who are illusions.

The roofs of the congested trees, writhing in some kind of agony private and eternal, made tenebrous and shifty silhouettes against the sky, like shapes cut out of black paper by a maniac who pushes them with his thumb this way and that, irritably, on a concave surface of blue steel. Resin oozed unseen from the upper branches to the trunks swathed in creepers that clutched and interlocked with tendrils venomous, frantic and faint. Down below, by force of habit, the lush herbage went through the farce of growth—that farce old and screaming, whose trite end is decomposition.

Within the hut the form of the white man, corpulent and pale, was covered with a mosquito-net that was itself illusory like everything else, only more so. Flying squadrons of mosquitoes inside its meshes flickered and darted over him, working hard, but keeping silence so as not to excite him from sleep. Cohorts of yellow ants disputed him against cohorts of purple ants, the two kinds slaying one another in thousands. The battle was undecided when suddenly, with no such warning as it gives in some parts of the world, the sun blazed up over the horizon, turning night into day, and the insects vanished back into their camps.

The white man ground his knuckles into the corners of his eyes, emitting that snore final and querulous of a middle-aged man awakened rudely. With a gesture brusque but flaccid he plucked aside the net and peered around. The bales of cotton cloth, the beads, the brass wire, the bottles of rum, had not been spirited away in the night. So far so good. The faithful servant of his employers was now at liberty to care for his own interests. He regarded himself, passing his hands over his skin.

"Hi! Mahamo!" he shouted. "I've been eaten up!"

The islander, with one sinuous motion, sprang from the ground, through the mouth of the hut. Then, after a glance, he threw high his hands in thanks to such good and evil spirits as had charge of his concerns. In a tone half of reproach, half of apology, he murmured—

"You white men sometimes say strange things that deceive the heart."

"Reach me that ammonia bottle, d'you hear?" answered the white man. "This is a pretty place you've brought me to!" He took a draught. "Christmas Day, too! Of all the—But I suppose it seems all right to you, you funny blackamoor, to be here on Christmas Day?"

"We are here on the day appointed, Mr Williams. It is a feast-day of your people?"

Mr Williams had lain back, with closed eyes, on his mat. Nostalgia was doing duty to him for imagination. He was wafted to a bedroom in Marylebone, where in honour of the Day he lay late dozing, with great contentment; outside, a slush of snow in the street, the sound of church-bells; from

108

below a savour of especial cookery. "Yes," he said, "it's a feast-day of my people."

"Of mine also," said the islander humbly.

"It is though? But they'll do business first?"

"They must first do that."

"And they'll bring their ivory with them?"

"Every man will bring ivory," answered the islander, with a smile gleaming and wide.

"How soon'll they be here?"

"Has not the sun risen? They are on their way."

"Well, I hope they'll hurry. The sooner we're off this cursed island of yours the better. Take all those things out," Mr Williams added, pointing to the merchandise, "and arrange them—neatly, mind you!"

In certain circumstances it is right that a man be humoured in trifles. Mahamo, having borne out the merchandise, arranged it very neatly.

While Mr Williams made his toilet, the sun and the forest, careless of the doings of white and black men alike, waged their warfare implacable and daily. The forest from its inmost depths sent forth perpetually its legions of shadows that fell dead in the instant of exposure to the enemy whose rays heroic and absurd its outposts annihilated. There came from those inilluminable depths the equable rumour of myriads of winged things and crawling things newly roused to the task of killing and being killed. Thence detached itself, little by little, an insidious sound of a drum beaten. This sound drew more near.

Mr Williams, issuing from the hut, heard it, and stood gaping towards it.

"Is that them?" he asked.

"That is they," the islander murmured, moving away towards the edge of the forest.

Sounds of chanting were a now audible accompaniment to the drum.

"What's that they're singing?" asked Mr Williams.

"They sing of their business," said Mahamo.

"Oh!" Mr Williams was slightly shocked. "I'd have thought they'd be singing of their feast."

"It is of their feast they sing."

It has been stated that Mr Williams was not imaginative. But a few years of life in climates alien and intemperate had disordered his nerves. There was that in the rhythms of the hymn which made bristle his flesh.

Suddenly, when they were very near, the voices ceased, leaving a legacy of silence more sinister than themselves. And now the black spaces between the trees were relieved by bits of white that were the eyeballs and teeth of Mahamo's brethren.

"It was of their feast, it was of you, they sang," said Mahamo.

"Look here," cried Mr Williams in his voice of a man not to be trifled with. "Look here, if you've—"

He was silenced by sight of what seemed to be a young sapling sprung up from the ground within a yard of him—a young sapling tremulous, with a root of steel. Then a thread-like shadow skimmed the air, and another spear came impinging the ground within an inch of his feet.

As he turned in his flight he saw the goods so neatly arranged at his orders, and there flashed through him, even in the thick of the spears, the thought that he would be a grave loss to his employers. This—for Mr Williams was, not less than the goods, of a kind easily replaced—was an illusion. It was the last of Mr Williams' illusions.

MAX BEERBOHM

110

NOËL COWARD
1899–1973

THE ARCHERS

DAN: Where have you been lately?

DORIS: To feed the cows.

DAN: Very big, cows.

DORIS: I also fed the chickens.

DAN: Very small, chickens.

DORIS: And you?

DAN: Oh, here and there, you know. Borchester.

DORIS: Did you see the Town Hall by moonlight? They say it's . . . very exciting by moonlight.

DAN: Rather disappointing, I found.

DORIS: I'm sorry.

DAN: It's hardly your fault. Or is it? All those fake beams.

DORIS: Horrid.

DAN: Very.

DORIS: I suppose you called in at "The Bull"?

DAN: Yes.

DORIS: Very beery, "The Bull".

DAN: Yes. Very beery.

DORIS: Oh, Dan! Where did we go wrong?

MAUD GRACECHURCH

111

LEN DEIGHTON
1929–

FUNERAL UNDER WATER

Dawn spewed over the Thames like a plate of green figs. The river's oily lapping mingled with the cries of the seagulls from the nearby vivisection centre. Somewhere in Piccadilly, a barge hooted.

I turned to Macready, overlord of Britain's worst-kept secret service, who was setting his watch right by a pail of bilge. Drawing his Clamp and Nettlescrew point-two-point, he sent shot after shot smashing into the timepiece and we both caught the unmistakably musty smell of spam fritters.

"Bugged! The filthy Bolshevik hyenas!"

I sensed a note of criticism in his voice.

It was our first case together, and we were just finishing the last bottle in it, when he handed me a record. I looked at it carefully. It was round and black with tiny grooves and a hole in the middle. The label read, "The Royal Family's Greatest Hits", and the last track, an unusual rendering of "Mull of Kintyre" by the Balmoral Corgi Ensemble, contained the coded message that was to send me winging my way across Europe to the beleaguered city of Berlin.

Berlin is a wart on the German belly. I mentioned this to the steward as we came into land and he slewed over to one side trailing smoke. Unpredictable race, the Germans.

The plane was long and thin with bits sticking out of the sides, and I was sorry to leave the cheery glow of its open log fire to step out on to the treacly bitumen of the airport lounge.

The customs officials poured quicklime into my shoes, ran lasers over my evening wear and dropped my cases into the central-heating duct, which distributed them throughout the building. I had come across German efficiency before, however, and was more concerned with my mission. I looked up and down for my contact, located it in my turnup and pressed it back into my eyeball. Then I tried to spot the man I had been sent to meet.

He was clinging to the Arrivals Board wearing a copy of *The Times* and reading a carnation. Our latest recruits are all like that. It's a wonder they still write about us. He slipped me an uncoded message in giant neon which sent me speeding across town in a taxi.

When we arrived I paid the driver and he smashed his fist into my glasses. At first I thought he wanted a tip, then I noticed the hammer and sickle on his cuff links. Lashing out with the poisoned tip of a *New Statesman*, I turned to run, but my corduroy twills exploded about my ankles. The braces had been sawn half through. Oblivion beckoned and I felt myself collapsing like a punctured brick.

At first, when I came to, I could make no sense of my surroundings. Then it all became only too familiar. I was sellotaped to a gas-fuelled effigy of Karl Marx whilst freshly bronzed youths in the tights and sequins of the KGB menaced me with party blowers. The usual situation. As much a part of the modern spy's everyday round as recipes for goulash.

A massive steel door grated open on badly oiled hinges and a well-oiled man entered. He was smoking a Cuban cigar held in an exquisitely carved mouth.

"You are a pawn in a large wheel," he spat. In the steam of his glance I spelt danger. He rubbed it out and pressed the glowing end of his cigar into my nostril. It hissed.

"What do you want me for?" I gritted, and his reply was like the cold steel of an apfelstrudel.

"An ashtray."

Once again, oblivion beckoned.

When I came to, I was eating sausages in one of the famous all-night sausage bars near the Wall. After my recent experiences, those sausages tasted like nectar to me.

I sent them back.

A scented man in open-necked jeans approached. He held out a hand. I inserted a coin and he spoke.

"Quickly, we have no time. Your contact is . . ."

A look of surprise flashed across his face. The kind of surprise you get when you finish a spy story without having understood a word. Slowly, the colour drained out of his denims and he collapsed with a low belch.

Fighting back the cheese sandwich which sprang to my lips, I leapt to his feet. They were cold. They had been standing too long.

I searched the bar for his assailant and then I saw him by the counter.

"Who are you?" I asked, dreading the old familiar answer.

"I am a counter spy."

I felt the joke tear through my hip as I hit him under the arm and let my fingers sink in to his wallet. For the last time oblivion beckoned and this time I recognized him. Oblivion was Macready. In his hand a smoking P45 with my name on it. I was finished without having understood a word.

The Labour Exchange was dark and crowded with lots of ex-spies queueing at the counter.

BARRY BROWN

114

CHARLES DICKENS
1812–70

from THE HAUNTED MAN
A Christmas Story

PART I
THE FIRST PHANTOM

Don't tell me that it wasn't a knocker. I had seen it often enough, and I ought to know. So ought the three o'clock beer, in dirty highlows, swinging himself over the railing, or executing a demoniacal jig upon the doorstep; so ought the butcher, although butchers as a general thing are scornful of such trifles; so ought the postman, to whom knockers of the most extravagant description were merely human weaknesses, that were to be pitied and used. And so ought, for the matter of that, etc., etc., etc.

But then it was *such* a knocker. A wild, extravagant, and utterly incomprehensible knocker. A knocker so mysterious and suspicious that Policeman X 37, first coming upon it, felt inclined to take it instantly in custody, but compromised with his professional instincts by sharply and sternly noting it with an eye that admitted of no nonsense, but confidently expected to detect its secret yet. An ugly knocker; a knocker with a hard, human face, that was a type of the harder human face within. A human face that held between its teeth a brazen rod. So hereafter in the mysterious future should be held, etc., etc.

But if the knocker had a fierce human aspect in the glare of day, you should have seen it at night, when it peered out of the gathering shadows and suggested an ambushed figure; when the light of the street lamps fell upon it, and wrought a play of sinister expression in its hard outlines; when it seemed to wink meaningly at a shrouded figure who, as the night fell darkly, crept up the steps and passed into the mysterious house; when the swinging door disclosed a black passage into which the figure seemed to lose itself and become a part of the mysterious gloom; when the night grew boisterous and the fierce wind made furious charges at the knocker, as if to wrench it off and carry it away in triumph. Such a night as this.

It was a wild and pitiless wind. A wind that had commenced life as a gentle country zephyr, but wandering through manufacturing towns had become demoralized, and reaching the city had plunged into extravagant dissipation and wild excesses. A roisting wind that indulged in Bacchanalian shouts on the street corners, that knocked off the hats from the heads of helpless passengers, and then fulfilled its duties by speeding away, like all young prodigals—to sea.

He sat alone in a gloomy library listening to the wind that roared in the chimney. Around him novels and story-books were strewn thickly; in his lap he held one with its pages freshly cut, and turned the leaves wearily until his eyes rested upon a portrait in its frontispiece. And as the wind howled on more fiercely, and the darkness without fell blacker, a strange and fateful likeness to that portrait appeared above his chair and leaned upon his shoulder. The Haunted Man gazed at the portrait and sighed. The figure gazed at the portrait and sighed too.

"Here again?" said the Haunted Man.

"Here again," it repeated in a low voice.

"Another novel?"

"Another novel."

"The old story?"

"The old story."

"I see a child," said the Haunted Man, gazing from the pages of the book into the fire—"a most unnatural child, a model infant. It is prematurely old and philosophic. It dies in poverty to slow music. It dies surrounded by luxury to slow music. It dies with an accompaniment of golden water and rattling carts to slow music. Previous to its decease it makes a will; it repeats the Lord's Prayer, it kisses the 'boofer lady'. That child—"

"Is mine," said the phantom.

"I see a good woman, undersized. I see several charming women, but they are all undersized. They are more or less imbecile and idiotic, but always fascinating and undersized. They wear coquettish caps and aprons. I observe that feminine virtue is invariably below the medium height, and that it is always babyish and infantine. These women—"

"Are mine."

"I see a haughty, proud, and wicked lady. She is tall and queenly. I remark that all proud and wicked women are tall and queenly. That woman—"

"Is mine," said the phantom, wringing his hands.

"I see several things continually impending. I observe that whenever an accident, a murder, or death is about to happen, there is something in the furniture, in the locality, in the atmosphere that foreshadows and suggests it years in advance. I cannot say that in real life I have noticed it—the perception of this surprising fact belongs—"

"To me!" said the phantom. The Haunted Man continued, in a despairing tone:

"I see the influence of this in the magazines and daily papers: I see weak imitators rise up and enfeeble the world with senseless formula. I am getting tired of it. It won't do, Charles: it won't do!" and the Haunted Man buried his head in his hands and groaned. The figure looked down upon him sternly: the portrait in the frontispiece frowned as he gazed.

"Wretched man," said the phantom, "and how have these things affected you?"

"Once I laughed and cried, but then I was younger. Now, I would forget them if I could."

"Have then your wish. And take this with you, man whom I renounce. From this day henceforth you shall live with those whom I displace. Without forgetting me, 'twill be your lot to walk through life as if we had not met. But first you shall survey these scenes that henceforth must be yours. At one tonight, prepare to meet the phantom I have raised. Farewell!"

The sound of its voice seemed to fade away with the dying wind, and the Haunted Man was alone. But the firelight flickered gaily, and the light danced on the walls making grotesque figures of the furniture.

"Ha, ha!" said the Haunted Man, rubbing his hands gleefully; "now for a whisky punch and a cigar."

BRET HARTE

from THE DRY PICKWICK

The long day wore its gradual length away as the four Pickwickians were dragged over muddy roads, past mournful fields and leafless woods across the face of what had once been Merry England. Not till the daylight had almost faded did they find themselves, on reaching a turn in the road, in the familiar neighbourhood of the Manor Farm of Dingley Dell.

"There's Wardle," cried Mr Pickwick, waking up to a new alacrity and making sundry attempts at waving signals with an umbrella. "There's Wardle, waiting at the corner of the road."

There, right enough, was the good old gentleman, his stout figure unmistakable, waiting at the corner of the road. Close by was a one-horse cart, evidently designed for the luggage, beside which stood a tall thin boy, whose elongated figure seemed to Mr Pickwick at once extremely strange and singularly familiar.

"You're late," said Mr Wardle in a slightly testy tone. "I've waited at this infernal corner the best part of an hour. What sort of journey did you have?"

"Abominable," said Mr Pickwick.

"Always that way at this infernal time of the year," said Wardle. "Here, Joe, make haste with that luggage. Drive it on in the cart. We'll walk up."

"Joe!" repeated Mr Pickwick with a glance of renewed wonder and partial recognition at the tall thin boy whose long legs seemed to have left his scanty trousers and his inadequate stockings far behind in their growth. "Is that Joe? Why, Joe was—"

"Was the 'Fat Boy'," interrupted Wardle. "Exactly so. But when I had to cut his beer off he began to grow. Look at him!"

"Does he still sleep as much as ever?" asked Mr Tupman.

"Never!" said Mr Wardle.

The cart having set off at a jog-trot for the Manor Farm the five gentlemen, after sundry adjustments of mufflers, gaiters and gloves, disposed themselves to follow.

"And how are you, Wardle?" asked Mr Pickwick as they fell in side by side.

"Not so well," said Mr Wardle.

"Too bad," said Mr Pickwick.

"I find I don't digest as well as I used to."

"Dear me!" said Mr Pickwick, who has passed more than half a century of life without being aware that he digested at all, and without connecting that interesting process with the anatomy of Wardle or of any other of his friends.

"No," continued Wardle, "I find that I have to keep away from starch. Proteins are all right for me, but I find that nitrogenous foods in small quantities are about all that I can take. You don't suffer from inflation at all, do you?"

"Good Lord, no!" said Mr Pickwick. He had no more idea of what inflation was than of the meaning of nitrogenous food. But the idea of itself was enough to make him aghast.

They walked along for some time in silence.

Presently Mr Wardle spoke again. "I think that the lining of my oesophagus must be punctured here and there," he said.

"Good heavens!" exclaimed Mr Pickwick.

"Either that or some sort of irritation in the alimentary canal. Ever have it?"

119

"My dear sir!" said Mr Pickwick.

"It's this damn bootleg stuff," said Mr Wardle.

Mr Pickwick turned as he walked to take a closer look at his old and valued friend, whose whole manner and person seemed, as it were, transformed. He scrutinized closely the legs of Mr Wardle's boots, but was unable to see in those stout habiliments any suggested cause for the obvious alteration of mind and body which his friend had undergone. But when he raised his eyes from Wardle's boots to Wardle's face, he realized that the change was great. The jolly rubicund features had faded to a dull, almost yellow complexion. There were pouches beneath his eyes and heavy lines in the once smooth cheeks.

Musing thus on the obvious and distressing changes in his old friend, Mr Pickwick found himself arriving once more in sight of the Manor Farm, a prospect which even on such a gloomy day filled him with pleasant reminiscences. The house at any rate had not changed. Here was still the same warm red brick, the many gables and the smoking chimneys of that hospitable home. Around and beside it were the clustering evergreens and the tall elm trees which had witnessed the marksmanship of Mr Winkle in the slaughter of rooks. Mr Pickwick breathed a sigh of satisfaction at the familiar and pleasant prospect. Yet even here, in a nearer view, he could not but feel as if something of the charm of past years had vanished. The whole place seemed smaller, the house on a less generous scale, the grounds far more limited, and even the spruce trees fewer and the elms less venerable than at his previous visit.

In fact Dingley Dell seemed somehow oddly shrunken from what it had been. But Mr Pickwick, who contained within himself like all great intellects the attitude of the philosopher, resolutely put aside this feeling, as one always familiar in visits paid to scenes of former happiness.

Here at least as he entered the good old house was the same

120

warm and hearty welcome as of yore. The old lady, Mr Wardle's mother, her deafness entirely laid aside, greeted Mr Pickwick and his younger companions with affectionate recognition: while the charming Emily Wardle and the dashing Arabella Allen appeared in a bevy of pretty girls for the especial welcome and the complete distraction of the susceptible hearts of Messrs Snodgrass and Winkle. Here too, as essential members of the Christmas party, were the two young medical students, those queer combinations of rowdiness and good-humour, Mr Bob Sawyer and Mr Benjamin Allen, the brother of the fair Arabella.

Mr Wardle, also, as he re-entered his home and assumed his duties as host, seemed to recover in great measure his genial good-nature and high spirits.

"Now, then, mother," he exclaimed, "our friends I am sure are thirsty; before they go to their rooms let us see what we can offer them in the way of wine. Joe—where's that boy?—a couple of bottles of the red wine, the third bin in the cellar, and be smart about it." The tall thin boy, whom the very word "wine" seemed to galvanize out of his mournful passivity into something like energy, vanished in the direction of the cellar, while Mr Pickwick and his companions laid aside their outer wraps and felt themselves suddenly invaded with a glow of good-fellowship at the mere prospect of a "drink". Such is the magic anticipation that the Pickwickians already felt their hearts warm and their pulses tingle at the very word.

"Now, then," said the hospitable Wardle, "bustle about, girls—glasses—a corkscrew—that's right—ah, here's Joe. Set it on the sideboard, Joe."

The cork of the first bottle came out with a "pop" that would have done credit to the oldest vintage of the Rhine, and Mr Wardle proceeded to fill the trayful of glasses with the rich red liquid.

"What is it?" asked Mr Pickwick, beaming through his spectacles at the fluid through which the light of the blazing fire upon the hearth reflected an iridescent crimson. "What is it—Madeira?"

"No," said Mr Wardle, "it's a wine that we made here at home."

"Ah," said Mr Pickwick. Volumes could not have said more.

"It's made," continued the hospitable old gentleman, passing round the glasses as he talked, "from cranberries. I don't know whether one would exactly call it a claret—"

"No," said Mr Pickwick, as he sipped the wine—"hardly a claret."

"No," said Wardle, "a little more of a burgundy taste—"

"Yes," said Mr Pickwick, "a little more of a Burgundy taste."

"Drink it," said Mr Wardle.

"I am," said Mr Pickwick, "but I like to sip it rather slowly, to get the full pleasure of it."

"You like it?" said Mr Wardle eagerly.

"It is excellent," said Mr Pickwick.

"Then let me fill up your glass again," said Wardle. "Come along, there's lots more in the cellar. Here. Winkle, Tupman, your glasses."

There was no gainsaying Mr Wardle's manner. It had in it something of a challenge which forbade the Pickwickians from expressing their private thoughts, if they had any, on the merits of Mr Wardle's wine. Even Mr Pickwick himself found the situation difficult. "I think, perhaps," he said as he stood with a second bumper of wine untasted in his hand, "I will carry this up to my room and have the pleasure of drinking it as I dress for dinner." Which no doubt he did, for at any rate the empty glass was found in due course in Mr Pickwick's bedroom. But whether or not certain splashes of red in the snow beneath Mr Pickwick's bedroom window may have been connected with the emptiness of the glass we are not at liberty to say.

STEPHEN LEACOCK

SIR ARTHUR CONAN DOYLE
1859–1930

THE STOLEN CIGAR CASE

I found Hemlock Jones in the old Brook Street lodgings, musing before the fire. With the freedom of an old friend I at once threw myself in my usual familiar attitude at his feet, and gently caressed his boot. I was induced to do this for two reasons: one that it enabled me to get a good look at his bent, concentrated face, and the other that it seemed to indicate my reverence for his superhuman insight. So absorbed was he even then, in tracking some mysterious clue, that he did not seem to notice me. But therein I was wrong—as I always was in my attempts to understand that powerful intellect.

"It is raining," he said, without lifting his head.

"You have been out, then?" I said quickly.

"No. But I see that your umbrella is wet, and that your overcoat has drops of water on it."

I sat aghast at his penetration. After a pause he said carelessly, as if dismissing the subject: "Besides, I hear the rain on the window. Listen."

I listened. I could scarcely credit my ears, but there was the soft pattering of drops on the panes. It was evident there was no deceiving this man!

"Have you been busy lately?" I asked, changing the subject. "What new problem—given up by Scotland Yard as inscrutable—has occupied that gigantic intellect?"

He drew back his foot slightly, and seemed to hesitate ere he returned it to its original position. Then he answered wearily: "Mere trifles—nothing to speak of. The Prince Kupoli has been here to get my advice regarding the disappearance of certain rubies from the Kremlin; the Rajah of Pootibad, after vainly beheading his entire bodyguard, has been obliged to seek my assistance to recover a jewelled sword. The Grand Duchess of Pretzel-Brauntswig is desirous of discovering where her husband was on the night of February 14; and, last night"—he lowered his voice slightly—"a lodger in this very house, meeting me on the stairs, wanted to know why they didn't answer his bell."

I could not help smiling—until I saw a frown gathering on his inscrutable forehead.

"Pray remember," he said coldly, "that it was through such an apparently trivial question that I found out Why Paul Ferroll Killed His Wife, and What Happened to Jones!"

I became dumb at once. He paused for a moment, and then, suddenly changing back to his usual pitiless, analytical style, he said: "When I say these are trifles, they are so in comparison to an affair that is now before me. A crime has been committed and, singularly enough, against myself. You start," he said; "you wonder who would have dared to attempt it. So did I; nevertheless, it has been done. *I* have been *robbed!*"

"*You* robbed! You, Hemlock Jones, the Terror of Peculators!" I gasped in amazement, arising and gripping the table as I faced him.

"Yes! Listen. I would confess it to no other. But *you* who have followed my career, who know my methods; you, for whom I have partly lifted the veil that conceals my plans from ordinary humanity; you, who have for years rapturously accepted my confidences, passionately admired my inductions and inferences, placed yourself at my beck and call, become my slave, grovelled at my feet, given up your practice except those few unremunerative and rapidly decreasing patients to whom, in moments of abstraction over *my* problems, you have administered strychnine for quinine, and arsenic for Epsom salts; you, who have sacrificed anything and everybody to me—*you* I make my confidant!"

I arose and embraced him warmly, yet he was already so engrossed in thought that at the same moment he mechanically placed his hand upon his watch chain as if to consult the time. "Sit down," he said. "Have a cigar?"

"I have given up cigar smoking," I said.

"Why?" he asked.

I hesitated, and perhaps coloured. I had really given it up because, with my diminished practice, it was too expensive. I could afford only a pipe. "I prefer a pipe," I said laughingly. "But tell me of this robbery. What have you lost?"

He arose and, planting himself before the fire with his hands under his coat-tails, looked down upon me reflectively for a moment. "Do you remember the cigar case presented to me by the Turkish Ambassador for discovering the missing favourite of the Grand Vizier in the fifth chorus girl at the Hilarity Theatre? It was that one. I mean the cigar case. It was encrusted with diamonds."

"And the largest one had been supplanted by paste," I said.

"Ah," he said, with a reflective smile, "you know that?"

"You told me yourself. I remember considering it a proof of your extraordinary perception. But, by Jove, you don't mean to say you have lost it?"

He was silent for a moment. "No—it has been stolen, it is true—but I shall still find it. And by myself alone! In your profession, my dear fellow, when a member is seriously ill, he does not prescribe for himself, but calls in a brother doctor. Therein we differ. I shall take this matter in my own hands."

"And where could you find better?" I said enthusiastically. "I should say the cigar case is as good as recovered already."

"I shall remind you of that again," he said lightly. "And now, to show you my confidence in your judgement, in spite of my determination to pursue this alone, I am willing to listen to any suggestions from you."

He drew a memorandum book from his pocket and, with a grave smile, took up his pencil.

I could scarcely believe my senses. He, the great Hemlock Jones, accepting suggestions from a humble individual like

125

myself! I kissed his hand reverently, and began in a joyous, tone:

"First, I should advertise, offering a reward; I should give the same intimation in hand-bills, distributed at the 'pubs' and the pastry-cooks'. I should next visit the different pawn-brokers; I should give notice at the police station. I should examine the servants. I should thoroughly search the house and my own pockets. I speak relatively," I added, with a laugh. "Of course I mean *your* own."

He gravely made an entry of these details.

"Perhaps," I added, "you have already done this?"

"Perhaps," he returned enigmatically. "Now, my dear friend," he continued, putting the note-book in his pocket and rising, "would you excuse me for a few moments? Make yourself perfectly at home until I return; there may be some things," he added with a sweep of his hand towards his heterogeneously-filled shelves, "that may interest you and while away the time. There are pipes and tobacco in that corner."

Then nodding to me with the same inscrutable face he left the room. I was too well accustomed to his methods to think much of his unceremonious withdrawal, and made no doubt he was off to investigate some clue which had suddenly occurred to his active intelligence.

Left to myself I cast a cursory glance over his shelves. There were a number of small glass jars containing earthy substances labelled, "Pavement and Road Sweepings", from the principal thoroughfares and suburbs of London, with the sub-directions "for identifying foot-tracks". There were several other jars labelled, "Fluff from Omnibus and Road-Car Seats", "Cocoanut Fibre and Rope Strands from Mattings in Public Places", "Cigarette Stumps and Match Ends from Floor of Palace Theatre, Row A, 1 to 50". Everywhere were evidences of his wonderful man's system and perspicacity.

I was thus engaged when I heard the slight creaking of a

door, and I looked up as a stranger entered. He was a rough-looking man with a shabby overcoat and a still more disreputable muffler around his throat and the lower part of his face. Considerably annoyed at his intrusion, I turned upon him rather sharply, when, with a mumbled, growling apology for mistaking the room, he shuffled out again and closed the door. I followed him quickly to the landing and saw that he disappeared down the stairs. With my mind full of the robbery, the incident made a singular impression upon me. I knew my friend's habit of hasty absences from his room in his moments of deep inspiration; it was only too probable that, with his powerful intellect and magnificent perceptive genius concentrated on one subject, he should be careless of his own belongings, and no doubt even forget to take the ordinary precaution of locking up his drawers. I tried one or two and found that I was right—although for some reason I was unable to open one to its fullest extent. The handles were sticky, as if some one had opened them with dirty fingers. Knowing Hemlock's fastidious cleanliness, I resolved to inform him of this circumstance, but I forgot it, alas! until—but I am anticipating my story.

His absence was strangely prolonged. I at last seated myself by the fire, and lulled by warmth and the patter of the rain on the window, I fell asleep. I may have dreamt, for during my sleep I had a vague semi-consciousness as of hands being softly pressed on my pockets—no doubt induced by the story of the robbery. When I came fully to my senses, I found Hemlock Jones sitting on the other side of the hearth, his deeply-concentrated gaze fixed on the fire.

"I found you so comfortably asleep that I could not bear to awaken you," he said with a smile.

I rubbed my eyes. "And what news?" I asked. "How have you succeeded?"

"Better than I expected," he said, "and I think," he added, tapping his note-book, "I owe much to *you*."

Deeply gratified, I awaited more. But in vain. I ought to

have remembered that in his moods Hemlock Jones was reticence itself. I told him simply of the strange intrusion, but he only laughed.

Later, when I arose to go, he looked at me playfully. "If you were a married man," he said, "I would advise you not to go home until you had brushed your sleeve. There are a few short, brown sealskin hairs on the inner side of your forearm—just where they would have adhered if your arm had encircled a sealskin coat with some pressure!"

"For once you are at fault," I said triumphantly; "the hair is my own, as you will perceive; I have just had it cut at the hairdresser's, and no doubt this arm projected beyond the apron."

He frowned slightly, yet, nevertheless, on my turning to go he embraced me warmly—a rare exhibition in that man of ice. He even helped me on with my overcoat, and pulled out and smoothed down the flaps of my pockets. He was particular, too, in fitting my arm in my overcoat sleeve, shaking the sleeve down from the armhole to the cuff with his deft fingers. "Come again soon!" he said, clapping me on the back.

"At any and all times," I said enthusiastically; "I only ask ten minutes twice a day to eat a crust at my office, and four hours' sleep at night—and the rest of my time is devoted to you always—as you know."

"It is indeed," he said with his impenetrable smile.

Nevertheless, I did not find him at home when I next called. One afternoon, when nearing my own home, I met him in one of his favourite disguises—a long blue swallow-tailed coat, striped cotton trousers, large turnover collar, blacked face and white hat, carrying a tambourine. Of course to others the disguise was perfect, although it was known to myself, and I passed him—according to an old understanding between us—without the slightest recognition, trusting to a later explanation. At another time, as I was making a professional visit to the wife of a publican at the East End, I saw him, in the disguise of a broken-down artisan, looking into the window of an adjacent pawnshop. I was delighted to see that he was evidently following my suggestions, and in my joy I ventured to tip him a wink; it was abstractedly returned.

Two days later I received a note appointing a meeting at his lodgings that night. That meeting, alas! was the one memorable occurrence of my life, and the last meeting I ever had with Hemlock Jones! I will try to set it down calmly, though my pulses still throb with the recollection of it.

I found him standing before the fire, with that look upon his face which I had seen only once or twice in our acquaintance—a look which I may call an absolute concentration of inductive and deductive ratiocination—from which all that was human, tender, or sympathetic was absolutely discharged. He was simply an icy, algebraic symbol! Indeed his whole being was concentrated to that extent that his clothes fitted loosely, and his head was absolutely so much reduced in size by his mental compression that his hat tipped back from his forehead and literally hung on his massive ears.

After I had entered he locked the doors, fastened the windows, and even placed a chair before the chimney. As I watched these significant precautions with absorbing interest, he suddenly drew a revolver and, presenting it to my temple, said in low, icy tones:

"Hand over that cigar case!"

Even in my bewilderment my reply was truthful, spontaneous and involuntary. "I haven't got it," I said.

He smiled bitterly, and threw down his revolver. "I expected that reply! Then let me now confront you with something more awful, more deadly, more relentless and convincing than that mere lethal weapon—the damning, inductive and deductive proofs of your guilt!" He drew from his pocket a roll of paper and a note-book.

"But surely," I gasped, "you are joking! You could not for a moment believe—"

"Silence! Sit down!" I obeyed.

"You have condemned yourself," he went on pitilessly. "Condemned yourself on my processes—processes familiar to you, applauded by you, accepted by you for years! We will go back to the time when you first saw the cigar case. Your expressions," he said, in cold, deliberate tones, consulting his paper, "were, 'How beautiful! I wish it were mine.' This was your first step in crime—and my first indication. From 'I *wish* it were mine' to 'I *will* have it mine,' and the mere detail, '*How can* I make it mine,' the advance was obvious. Silence! But, as in my methods it was necessary that there should be an overwhelming inducement to the crime, that unholy admiration of yours for the mere trinket itself was not enough. You are a smoker of cigars."

"But," I burst out passionately, "I told you I had given up smoking cigars."

"Fool!" he said coldly, "that is the *second* time you have committed yourself. Of course you told me! What more natural than for you to blazon forth that prepared and unsolicited statement to *prevent* accusation. Yet, as I said before, even that wretched attempt to cover up your tracks was not enough. I still had to find that overwhelming, impelling motive necessary to affect a man like you. That motive I found in the strongest of all impulses—Love, I suppose you would call it," he added bitterly—"that night you called! You had brought the most conclusive proofs of it on your sleeve."

"But—," I almost screamed.

"Silence!" he thundered. "I know what you would say. You would say that even if you had embraced some Young Person in a sealskin coat, what had that to do with the robbery? Let me tell you, then, that that sealskin coat represented the quality and character of your fatal entanglement! You bartered your honour for it—that stolen cigar case was the purchaser of the sealskin coat!

"Silence! Having thoroughly established your motive, I

130

now proceed to the commission of the crime itself. Ordinary people would have begun with that—with an attempt to discover the whereabouts of the missing object. These are not *my* methods."

So overpowering was his penetration that, although I knew myself innocent, I licked my lips with avidity to hear the further details of this lucid exposition of my crime.

"You committed that theft the night I showed you the cigar case and after I had carelessly thrown it in that drawer. You were sitting in that chair and I had arisen to take something from that shelf. In that instant you secured your booty without rising. Silence! Do you remember when I helped you on with your overcoat the other night? I was particular about fitting your arm in. While doing so I measured your arm with a spring tape measure, from the shoulder to the cuff. A later visit to your tailor confirmed that measurement. It proved to be the *exact distance between your chair and that drawer!*"

I sat stunned.

"The rest are mere corroborative details! You were again tampering with the drawer when I discovered you doing so! Do not start! The stranger that blundered into the room with a muffler on—was myself? More, I had placed a little soap on the drawer handles when I purposely left you alone. The soap was on your hands when I shook it at parting. I softly felt your pockets, when you were asleep, for further develop-ments. I embraced you when you left—that I might feel if you had the cigar case or any other articles hidden on your body. This confirmed me in the belief that you had already disposed of it in the manner and for the purpose I have shown you. As I still believed you capable of remorse and confess-ion, I twice allowed you to see I was on your track: once in the garb of an itinerant negro minstrel, and the second time as a workman looking in the window of the pawnshop where you pledged your booty."

"But," I burst out, "if you had asked the pawnbroker, you would have seen how unjust—"

131

"Fool!" he hissed, "that was one of *your* suggestions—to search the pawnshops! Do you suppose I followed any of your suggestions—the suggestions of a thief? On the contrary, they told me what to avoid."

"And I suppose," I said bitterly, "you have not even searched your drawer?"

"No," he said calmly.

I was for the first time really vexed. I went to the nearest drawer and pulled it out sharply. It stuck as it had before, leaving a part of the drawer unopened. By working it, however, I discovered that it was impeded by some obstacle that had slipped to the upper part of the drawer, and held it firmly fast. Inserting my hand, I pulled out the impeding object. It was the missing cigar case! I turned to him with a cry of joy!

But I was appalled by his expression. A look of contempt was now added to his acute, penetrating gaze. "I have been mistaken," he said slowly; "I had not allowed for your weakness and cowardice! I thought too highly of you even in your guilt. But I see why you tampered with that drawer the other night. By some inexplicable means—possibly another theft—you took the cigar case out of pawn and, like a whipped hound, restored it to me in this feeble, clumsy fashion. You thought to deceive me—Hemlock Jones!—more, you thought to destroy my infallibility. Go! I give you your liberty. I shall not summon the three policemen who wait in the adjoining room—but out of my sight forever!"

As I stood once more dazed and petrified, he took me firmly by the ear and led me into the hall, closing the door behind him. This reopened presently, wide enough to permit him to thrust out my hat, overcoat, umbrella, and overshoes, and then closed against me forever!

I never saw him again. I am bound to say, however, that thereafter my business increased, I recovered much of my old practice, and a few of my patients recovered also. I became rich. I had a brougham and a house in the West End. But I often wondered, pondering on that wonderful man's penetration and insight, if, in some lapse of consciousness, I had not really stolen his cigar case!

BRET HARTE

THE CASE OF THE DANISH PRINCE

ACT I

Baker Street, No. 221b.
Enter SHERLOCK *and* DOCTOR WATSON.
SHERL: Were all the fiery demons in the nether world
    To blow their poisonous smoke into London,
    Compound it with a yellow hue and take
    Away our light, they could not make a fouler day
    Than we have now.
WATS: It's foggy out?
SHERL: It is.
    A wretched, vile and tedious kind of morning,
    And nothing in the post but thanks from Scotland.
    That I did solve the sudden death of Duncan,
    Not to mention Banquo. No doubt by now
    You've written up the case and had it published?
WATS: A little five-act tragedy, with notes
    On some of the more striking details.
SHERL: And blood,
    And fights, deaths, witches, ghosts and all
    The melodrama that you inflict on logic,
    I'll be bound. Once I'd seen the importance
    Of having, not two murderers, but three,
    The rest was simple. Have you read the paper?
WATS: Only the *Morning Post*. King Lear's

133

Still lost. A fascinating trial in Venice.
A case of changed identity in Verona,
And sundry goings on in Windsor. Nothing else.
(*A noise on the stairs.*)

SHERL: But here, unless I'm much mistook, comes one
That needs our aid. A case at last!
(*Enter to them* HAMLET.)

HAM: Which one—

SHERL: Of us is Holmes? 'Tis I. This gentle here
Is Watson, my devoted friend and colleague.

HAM: Good morrow to you both. You do not know me—

SHERL: Apart from knowing that you are a prince,
From Denmark, I would hazard, and a solitary,
That you take snuff, have lately been at sea,
Were frightened by a horse at five and now
Are sitting for your portrait, you are a stranger.

WATS: Good heavens, Holmes!

HAM: Do you have magic powers?

SHERL: Sheer observation. You do wear a crown
And are a prince. You have a Danish accent,
Your shoes have late been knotted by a seaman,
There's snuff upon your ruff, and on your doublet
Some Prussian Blue flicked by a careless painter.
That you do not frequent society
Was clear because you did not knock the door
When entering, and then did leave it standing ope.

WATS: But, Sherlock, what about his childhood fright!

SHERL: Come, come, dear Watson! Lives there yet a man
Who was not frightened by a horse at five?

HAM: All that you say is true, and yet I fear
You cannot guess my problem. To be brief,
My father was the King of Denmark, where
Now reigns his brother, my uncle, Claudius,
With as his wife my mother, the late Queen
And Queen again. Sir, I implore your aid.

SHERL: The grammar's convoluted, but I think

134

I have the picture. I have the answer too.
The wrong man reigns—*you* should have climbed the
                                                   throne.
HAM: No, no, that's Danish law, to instate the brother,
    Not the son. What I seek to know
    Is how my father was so cruelly murdered?
SHERL: Your father murdered? Are you sure of this?
HAM: Quite sure. My father's ghost has told me so.
SHERL: I see. (*Aside*) Quick, Watson, get your gun. This man's
    A raving lunatic. (*To* HAMLET) You have a suspect?
HAM: I fear the foulest of my uncle, Claudius.
SHERL: No evidence?
HAM: Except that he poured poison
    Into the ear of my poor sleeping father.
SHERL: How know'st thou this?
HAM: The ghost did tell me so.
SHERL: Hmm. (*Aside*) A talkative ghost. Would that he were
    Admissible in a court of British justice.
    (*To* HAMLET) This case is not without its points of
                                                   interest.
    Within a day or two, sweet prince, I may well be
    With you in Denmark.
HAM: My thanks! (*Exit.*)
SHERL: Or there again
    I may well not. I've better things to do
    Than listen to the babblings of mad youths.
    (*Enter* CLAUDIUS, *disguised.*)
CLAUD: Have I the honour to address the well-known
                                                   Holmes?
SHERL: You do not. This is my trusty colleague Watson.
WATS: Hello.
CLAUD: Hello. And was that man outside
    Young Hamlet, Prince of Denmark?
SHERL: So he said.
CLAUD: And did he spin you some far-fangled tale
    Of how his uncle has contrived his father's death?

SHERL: That was the drift.

CLAUD: Pay him no heed. He has
    A most ingenious mind, but little sense.

SHERL: Indeed, Your Majesty?

CLAUD: You guessed?

SHERL: Of course.
    You too did leave the door ajar, and wear a crown
    Are there many more like you at home?

CLAUD: Nevertheless I swear there's nothing to it.
    Remember—you come to Elsinore at your peril.
    (*Exit* CLAUDIUS.)

SHERL: Better and better! I think it would not hurt
    To spend a day or two at Elsinore.
    Watson, look up the boats and see which leaves
    Tomorrow morning on the Danish line.

WATS: Right ho.

ACTS II, III, IV AND V

Denmark.
Enter SHERLOCK HOLMES *and* WATSON.

WATS: A draughty castle this, Holmes, where a man
    Could catch his death of cold. I'm glad I brought
    My tartan rug.

SHERL: I thought your kilt looked odd. . . .
    I wouldn't be surprised if Hamlet's father
    Froze to death. But look! What shape is this?
    (*Enter* HAMLET'S FATHER'S GHOST.)

GHOST: For you to be in Denmark is not meet.
    Go now, and get you back to Baker Street.
    (GHOST *vanishes.*)

WATS: I think he's right, Holmes; I do fear that he
    Came from the other world to give us warning!

SHERL: (*With lens*) Then why did he leave prints in this soft
                                                            earth
    Of hunting boots, size ten, one broken heel

And marks of clay upon the instep? Tell me that.
(*Enter* HAMLET.)

HAM: 'Tis good to see you, Mr Holmes, Have you
    Found aught that might reveal the murderer?

SHERL: A clue or two. But tell me, Prince, is there
    A man who served your father at the court
    Of whom I might a few light questions ask?

HAM: Alas, alas, one such there was, but he
    —Polonius, I mean—has just been stabbed i'th'arras.

WATS: Sounds painful. In this a Danish malady?

SHERL: And does he live?

HAM: No, sir, his life has ebbed.

SHERL: Most interesting. And tell me, Hamlet, too,
    If Claudius should die, have you a queen?

HAM: I would have had, in fair Ophelia.

SHERL: You would have had? You mean—

HAM: She's also dead.

WATS: I told you that the castle was unhealthy.

SHERL: I think I start to see some light amid the gloom.
    I'll take a walk and meet back in our room.

A graveyard with diggers.
Enter SHERLOCK HOLMES.

SHERL: Good fellows, may I talk to you and ask
    What is't you do?

1ST DIG: Why, sir, 'tis meet we dig, though 'tis not meat
    We dig, but bones, of that we make no bones,
    And then into this hole we place the bones,
    Though being bones they are not whole. . . .

SHERL: Here's five bob.

2ND DIG: To answer questions?

SHERL: No, to stop thy puns.
    Here's five bob more to answer questions with.
    Now, tell me straight, is business good or bad?

1ST DIG: Not bad, not good. Not good for us, but good
    For those that stay alive. 'Tis many a year

Since we did have good digging, people live so long.

SHERL: Except for Hamlet's father.

2ND DIG: A one-off job.
   Since then, nothing. Still, it may pick up.
   Ours is a dying business—

SHERL: I said, no puns!

1ST DIG: We're sorry, guv. That's one of our favourite ones.

In Elsinore Castle.
Enter SHERLOCK HOLMES *and* WATSON.

SHERL: You know my methods, Watson; when in doubt
   Eliminate th'improbable—what is left
   Must be the truth howe'er unlike it seems.

WATS: So you have always said, but still I am
   In some uncertainty over the murderer's name.
   Who was it?

SHERL: I'll tell you presently.
   But first I expect some news. This may be it.
   (*Enter to them* FORTINBRAS.)

FORT: Alack! What a dreadful day! The heavens themselves
   Could no more cease from weeping than the sea—

SHERL: Come, pull yourself together. I have not time
   To listen to long speeches. What's your news?

FORT: Hamlet is dead!

SHERL: I thought as much. Go on.

FORT: And Claudius! Laertes! Also Gertrude!

SHERL: The whole bang shoot, in fact. That's life.
   Or, as my digger friend would say, that's death.

WATS: You have an Australian friend?

SHERL: Sometimes, Watson,
   I wonder if I'm really in detection.
   Or the better half of an awful music hall act.

FORT: O heavens, weep!—

WATS: He's off again.

SHERL: You asked
   Just now what was the murderer's name.

I told you. Eliminate all else
And what is left. . . .
WATS: You mean, it's Fortinbras?
SHERL: No, no, he's just the man who brings the news.
   The gravediggers. Their trade was bad and threatened by
   Redundancy, so they conceived a plot.
   To slay the highest in the land and profit
   By their piecework. Only one mistake they made,
   To imitate the ghost and wear their boots the while.
   I wrote a monograph on soles you may have read.
WATS: May God have mercy.
SHERL: Mercy on what?
WATS: Their soles.
SHERL: That settles it—let's leave this cursed place
   Where none do ope their mouths but they do utter puns.
   Besides, I have a telegram from Lestrade in the Yard,
   Begging for my help in some new case.
WATS: What says he now?
SHERL: "Othello's wife is dead.
   We found her lying lifeless on her bed."
WATS: No sooner is one case accounted for,
   Than we go chasing after—
SHERL: Don't say it!
WATS: —some Moor.
   (SHERLOCK HOLMES *knocks* WATSON *to the ground.*
   Exeunt omnes.
   Curtain)

MILES KINGTON

LAWRENCE DURRELL
1912–

VOLUPTIA

In my mind, I was thinking. Alexandria, Queen of Cities, gathered round me as if it were a violet dusk. Mauve clouds like sheered seaweed filtered across the sky. Somewhere, over boxes of nougat, ambassadors wrangled. I scratched a love-bite on my shoulder and gazed down at my pallid body, clad in its tartan underdrawers, stretched out before me, a long, sad groan of fate. O, how lonely I felt. I called Ali, in my best Greek, to bring me a nectarine of Scythian *krash*. I was so subtracted I forgot he was deaf, and probably knew no Greek anyway. But he KNEW, even as I held up a finger which hung in the velvet air like a tendril of verbena.

Then Voluptia was there. She laid a hand over my ears, and whispered softly. I could not hear her. I gazed upon her dank lips, rubbed with old kisses, those obfuscating osculations suspended there, recalled on the instant she reappeared. That her words were endearments of love (L-O-V-E) I was sure. Then, with a brisk chattering snatch of laughter, she sat: as delicately as a mushroom on the green sward.

"Darley!" she whispered.

"Voluptia!" I murmured.

"Darley!" she said.

Then I noticed she had lost her nose! I stared spellbound at the hole like a fox's hide which lay gaping between her eyes. A long moment wound itself away; I knew she would tell me. "I've had a tiresome day," she began. Ali came in with my *krash*, and I signalled one for her in my second-best Greek. "First," she whispered, "let us drink to . . .love!" "Life!" I said.

She arranged herself into a pattern of Byzantine order, her clothes fighting for their colour with the grass. "I lost an ear

140

this morning," she uttered at last. "Hamid cut it off in pique. Then the left eye Memlik dashed out at lunchtime, because I wouldn't take him on Mountolive's spider-shoot." But it was still the nose that took me by surprise. I looked at her, trying to fathom the labyrinths of her silence. What can I give you, I cogitated with myself, but sympathy? (As Pursewarden—the devil—wrote: TO ALL WHO SUFFER SHALL COME . . .SUFFER-ING.)

The heat popped and eddied in my eardrum; I watched lazily as a bead of sweat formed on the skin of my baggy, shapeless hand. "Let us make love," I outspake at last, "even on a punt, even on Mareotis, which by now must be the colour of gunmetal, the texture of boiled offal. Now!" I feared that she would feel unwanted.

"No," she responded, vivid in grass, "I must tell you the story, and without obfuscation. There are three versions so far, as many as there are persons, and there might be more if we wait. If we have time to wait. You see, it is so cruel, not really knowing WHY!"

"Yes," I muttered. My heart was drenched in brilliants of violet love. But before she could even begin her first explanation, there was the sound of footfalls, many footfalls. Scobie dashed in on us, his glass lips blubbering. Behind, the soft-footed Ali beat out his lighter yet fundamentally arrogant note. He stood protective as Scobie, disagreeably abnormal, spoke in a tottering voice.

"Sorry, Darley," he said, avoiding looking directly at the nipples on my chest, "but I've got to cart Voluptia off to chokey. She's been interfering down in the circumcision booths. There've been complaints."

Voluptia, to give her credit, resisted.

"YA SCOBIE," I yelled, "are you sure you're not under the influence?" After a moment he nodded, closing his eyes. Then musingly he *loquitur*: "Sometimes the mind strays further than life allows. It is easy to excuse, but one's duty is in the end to judge. Alas, our pitiless city demands. . . ."

141

Voluptia rose. I glanced at her warningly. There was a terrible mêlée. I became another person, utterly different from the person I'm usually talking to. In the frantic struggle, Scobie sweated, and Voluptia had her foot pinned to the floor by a Bimbashi's dagger. I was aghast!

Then she had all her clothes pulled off. UNDERNEATH SHE WAS DRESSED AS A MAN! "Voluptia!" Scobie cried out, his voice stark, nude. "She eschews definition," he finally said. Voluptia, wax pale, moaned on the note of a distant sirocco. Then she broke from Scobie's grip and her lips touched my ankle. She murmured, brokenly, half a dozen lines from Cavafy, their spirit untranslatable. Scobie watched and uttered: "Sex speaks rapidly between unbridgeable cultures." Then Scobie took her, not as a lawgiver takes a lawbreaker but as a dragoman leads a spirited horse. "Allah be praised!" said Ali by dumb-sign as he left with his prisoner. Prisoner! (As Pursewarden writes: we are all prisoners.) I heard her go, soft-footed to the last.

"Another Scythian *krash*," I signalled, my head askew on my shoulders. Mareotis grinned back at me under the puce moon. I felt almost sick. Alexandria! Her voice came again from below, swept up on the hot airs of the city. "*Chéri!*" she cried, and I could sense the vibration of those firm slashing breasts, "We must all go back."

Sweaty, my tartan undershorts clung coldly to my alabaster thighs. Again I was lonely. I wanted to press someone's elbow, but there was only Ali; and after some thought I simply pressed my own. Outside smugglers drove past in old cars; somewhere, over boxes of nougat, ambassadors still wrangled. A smell of decay, the smell that goes indeed with perfection, came up from the city. Excited, my nostrils quivered. For then it came to me, throbbingly out of the desert, over Mareotis, over minaret and palm, through the circumcision booths, through the pierced cheeks of the demon dancers, straight as a glinting arrow through the musk and maze of what we think of as reality. As Pursewarden said:

Love is a four-letter word! In a feeling of exultation, I rubbed my hands together, thankful that, despite the company I mixed with, I still had them to rub.

MALCOLM BRADBURY

T. S. ELIOT
1888–1965

CHARD WHITLOW

Mr Eliot's Sunday Evening Postscript

As we get older we do not get any younger.
Seasons return, and today I am fifty-five,
And this time last year I was fifty-four,
And this time next year I shall be sixty-two.
And I cannot say I should like (to speak for myself)
To see my time over again—if you can call it time:
Fidgeting uneasily under a draughty stair,
Or counting sleepless nights in the crowded tube.

There are certain precautions—though none of them very
    reliable—
Against the blast from bombs and the flying splinter.
But not against the blast from heaven, *vento dei venti*,
The wind within a wind unable to speak for wind;
And the frigid burnings of purgatory will not be touched
By any emollient.
            I think you will find this put,
Better than I could ever hope to express it,
In the words of Kharma: "It is, we believe,
Idle to hope that the simple stirrup pump

143

Will extinguish hell."

                  Oh, listeners,
And you especially who have turned off the wireless,
And sit in Stoke or Basingstoke listening appreciatively to
    the silence,
(Which is also the silence of hell), pray, not for your skins,
    but your souls.

And pray for me also under the draughty stair.
As we get older we do not get any younger.

And pray for Kharma under the holy mountain.

HENRY REED

A LIFE OF T. S. ELIOT

ACKNOWLEDGEMENTS

How can I begin to thank
Professor Pomattox, or Doctor Frack,
The Misses Fischbein, or Monsignor Blum?
Words lose their meaning, and grow slack.

Some typed upon Remingtons in obscure rooms.
Some made suggestions.
Some read the proofs. Some wept. One smiled:
"The world is full of questions."

Mrs Crupper came and went
With tiny jars of liniment.

The finished pages flutter to the floor.
La lune éternue et s'endort.

All this, and so much more,
And so much more.
MICHAEL FRAYN

from THE SWEENIAD

THE VOICE OF SWEENEY

Sunday is the dullest day, treating
Laughter as a profane sound, mixing
Worship and despair, killing
New thought with dead forms.
Weekdays give us hope, tempering
Work with reviving play, promising
A future life within this one.
Thirst overtook us, conjured up by Budweisserbrau
On a neon sign: we counted our dollar bills.
Then out into the night air, into Maloney's Bar,
And drank whisky, and yarned by the hour.
Das Herz ist gestorben,[1] swell dame, echt Bronx.
And when we were out on bail, staying with the Dalai
    Lama,
My uncle, he gave me a ride on a yak,
And I was speechless. He said, Mamie,
Mamie, grasp his ears. And off we went
Beyond Yonkers, then I felt safe.
I drink most of the year and then I have a Vichy.

    Where do we go from here, where do we go,
Out of the broken bottles? Pious sot!
You have no guide or clue for you know only
Puce snakes and violet mastodons, where the brain beats,
And a seltzer is no answer, a vomit no relief.
And the parched tongue no feel of water. Only

145

There is balm in this YMCA
(Claim now the balm inside this YMCA),
And you will see that there is more in life than
Those vigils at the doors of pubs in the morning,
Or bootings from the doors of pubs at closing-time.
I will show you fear in a pile of half-bricks.

> *Wer reitet so spät*
> *Durch Nacht und Wind?*
> *Es ist der Vater mit seinem Kind.*[2]

"You called me 'Baby Doll' a year ago;
You said that I was very nice to know,"
Yet when we came back late from that Wimbledon
    dance-hall,
Your arms limp, your hair awry, you could not
Speak, and I likewise, we were neither
Living nor dead, and we knew nothing.
Gazing blankly before us in the carriage.
"Bank Station! All change! *Heraus! Heraus!*"

  (Cloax is the vilest drink, gouging
Pockets out of your giblets, mixing
Frenzy and remorse, blending
Rot-gut and white-ants.
Jalap has a use, laundering
Colons with refreshing suds, purging
The lower soul with gentle motion.)

  Count Cagliostro,[3] famous impostor,
Often in gaol, nevertheless
Enjoyed a great career, adored by the ladies.
Sold them love and youth elixirs. Said he,
Take this powder, "Lymph of Aphrodite",
("In delay there lies no plenty."[4] See!)
Made with belladonna, that lightens up your eyes,
Enhances your fascinations.
Much more than this, now listen, it gives you power

To peep into the past and future, crystalline bright.
Just a pinch, you witness the fall of ancient Troy.
Another small pinch, a deep breath, before your eyes
The Apocalypse! Just watch *me* taste.
Lo! The Four Horsemen and the Beast, as plain as the stars!
Goodbye, Marquise. If you see her Majesty the Queen,
Tell her I have the Diamond Necklace,[5]
It's hidden in my *cabinet de toilette*.

   Earthly Limbo,
Chilled by the raw mist of a January day,
A crowd flowed down King's Parade, so ghostly,
Mowed down by the centuries, so ghostly.
You barely heard the gibbering and the squeaks
As each man gazed in front with staring eyes,
Flowed past Caius Insurance Offices
To where the clock in Trinity Great Court
Marked off the hours with male and female voice.
There I saw one I knew, and hailed him shouting,
   Muravieff-Amursky!
You who were with me up at Jesus,
And fought in my battalion at Thermopylae!
Your brain-box stopped an arrow, you old cadaver.
Are you Hippolytus,[6] killed by your horses' hoofs,
Revivified by Aesculapius?
"I sometimes think there never blows so red
The Rose as where some buried Caesar bled."[7]
"If Winter comes can Spring be far behind?"[8]

NARRATOR
His words are very indistinct—perhaps it's atmospherics?
He's quoting from the *Daily Telegraph*, and now there's a
   piece that sounds as if it might be Herrick's—
Ah, there he is once more, completely audible again,
Summing up his views, I think, though he seems to be in
   pain!

147

This is the vacant mind,
This is the barren mind,
Empty, bereft of intellect,
Can nothing fill the yawning void?
Is there no voodoo, charm, or pious platitude
To save the world from thought?

. . . . .

But you must believe in *some*thing!
Can't you see it's only alle*gor*ical!
And what would happen to society?

. . . . .

Iudica me, Deus, et discérne causam meam de gente non sancta:
    ab hómine iníquo, et dolóso érue me.[9]
Boomalay, boomalay, boomalay, boom![10]
L'Érèbe les eût pris pour ses coursiers funèbres,[11]

聖人因而興制不事心焉 [12]

[13]

••• ——— ••• [14]

[15]

"Love thy neighbour as thyself,"
"Couldn't you bring better weather with you?" and,
Above all,
"Please adjust your dress before leaving."[16]

. . . . .

Up and down the City Road
In and out the "Eagle",
That's the way the money goes,
Pop, goes the weasel.

. . . . .

Aspérges me Dómine hyssópo, et mundábor; lavábis me et super
    nivem dealbábor.[17]

148

Eeny, meeny, miney mo,
Catch a nigger by his toe,
By his toe,
                Miney mo
                –ney mo
                        o!

This is what the curate said,
This is what the curate said,
This is what the curate said,
   Not with a fart but a simper.

NARRATOR

We thank you, Sir, you are most kind
To read us extracts from your masterpiece, "The Vacant
   Mind",
The poem that revolutionized the poet's point of view
Way back in '22.
Once more you lower your trajectory,
Exploding harmless shells in vicarage and rectory,
And causing piddling thrills in college and refectory.
"What does it mean?" Here's someone says he knows,
But asks our leave to spread himself in prose.

NOTES

[1] Schiller, *Das Mädchens Klage.*

[2] Goethe, *Erlkönig.*

[3] Count Cagliostro (1743–95), Italian alchemist, whose real name
was Giuseppe Balsamo. (See Note 5 below.)

[4] Shakespeare, *Sweet and Twenty.*

[5] The Affair of the Diamond Necklace (1778–86). A mysterious
incident which involved Marie Antoinette. In the sensational trial
which ensued, Cagliostro was acquitted.

Here Cagliostro figures as the Prophet of the Age of Unreason,
which he foretold would begin in earnest in 1922.

[6] Hippolytus, son of Theseus by Hippolyta, Queen of the Amazons. He was falsely suspected of having attempted the dishonour of Theseus' second wife, Phaedra. Poseidon, at the instigation of Theseus, sent forth a bull from the water at which the horses drawing Hippolytus' chariot took fright, overturned the chariot, and dragged Hippolytus along the ground until he was dead. Artemis, however, induced Aesculapius to restore him to life again.

Originally a Vegetation Myth, but here, for the sake of poetical consistency, Aesculapius administers arsenic instead of elixir to Hippolytus.

[7] Fitzgerald, *Omar Khayyám*. "The Rose" = Pernicious Anaemia.

[8] Shelley, *Ode to the West Wind*. For "Winter" read "Spring" and vice versa.

[9] Roman Catholic *Liturgy of the Mass*. Here read in Anglican (or "Pickwickian") sense.

[10] Vachel Lindsay, *The Congo*. Last words of St Mumbo Jumbo.

[11] Baudelaire, *Les Chats*. Euphony only (no relevance).

[12] From *Lü Shih Ch'un Ch'un*. "The Sage follows nature in establishing social order, and does not invent principles out of his own head."

Since this is a rational statement in authentic Chinese it is thought to have slipped in by mistake for a quotation from Mr Pound.

[13] From an ancient Egyptian inscription. Literally, "Thy breath of life is sweet in my nostril."

"Life" here is an occult symbol for death.

[14] The famous Morse signal of distress sent out by the *Titanic* on 14 April 1912. Here it is sent out by the inhabitants of the "Unreal City". No one answers it.

[15] "Hydor", water, short for "Ariston Men Hydor", i.e. "Take more water with it." A message in manual code from Microcephalos, the deaf-and-dumb soothsayer of Thebes, to Tiresias (who was blind anyway) on the morning after a feast. Here it signifies the Seven Types of Ambiguity.

[16] Reproduced by permission of the Westminster City Council.

[17] *Liturgy of the Mass*. See Note 9 above.

"The Vacant Mind" contains allusions and adaptions from thirty-five different writers in twenty languages, including Pali, Sanskrit, Aramaic, Tagálog, Swahili, and Bêche-de-mer.

MYRA BUTTLE

THE WASTED LAND
by T. S. Tambiguiti

April is a very unkind month, I am telling you.
Oh yes. And Summer was surprising us very much,
Coming over the Tottenham Court Road.
What are the roots that grab around you,
What are the branches that grow, actually,
Out of all this? Can't you tell me that?
You know only a heap of images all broken up.
Under the brown fog of a winter dawn,
A crowd was flowing over London Bridge, so many.
So many people there were crossing that bridge
It was looking like Calcutta.
There I was seeing somebody I knew and crying out
Rhanji! Rhanji! You who were with me
In that correspondence course they were giving
About how to repair railway engines
At home. Did you pass? But that was
A long time ago, oh yes, a long time ago.
Oh the moon shone very brightly on Mrs Murray
Who lived in Surrey.
She washed her feet in chicken curry.
Twit twit twit twit
Jug jug jug jug
Moo
It is unreal, this place, I am telling you that
Do you listen to what I am telling you?
Burning burning burning burning burning
The whole bindaloo is burning, Ghita,
While you are talking to that silly Mrs Chatterjee.
These fragments I have shored against my ruins.
Hurry up please, you must be going home now.

Hurry up please, please hurry up.
Good night Rhanji. Good night Satyajit.
Good night Rabindranath. Good night Assistant
District Commissioner Cunningham-Price-Alyston.
Good night. Oh yes. It's goodnight that I am saying.
Good night. Good night. Tambiguiti is mad again.
Good night.
Shantih shantih shantih.
It's only a shantih in old
Shantih town.

EDWARD PYGGE

EDWARD FITZGERALD
1809–83

MARY, MARY

I

"Come," cried the Voice, "it is already Spring"
(Methought the Sentence had an angry Ring),
   "Come and inspect my Garden, if you will,
But cease awhile this idle Questioning!"

II

And straight I answered, sad and overcast,
"Why, then my Occupation would be past;
   If Life be but a Riddle, I will put
Insoluble Conundrums to the last!

III

   "What better Task my Time could occupy
Than solving Horticulture's Mystery—
   From Cultivators of Experience
To learn the How, the Wherefore, and Why?

IV

   "Myself when young would deftly ply the Hoe,
Or plant Potatoes in a stately Row,
   For Information once again I ask—
Oh, how, my Mary, does your Garden grow?

V

"By Day with a painful Diligence I sought
To make my Seedlings flourish as they ought,
   And still by Night the execrable Cat
Would bring my Hardy Annuals to Nought!

VI

   "But, since by Fate's inscrutable Decree
You gain Success that never comes to Me,
   If you will tell me how the Trick is done
Profound indeed my Gratitude will be!"

VII

The angry Voice made answer: "Foolish Man!
Learn that I garden on another Plan;
   Oh, leave your Seedlings and Potato-plots,
And follow my example . . . if you can!

VIII

"From every Bed perpetually swells
The Silvery Music of Melodious Bells,
   While, to enhance the Beauty of the Scene,
The Ground is carpeted with Cockle-shells.

IX

"A simple Strain of Tinkling Harmonies,
A little Ground, whereon the Cockle lies,
   Some pretty Maidens, standing in a Row,
And lo! the Garden is a Paradise!"

ANTHONY C. DEANE

IAN FLEMING
1908–64

BOND STRIKES CAMP

Shadows of fog were tailing him through the windows of his Chelsea flat; the blonde had left a broken rosette of lipstick on the best Givan's pillowcase—he would have to consult last night's book-matches to find out where he had grabbed her. It was one bitch of a morning. And, of course, it turned out to be the day! For there was always one breakfast in the month when a very simple operation, the boiling of an egg so that the yolk should remain properly soft and the white precisely hard, seemed to defeat his devoted housekeeper, May. As he decapitated the fifth abort on its Wedgwood launching-pad he was tempted to crown her with the sixteen-inch pepper mill. Three minutes and fifty-five seconds later by his stopwatch and the sixth egg came up with all systems go. As he was about to press the thin finger of wholemeal toast into the prepared cavity the telephone rang. It was probably the blonde: "Don't tell me: it all comes back—you're the new hat-check from 'The Moment of Truth'," he snarled into the receiver. But the voice which cut in was that of his secretary, Miss Ponsonby. "He wants you now, smart pants, so step on the Pogo."

Swearing pedantically, Bond pulled away from his uneaten egg and hurried from the flat to the wheel of his souped-up Pierce Arrow, a Thirty-one open tourer with two three-piece windscreens. A sulphurous black rain was falling and he nearly took the seat off a Beatnik as he swerved into Milner. It was that kind of a Christmas. Thirteen minutes later his lean body streaked from the tonneau-cover like a conger from its hole and he stood outside M.'s door with Lolita Ponsonby's great spaniel eyes gazing up at him in dog-like devotion.

"Sorry about the crossed line," he told her. "I'll sock you a lunch if they don't need you at Crufts." Then the green lights showed and he entered.

'Sit down, 007.' That was Grade C welcome indicating the gale warning. There had been several lately. But M. did not continue. He surveyed Bond with a cold, glassy stare, cleared his throat and suddenly lowered his eyes. His pipe rested unlit beside the tobacco in the familiar shell-cap. If such a thing had been possible, Bond would have sworn he was embarrassed. When at length he spoke, the voice was dry and impersonal. "There are many things I have asked you to do, Bond; they have not always been pleasant but they have been in the course of duty. Supposing I were to ask you to do something which I have no right to demand and which I can

155

justify only by appealing to principles outside your service obligations. I refer to your patriotism. You are patriotic, Bond?"

"Don't know, sir, I never read the small-print clauses."

"Forgive the question, I'll put it another way. Do you think the end justifies the means?"

"I can attach no significance of any kind to such expressions."

M. seemed to reflect. The mood of crisis deepened.

"Well, we must try again. If there were a particularly arduous task—and I called for a volunteer—who must have certain qualifications—and only one person had those qualifications—and I asked him to volunteer. What would you say?"

"I'd say stop beating about the bush, sir."

"I'm afraid we haven't even started."

"Sir?"

"Do you play chess, Bond?"

"My salary won't run to it."

"But you are familiar with the game?"

"Tolerably." As if aware that he was in the stronger position, Bond was edging towards insolence.

"It has, of course, been thoroughly modernized; all the adventure has been taken out of it; but the opening gambits in which a piece used to be sacrificed for the sake of early development proved unsound and therefore abandoned. But it is so long since they have been tried that many players are unfamiliar with the pitfalls and it is sometimes possible to obtain an advantage by taking a risk. In our profession, if it be a profession, we keep a record of these forgotten traps. Ever heard of Mata Hari?"

"The beautiful spy?" Bond's voice held derision. The school prefect sulking before his housemaster.

"She was very successful. It was a long time ago." M. still sounded meek and deprecating.

"I seem to remember reading the other day that a concealed

microphone had replaced the *femme fatale*."

"Precisely. So there is still a chance for the *femme fatale*."

"I have yet to meet her."

"You will. You are aware there is a Russian military mission visiting this country?"

Bond let that one go into the net.

"They have sent over among others an elderly general. He looks like a general, he may well have been a general, he is certainly a very high echelon in their KGB. Security is his speciality; rocketry, nerve gases, germ warfare—all the usual hobbies." M. paused. "And one rather unusual one."

Bond waited, like an old pike watching the bait came down.

"Yes. He likes to go to night clubs, get drunk, throw his money about and bring people back to his hotel. All rather old-fashioned."

"And not very unusual."

"Ah." M. looked embarrassed again. "I'm just coming to that. We happen to know quite a bit about this chap, General Count Apraxin. His family were pretty well known under the old dispensation though his father was one of the first to join the party; we think he may be a bit of a throw-back. Not politically, of course. He's tough as they come. I needn't tell you Section A make a study of the kind of greens the big shots go in for. Sometimes we know more about what these people are like between the sheets than they do themselves; it's a dirty business. Well, the General is mad about drag."

"Drag, sir?"

M. winced. "I'm sorry about this part, Bond. He's 'so'—'uno di quelli'—'one of those'—a sodomite."

Bond detected a glint of distaste in the cold blue eyes.

"In my young days," M. went on, "fellows like that shot themselves. Now their names are up for every club. Particularly in London. Do you know what sort of a reputation this city has abroad?" Bond waited. "Well, it stinks. These foreigners come here, drop notes of assignation

157

into sentries' top-boots, pin fivers on to guardsmen's bear-skins. The Tins are livid."

"And General Apraxin?" Bond decided to cut short the Wolfenden.

"One of the worst. I told you he likes drag. That's—er—men dressed up as women."

"Well, you tell me he's found the right place. But I don't quite see where we come in."

M. cleared his throat. "There's just a possibility, mind, it's only a possibility, that even a top KGB might be taken off guard—if he found the company congenial—perhaps so congenial that it appealed to some secret wish of his imagination—and if he talked at all (mind you, he is generally absolutely silent), well then anything he said might be of the greatest value—anything—it might be a lead on what he's really here for. You will be drawing a bow at a venture. You will be working in the dark."

"Me, sir?"

M. rapped out the words like a command. "007, I want you to do this thing. I want you to let our people rig you up as a moppet and send you to a special sort of club and I want you to allow yourself to be approached by General Apraxin and sit at his table and if he asks you back to his hotel I want you to accompany him and any suggestion he makes I request you to fall in with to the limit your conscience permits. And may your patriotism be your conscience, as it is mine."

It was a very odd speech for M. Bond studied his fingernails. "And if the pace gets too hot?"

"Then you must pull out—but remember. T. E. Lawrence put up with the final indignity. I knew him well, but knowing even that, I never dared to call him by his Christian name."

Bond reflected. It was clear that M. was deeply concerned. Besides, the General might never turn up. "I'll try anything once, sir."

"Good man." M. seemed to grow visibly younger.

"As long as I'm not expected to shake a powder into his drink and run away with his wallet."

"Oh, I don't think it will come to that. If you don't like the look of things, just plead a headache; he'll be terrified of any publicity. It was all Section A could do to slip him a card for this club."

"What's its name?"

M. pursed his lips. "The Kitchener. In Lower Belgrave Mews. Be there about eleven o'clock and just sit around. We've signed you in as 'Gerda'."

"And my—disguise?"

"We're sending you off to a specialist in that kind of thing—he thinks you want it for some Christmas 'do'. Here's the address."

"One more question, sir. I have no wish to weary you with details of my private life but I can assure you I've never dressed up in 'drag' as you call it since I played Katisha in 'The Mikado' at my prep school. I shan't look right, I shan't move right, I shan't talk right; I shall feel about as convincing arsing about as a night-club hostess as Randolph Churchill."

M. gazed at him blankly and again Bond noticed his expression of weariness, even of repulsion. "Yes, 007, you will do all of those things and I am afraid that is precisely what will get him."

Bond turned angrily but M.'s face was already buried in his signals. This man who had sent so many to their deaths was still alive and now the dedicated bachelor who had never looked at a woman except to estimate her security risk was packing him off with the same cold indifference into a den of slimy creatures. He walked out of the room and was striding past Miss Ponsonby when she stopped him. "No time for that lunch, I'm afraid. You're wanted in Armoury."

The Armoury in the basement held many happy memories for Bond. It represented the first moments of a new adventure, the excitement of being back on a job. There were the revolvers and the Tommy guns, the Smith and Wessons,

159

Colts, lugers, berettas, killer weapons of every class or nationality; blow-pipes, boomerangs, cyanide fountain-pens, Commando daggers and the familiar heap of aqualungs, now more or less standard equipment. He heard the instructor's voice. "Grind yer boot down his skin and crush his instep. Wrench off his testicles with yer free hand and with the fingers held stiffly in the V-sign gouge out his eyes with the other."

He felt a wave of home-sickness. "Ah, Bond, we've got some hardware for you. Check it over and sign the receipt," said the lieutenant of marines.

"Good God, what's this? It looks to me like a child's water-pistol."

"You're so right—and here's the water." He was given a small screw-top ink-bottle full of some transparent liquid. "Don't spill any on your bib and tucker."

"What'll it stop?"

"Anything on two legs if you aim at the eyes."

Bond consulted the address of his next "armourer". It was a studio off Kinnerton Street. The musical cough of the Pierce Arrow was hardly silent when the door was opened by a calm young man who looked him quickly up and down. Bond was wearing one of his many pheasant's-eye alpacas which exaggerated the new vertical line—single-breasted, narrow lapels, ton-up trousers with no turnups, peccary suede shoes. A short over-coat in cavalry twill, a black sting-ray tail of a tie, an unexpected width of shoulder above the tapering waist and the casual arrogance of his comma of dark hair low over the forehead under his little green piglet of a hat completed the picture of mid-century masculinity. The young man seemed unimpressed. "Well, well, how butch can you get? You've left it rather late. But we'll see what we can do."

He turned Bond towards the lighted north window and studied him carefully, then he gave the comma a tweak. 'I like the spit curl, Gerda, we'll build up round that. Now go in there and strip."

160

When he came out in his pants, the barracuda scars dark against the tan, a plain girl was waiting in a nurse's uniform. "Lie down, Gerda, and leave it all to Miss Haslip," said the young man. She stepped forward and began, expertly, to shave his legs and armpits. "First a shave, then the depilatory—I'm afraid, what with the fittings, you'll be here most of the day." It was indeed one bitch of a morning. The only consolation was that the young man (his name was Colin Mount) allowed him to keep the hair on his chest. "After all, nobody wants you *all* sugar."

After the manicure, pedicure and plucking of the eyebrows it was time to start rebuilding. Bond was given a jock-strap to contain his genitals; the fitting of an elaborate chestnut wig so as to allow the comma to escape under it was another slow process. And then the artificial eyelashes. Finally what looked like a box of tennis balls was produced from a drawer. "Ever seen these before?"

"Good God, what *are* they?"

"The very latest in falsies—foam-rubber, with electronic self-erecting nipples—pink for blondes, brown for brunettes. The things they think of! Which will you be? It's an important decision."

"What the hell do I care?"

"On the whole I think you'd better be a brunette. It goes with the eyes. And with your height we want them rather large. Round or pear-shaped?"

"Round, for Christ's sake."

"Sure you're not making a mistake?"

The falsies were attached by a rubber strap, like a brassière, which—in black moiré—was then skilfully fitted over them. "How does that feel? There should be room for a guy to get his hand up under the bra and have a good riffle." Then came the slinky black lace panties and finally the black satin evening skirt with crimson silk blouse suspended low on the shoulder, a blue mink scarf over all and then the sheerest black stockings and black shoes with red stilettos. Bond surveyed

161

himself in the long glass and experienced an unexpected thrill of excitement; there was no doubt he had a damned good figure.

"Well, you're no Coccinelle," said the young man, "but you'll certainly pass. Hip-square! Drag's a lot of fun you'll find. One meets quite a different class of person. Now go and practise walking till you drop. Then get some sleep, and after that, if you're good, we'll make up that pretty face and launch you at the local cinema."

After practising in high heels for a couple of hours, Bond went back to his couch and lay down exhausted. He dreamed he was swimming under water on a stormy day, the waves breaking angrily above him while, harpoon in hand, he followed a great sea-bass with spaniel eyes that seemed to turn and twist and invite him onward down an ever-narrowing, weed-matted gully.

When he awoke it was dark and he fell avidly on the Blue Mountain coffee and club sandwich Miss Haslip had brought him. "Now we'll start on the face—and here's your evening bag." Bond transferred his water-pistol, ink-bottle, Ronson lighter, gun-metal cigarette case and bill-folder and emptied the contents of his wallet; a vintage chart from the Wine and Food Society, an "Advanced Motorists'" certificate, another from the Subaqua Club, a temporary membership card of the Travellers, Paris, the Caccia, Rome, Puerto de Hierro, Madrid, Brook, Meadowbrook, Knickerbocker and Crazy Horse Saloon, Liguanea, Eagle, Somerset (Boston) and Boston (New Orleans), ending up with a reader's pass for the Black Museum. When he had done, Colin emptied the whole lot into a large envelope, which he told Bond to put in the glove compartment, and handed back the water-pistol and key-ring. "Try these instead," and Bond was given a powder-puff, a couple of lipsticks, some Kleenex, a package of cigarettes (Senior Service) with a long cane holder, some costume jewellery and a charm bracelet and a membership card in the name of Miss Gerda Blond for the Kitchener Social

162

Club, Lower Belgrave Mews, S.W.

In a compartment of his evening bag he found a pocket mirror, tortoiseshell comb, enamel compact and a box of eye make-up with a tiny brush. "When you get mad at someone it's a great relief to take this out and spit on it. The harder you spit, the more of a lady you'll seem." Mount showed him how to apply the little brush, the mascara and black eye-shadow. "When you don't know how to answer, just look down for a little—lower those eyelashes, that'll fetch them—and make with the holder. And do be careful in the loo. That's where nearly all the mistakes are made. Now we're off to the pictures."

"What are we going to see?"

"La Dolce Vita."

In the dark cinema Bond noticed a few interested glances in his direction. A man in the next seat put his hand on his knee. Bond knew the drill; a policewoman in Singapore had shown him. You take the hand tenderly in yours and extend his arm across your knee. Then you bring your other hand down hard and break the fellow's arm at the elbow. He had just got it all set up when the lights went on.

"I wanted you to see that picture, it gives you so many approaches," said Colin Mount. "You can try Ekberg—the big child of nature—or one of those sophisticated cats. Now off you go. Better take a taxi, that hearse of yours looks too draughty."

In Lower Belgrave Mews, Bond rang the bell, showed his card and was immediately admitted.

The Kitchener was discreetly decorated in the style of 1914 with a maze of red plush and some old war posters. The familiar, rather forbidding face with pouchy eyes and drooping moustache and the pointing finger, "Your King and country need you," recruited him wherever he looked. There were two upstairs rooms, in one of which people were dancing. The other held a few divans and tables and a little bar. They had once formed a large double drawing-room. On

163

the landing above, the bathrooms were labelled "Turks" and "Virgins".

Bond sat down at a table, ordered "Eggs Omdurman" washed down by a "Sirdar Special". He noticed several couples dancing sedately to the Cobbler's Song from "Chu Chin Chow" on a pick-up. There were posters of Doris Keane in *Romance* and Violet Loraine in *The Bing Boys* and of Miss Teddy Gerrard. The subdued lighting from pink lampshades, the roomy banquette, the liver-flicking welcome of his "Egg Omdurman" and the silken recoil of the "Sirdar Special" made him feel for the first time content with his preposterous mission. Had he not worn the kilt at Fettes? He was in it now, up to the sporran. All at once a woman's low voice interrupted his reverie. "Dance?" He lowered his eyes, as he had been told, and thought furiously. To refuse, in fact to tell her to get the hell out, was his first reaction—but that might arouse suspicion. He had better play along. "Thanks. I'd love to," he managed in a husky contralto and looked up past a mannish red waistcoat and tweed jacket into a pair of faintly mocking brown eyes. It was Lolita! Speechless with disaster, Bond wondered how long it would be before the story was all over the office. If only his disguise could last a couple of rounds. And then he remembered. Was he not 007 and licensed to kill with his water-pistol? He tensed himself and let the sweat dry on his forehead. In a moment he was hobbling on to the dance floor, where it was much darker, to the strains of "Japanese Sandman". His secretary seemed transformed: capably she manoeuvred him into an obscure corner where they rocked up and down as she began to hold him closer, sliding a leg between his and shifting her hand slowly and expertly down his spine. He began to wonder how the jock-strap would hold. Suddenly she drew back a little and looked him in the eyes. "What's your name?"

"Gerda"—he croaked—"Gerda Blond."

"It's your first visit to the Kitch, isn't it?—well, Gerda, I could fall for you in a big way. I bet you could give someone

164

a good butt in the eye with those charleys." She ran a finger gently up a full, firm breast and gave a start when the nipple shot up trigger-happy as a Sensitive Plant. "Gerda, I want to ask you a question." Bond lowered his eyes. "Have you ever slept with a woman?"

"Well, no, not exactly."

"Well, you're going to tonight."

"But I don't even know your name."

"Just call me Robin."

"But I'm not sure that I can tonight."

"Well, I am. And let me tell you; once you've been to bed with me you won't want anyone else. I know what men are like—I work for one. No girl ever wants a man once she's made it with a dike. It's the difference between a bullfight and an egg-and-spoon race."

"But I can't imagine what you see in me."

"Well, you've got a pretty good figure and I like that in-between colour, like a Braque still life, and I adore the wizard tits—and then you're not like the other mice, sort of virginal and stand-offish—and I'm crazy about the spit curl." She gave it a sharp tug.

"That's not a spit curl," pouted Bond. "That's my comma."

"Have it your way. And I like your husky voice and those droopy eyes and right now I'm imagining your little black triangle."

"Oh, belt up, Robin!"

"Come on, Gerda, we're going back to my place."

Miss Ponsonby began to lug him off the dance floor. Immediately, out of the corner of his eye, Bond caught sight of a stout figure in a dinner-jacket at another table, a bald head and fishy stare and a pair of enormous moustaches, even as a thick forefinger shot up like an obscene grub and began to beckon to him. A deep voice rumbled: "Would the two little ladies care to accept a glass of champagne?"

"Certainly not," snapped Miss Ponsonby. "Father would

turn in his vault."

"Thanks a lot. No objection," came Bond's husky contralto. His secretary wheeled round. "Why, you black bitch—you filthy little tart, I suppose you support a basketful of bastards at home all bleating their bloody heads off. Go along and I hope the old Tirpitz gives you a Lulu." She gave Bond a ringing slap across the eyes and burst into tears. As she left she turned to the new arrival. "You watch out with that bint. Mark my words. She'll do you in."

Bond held his smarting cheek. The foreign gentleman patted his arm and pulled him on to the banquette. "What a headstrong young lady—she gave me quite a turn. But here comes our champagne. I have ordered a magnum of Taittinger Blanc de blancs, '52—it never departs from a certain 'tenu'—independent yet perfectly deferential." He had a trace of guttural accent but what impressed Bond most were the magnificent whiskers. He had seen them only once before on a Russian, Marshal Budenny, Stalin's cavalry leader. They gave a raffish Eighth Army-turned-innkeeper look to the big-nosed military man and were perhaps symptomatic of the formidable General's atavism.

Bond collapsed on to the alcove divan and raised the paradisal prickle to his lips, remembering Monsieur Georges, the wine waiter at the Casino Royale who had called his attention to the brand in the first of his annual agonies.

"Perhaps I had better introduce myself," said the General. "I am a Yugoslav travelling salesman here to make certain business contacts and tonight is my evening of relaxation. All day I have been in conference and tomorrow I have to go down early in the morning to Salisbury Plain. Vladimir Mishitch. Just call me Vladimir; the accent is on the second syllable."

Bond noticed that he had not enquired his own name and finally volunteered with downcast eye, "My name is Gerda. I like travelling too but I'm afraid I haven't anything to sell."

"One never knows. 'La plus belle fille du monde, ne peut

166

donner que ce qu'elle a.' " The General stuck his hand into Bond's blouse and ran his fingers through the hair on his chest. "That's a nice rug you've got there, Gerda." Bond lowered his eyes again. "And that—that is pretty too. How do you call it?"

"That's my comma."

"I see. I'm afraid I make more use of the colon. Ha! ha!" Bond did not know whether to seem amused or bored, and said nothing. "Tell me, Gerda—" the General's voice took on a warmer colour. "Have you ever slept with a man?"

"Well no, not exactly."

"I thought not, Gerda—your little girl friend—the *paprikahühn*—she would not allow it, hein?"

"Well, it's something we've all got to do sooner or later."

"And I suggest you do it right now—for when you've been to bed with a real man, a man of age and experience, you won't ever want anyone else. It's like the Salle Privée at the Sporting Club after a tea with your PEN."

He inserted a torpedo-shaped Larranaga such as seldom reaches these shores into an amber holder and poured out the ice-cold champagne until Bond unaccountably found himself sitting on his lap in some disarray, while the General broke into stentorian song:

> How you gonna keep them
> Down on the farm
> After they've seen Paree!

Bond broke away.

"Aren't you going to have a dance with me?"

The General roared with laughter. "I have never learned to dance except our Yugoslav ones and those we dance only with comrades."

"I expect I could pick them up."

"Yes. Like I have picked up you. I will play one to you in my hotel and you will dance like an Ustashi."

"But they were all fascists, weren't they?"

167

The General laughed again. "They danced very well at the end of a rope. Like Homer's handmaidens—with twittering feet."

Bond found the allusion faintly disturbing. "It's too hot, let's go."

The General paid the bill from a bundle of fivers and hurried down the stairs; it was only, Bond noticed, a little after midnight. "We will take a taxi, Gerda, it is less likely to be followed."

"But why should anyone want to follow you, Vladimir?"

"Business is business; don't worry your pretty little head."

The taxi turned off St James's Street and stopped in a cul-de-sac. "But this is not a hotel."

"No, Gerda, furnished service flatlets. Mine is in the basement, so we go down these steps and don't have to face your night porters—so puritanical—and so expensive. Though anyone can see you're not an ordinary lady of the town." He covered a falsie in his large palm and cupped it hard. "Pip—pip."

"Leave me alone. I've got a headache."

"I have just the thing," said the General and paid off the taxi, almost flinging Bond in his tight skirt and high heels down the steps into the area. For the first time he felt a twinge of fear. To the taxi-driver he was one of London's many thousand fly-by-nights off to earn their lolly—yet no one else in the great indifferent city knew his whereabouts nor what manner of man was preparing to have his way with him. At home in Chelsea his black shantung pyjamas would be laid out, the evening papers and the *Book Collector* spread on his night table, and the digestive biscuits and Karlsbad plums, a bottle of San Pellegrino, a jigger of Strathisla. Lately he had taken to spinning himself to sleep with a roulette wheel or some Chopi xylophone music from the Transvaal asbestos mines. . . .

Vladimir opened a Yale and then a mortice-lock and let them into a typical furnished basement flat, a beige sitting-

168

room with a sombre bedroom beyond. The fog was beginning to probe again, like a second day's grilling by Interpol. "Here, swallow this for the headache—and have a glass of whisky—Teachers, Cutty Sark, Old Grandad or do you prefer vodka or slivovitz?"

"Old Grandad—and what about you?"

"Oh, I'll help myself to some vodka." It was a tiny error but a revealing one. But perhaps the General argued that a Yugoslav drank slivovitz enough at home.

Bond put a cigarette in his mouth and just remembered in time to let the General light it. He took the yellow pill which he had been given, palmed it and pretended to swallow it with a grimace. "I hate all these pills and things. I don't believe they're any good AT all."

The General raised his vodka. "To Friendship."

"To Friendship," chorused Gerda, lifting up her Old-Grandad-on-the-rocks. She was thinking fast. The purpose of the pill she hadn't swallowed must have been to make her sleepy but hardly to put her out. She had better play drowsy.

"Let's have another toast," said the General. "Who is your best friend?"

Bond remembered the gambit pawn. "Guy Burgess."

The General guffawed. "I'll tell him. He'll be delighted. He doesn't often get a message from such a pretty girl."

Bond lowered his eyes. "He was my lover."

"One can see that by the way you walk."

Bond felt a mounting wave of fury. He opened his bag, took out his mascara and spat viciously. The General looked on with approval. Bond produced another cigarette. "Here, catch." The General tossed over his lighter. Bond, with the eye-brush in one hand and the pack in the other, brought his legs neatly together as it fell on his lap.

"Where were you at school, Gerda?"

"Westonbirt."

"And so they teach you to catch like a man—what is a woman's lap for? She widens it to catch, not brings her legs

169

together. And when she drowns she floats upward not downward. Remember that. It may come in useful."

Bond felt trapped. "I'm so sleepy," he muttered. "I don't understand."

"Quick, in here." The General pushed him into the bedroom with its electric fire and dingy satin coverlet. "Undress and get into bed and then look under the pillow."

Bond took off his blouse and skirt while the General gallantly turned his back, but kept on his stockings, pants and "bra", then got out his water-pistol and filled it, dropped the pill behind the bed and finally climbed in and felt under the pillow. The first thing he found was a tube of some oily-looking substance, the next was a shoe-horn with a long cane handle, the last was a piece of paper with "No one is the worse for a good beating" printed in heavy capitals. "Ready," he called and lay quietly until the General in a blue quilted vicuna kimono came simpering in. Bond made a kissy noise and as the General climbed on to the bed and advanced his hairy handlebars reached out with the water-pistol and shot him full in the eye.

The General wiped his face with a silk handkerchief. "Temper, temper," he giggled as the liquid ran down his chin. "What a silly toy for a naughty little girl. Who do we think we are, a black mamba?" He picked up the shoe-horn and dealt Bond a vicious cut across the falsies.

"Help, help, murder," screamed Bond and once again as the General drew back his mind began to race furiously. Somewhere along the line he had been double-crossed. But when? He lay back drowsily. "Vladimir—it was only my joke. I'm so sorry. Now let me sleep."

"Soon you shall sleep—but we have all to earn our sleep. Now shall I beat you first or will you beat me?"

"I will beat you, Vladimir, or I shall certainly drop off before my turn comes. Besides I've never beaten anyone before."

"Tell that to Guy Burgess." The General handed over the

170

long shoe-horn and lay down on his stomach. You can kill a man with a short stick, Bond remembered. Get his head forward. Hold the stick in both hands and jab one end up under his Adam's apple. It had all seemed so easy in Armoury. But the General's broad shoulders were in the way. "How dare you speak to me like that." Bond jumped up and ran for the bathroom.

As he hoped, the General lumbered after him. "Come out, you young fool, I can't sit around here all night while you play hard to get. I'll miss my train to Porton."

Porton! The anthrax boys! Bond's nipples stiffened at the name. "I won't come out till I get my little present."

"Fifty pounds—if you'll go the limit."

"I want half now."

The ends of some five-pound notes protruded under the bathroom door. Bond pulled hard but the General, he guessed, must be standing on them on the other side. That meant he was right by the door which opened inward. Bond would have to fling it open, get Vladimir's head forward and ram his throat in one continuous movement. He was in peak training, his opponent would assume him to be half asleep—it could be done. He counted down from five (the nearest he ever got to a prayer), threw open the door and discovered the smiling General with his hands deep in his Kimono pockets and head thrown far back. There was a strong smell of cigar and Floris mouthwash. Still holding the shoe-horn in one hand, Bond lunged forward with the other, got hold of both ends of the handlebars to bring his head down and gave a tremendous tug. There was a screech of rending cardboard and the General gave a yell of pain; a gummy red patch was spreading where the whiskers had been. Bond stared into the cold blue eyes and this time they fell before him.

"I'm sorry, James," said M. "It was the only way I could get you."

171

Bond drew himself up; his eyes flashed fire, his comma glistened, his breasts firmed, the nipples roused and urgent; his long rangy body flared out above his black silk panties, he looked like Judith carving Holofernes. In two seconds of icy concentration he saw everything that had to be done.

"It's been going on so long. I've been through too much. Don't think I haven't fought against it."

Bond cut him short. "I thought fellows like you shot themselves." M. hung his head. "Have you got a gun—sir—?" M. nodded. Bond looked at his watch. "It's a quarter past two. You may employ what means you prefer but if I find out you are still alive by nine o'clock I shall alert every newspaper here, Tass and United Press—Moscow, Washington, Interpol and Scotland Yard, *Izvestia* and the *Kingston Gleaner* with the whole story. If it had been anyone else I might have urged you to leave the country but with modern methods of eliciting information you would be blown in a day."

"You're quite right, James. I've staked all and I've lost. I hope you'll believe me when I say it would have been for the first and last time."

"I believe you, sir."

"And now perhaps you'd better leave me, 007; I shall have one or two reports to make."

Bond flung on his blouse and skirt, worked into his stilettos and snatched up his bag and tippet.

"One last question, James. How did you guess?"

Bond thought of simply confessing that he hadn't guessed, even when the water-pistol had proved a dud. Right down to the Taittinger M.'s arrangements had been perfect. But that might look bad on his file. Then it came back to him. "You spoke of Homer's handmaidens with 'twittering feet' when Ulysses hanged them. That was in Lawrence of Arabia's translation. Robert Graves objected to it. I remembered that you had said Lawrence was your friend. It might have occurred to you that Graves could be mine."

172

M.'s face brightened and the sickening love-light shone once more. "Good lad!"

It made Bond want to spit in his mascara. "Sir." It was the guardsman's simple dismissal. Without a backward glance he let himself out and stamped up the area steps into the fog. In a few hours the finest Secret Service in the world would be without a head: Miss Ponsonby and Miss Moneypenny would lack an employer. All over the world transmitters would go silent, quiet men grip their cyanide or burn their cyphers, double agents look around for a publisher.

And he would go home in his black pyjamas, snoring up an alibi in his big double bed. There could be only one successor, one person only immediately fitted to take up all the threads, one alone who could both administrate and execute, plan and command. M., as he said, had played and lost. Come egg-time 007 Bond (James) would no longer be a mere blunt weapon in the hands of government. "M. est mort! Vive le B.!"

And when all the razzmatazz had subsided, he would put on his glad-rags and mosey round to the old Kitch. . . .

"Taxi!" The cab drew up to him in the dim light of St James's Street. "King's Road, corner of Milner," he rasped.

"Jump up front, lady, and I'll take you for nothing."

Bond jumped.

CYRIL CONNOLLY

OLIVER GOLDSMITH
1730–74

A SONG

When lovely woman, prone to folly,
    Finds that e'en ROWLAND's oils betray;
What charm can soothe her melancholy?
    What art can turn gray hairs away?

The only art gray hairs to cover,
    To hide their tint from every eye,
To win fresh praises from her lover,
    And make him offer—is to dye.

ANON

"WHEN LOVELY WOMAN STOOPS
TO FOLLY"

When lovely woman stoops to folly
The evening can be awfully jolly.

MARY DEMETRIADIS

THOMAS GRAY
(1716–71)

IF GRAY HAD HAD TO WRITE HIS ELEGY IN THE CEMETERY OF SPOON RIVER INSTEAD OF IN THAT OF STOKE POGES

The curfew tolls the knell of parting day,
    The whippoorwill salutes the rising moon,
And wanly glimmer in her gentle ray,
    The sinuous windings of the turbid Spoon.

Here where the flattering and mendacious swarm
    Of lying epitaphs their secrets keep,
At last incapable of further harm
    The lewd forefathers of the village sleep.

The earliest drug of half-awakened morn,
    Cocaine or hashish, strychnine, poppy-seeds
Or fiery produce of fermented corn
    No more shall start them on the day's misdeeds.

For them no more the whetstone's cheerful noise,
    No more the sun upon his daily course
Shall watch them savouring the genial joys,
    Of murder, bigamy, arson and divorce.

Here they all lie; and, as the hour is late,
    O stranger, o'er their tombstones cease to stoop,
But bow thine ear to me and contemplate
    The unexpurgated annals of the group.

There are two hundred only: yet of these
   Some thirty died of drowning in the river,
Sixteen went mad, ten others had DT's.
   And twenty-eight cirrhosis of the liver.

Several by absent-minded friends were shot,
   Still more blew out their own exhausted brains,
One died of a mysterious inward rot,
   Three fell off roofs, and five were hit by trains.

One was harpooned, one gored by a bull-moose,
   Four on the Fourth fell victims to lock-jaw,
Ten in electric chair or hempen noose
   Suffered the last exaction of the law.

Stranger, you quail, and seem inclined to run;
   But, timid stranger, do not be unnerved;
I can assure you that there was not one
   Who got a tithe of what he had deserved.

Full many a vice is born to thrive unseen,
   Full many a crime the world does not discuss,
Full many a pervert lives to reach a green
Replete old age, and so it was with us.

Here lies a parson who would often make
   Clandestine rendezvous with Claflin's Moll,
And 'neath the druggist's counter creep to take
   A sip of surreptitious alcohol.

And here a doctor, who had seven wives,
   And, fearing this *ménage* might seem grotesque,
Persuaded six of them to spend their lives
   Locked in a drawer of his private desk.

And others here there sleep who, given scope,
    Had writ their names large on the Scrolls of Crime,
Men who, with half a chance, might haply cope,
    With the first miscreants of recorded time.

Doubtless in this neglected spot is laid
    Some village Nero who has missed his due,
Some Bluebeard who dissected many a maid,
    And all for naught, since no one ever knew.

Some poor bucolic Borgia here may rest
    Whose poisons sent whole families to their doom,
Some hayseed Herod who, within his breast,
    Concealed the sites of many an infant's tomb.

Types that the Muse of Masefield might have stirred,
    Or waked to ecstasy Gaboriau,
Each in his narrow cell at last interred,
    All, all are sleeping peacefully below.

★ ★ ★

Enough, enough! But, stranger, ere we part,
    Glancing farewell to each nefarious bier,
This warning I would beg you take to heart,
    "There is an end to even the worst career!"

                                J. C. SQUIRE

177

GRAHAM GREENE
1904–

AN OPENING PARAGRAPH

As he watched the Caribbean night darken swiftly over the beach he could not help thinking of that other night which was gathering almost as quickly and might not end in any morning. Had he, he wondered, been in some way responsible for that darkness? Had he been guilty, here and there, of mistakes, perhaps even of crimes? He shivered slightly; the wind was cold here once the sun had gone. An unaccustomed feeling came over him; he wanted someone, not to advise or encourage him, but to forgive. Not Harold, not Duncan, but someone else. Scarcely realizing what he was doing, he felt his knees bending until they touched the sand; his hands were raised in a stiff, unnatural pose. He was praying.

D. A. J. S.

THE POTTING SHED

The time is ten years hence, a decade after the London opening of Graham Greene's The Potting Shed. *A Failed Drama Critic lies abed in his dingy lodgings, up to here in Scotch. Around him are the bleak and grimy symbols of his faith—the cobwebbed bust of Brecht, the mildewed model of the National Theatre, the yellowing autograph of Stanislavsky, the drab little pot of clotted Eulogy, the rusty Panning Pen. He looks somehow void and empty, though of course, as we know, he is up to here. A young Psychiatrist is interrogating him.*

P: But in that case why do you still go to the theatre?

C: (*Simply, if indistinctly*) It's my job. Once a critic, always a critic. It's my half of the promise. Sometimes I fall down during the Anthem and disappear for acts on end, and then they have to take my pen away for a while. But I always come back. The people need critics, and a whisky-critic's better than none.

P: Even if he's lost his vocation?

C: Even then. But don't misunderstand me. I'm not a bad critic. I go through the motions. I get out of bed every day at seven o'clock in the evening and go to the theatre. Sometimes there isn't a play on, but I go anyway, in case I'm needed. It's a matter of conscience. Have another slug of fire-water.

P: Not just now. Can you remember exactly where you lost your faith? When did you last have it with you?

C: I didn't lose it. It was taken away from me one night ten years ago at the old Globe Theatre, before they turned it into a car-park. John Gielgud was in the play. Very wrought-up he was, very curt and brusque—you know how he used to talk to other actors as if he was going to tip them? Irene Worth played his ex-wife. Then there was Gwen Ffrangcon-Davies, very fierce, and a clever little pouter called Sarah Long. And Redmond Phillips—he played a frocked sot on the brink of the shakes. He was the best of a fine lot. No, you couldn't complain about the acting. But somehow that made it worse. (*He sobs controllably.*)

P: (*Controllingly*) Tell me about the play. Force yourself back into the theatre. Slump now as you slumped then in D16.

C: (*In a hoarse whisper*) Graham Greene wrote it. It began with the death of a famous atheist, head of a rationalist clan. Greene made them out to be a bunch of decrepit puritans, so old-fashioned that they even enjoyed the company of dowdy dullards like Bertrand Russell. But fair enough: Greene's a Catholic, and the history of Catholicism shows that you can't make an omelette

179

without breaking eggheads. Anti-intellectual jokes are part of the recipe. At first I thought I was in for a whodunit. The old man's son—Sir John—was kept away from the death-bed because of something nameless that had happened to him in the potting shed at the age of fourteen. There were clues all over the place. For one thing, he had recently lost his dog. . . .

P: (*Shrewdly*) Dog is God spelled backwards.

C: The same crude thought occurred to me, but I rejected it (pity my complexity) as being unworthy of the author. How wrong I was! The hero's subsequent investigations into his past revealed that we were indeed dealing not with a whodunit but a God-dunit. He had hanged himself in the dread shed, and demonstrably died. And his uncle, the priest, had begged God to revive him. Make me an offer, haggled the Deity. My faith in exchange for the boy's life, said the priest, and so the repulsive bargain was struck. The boy lived and uncle lost his faith. My first impulse on hearing these farcical revelations was to protest by the only means at my disposal: a derisive hiccup. But then I looked about me and saw row after row of rapt, attentive faces. *They were taking it seriously*! And suddenly, in a blaze of darkness, I knew that my faith in the theatre and the people who attend it had been withdrawn from me.

P: But why?

C: You may not now remember the theatre as it was ten years ago. It seemed on the brink of renaissance. I was one of many who were newly flushed with a great conviction. We recklessly believed that a theatre was a place where human problems could be stated in human terms, a place from which supernatural intervention as a solution to such problems had at long last been ousted. Drama for us was an affirmation of humanism, and its basic maxim was not: "I die that you may live," but: "I *live* that you may live." *The Potting Shed*, financed by two normally intelligent managements at a highly reputable theatre, shot us back overnight to the dark ages.

P: But what about Gibbon? "The Catholic superstition, which is always the enemy of reason, is often the parent of the arts"?

C: Art that is not allied with reason is today the enemy of life. And now you must excuse me. You have kept me in bed long after my usual time for getting up. And I have a first-night to attend. The play, I understand, is a fearless indictment of a priest who refuses to accompany a murderer to the scaffold because of stupid, heretical, rationalist doubts about the efficacy of prayer to bring the man back to life. The bounder will no doubt be shown his error. Meanwhile (*He takes a deep draught of red-eye*), here's to good G.G.! Who said the Pope had no divisions?

(*He departs, half-clad and half-cut, to perform in a spirit of obedient humility the offices laid down for him by providence and the Society of West End Theatre Managers.*)

KENNETH TYNAN

DASHIELL HAMMETT
1894–1961

$106,000 MUD BUNNY

The little group in Gory Joe's on Powell convinced me. Something big was brewing. No sleuth with eyes could miss it. Around the table sat a transcontinental convocation of crooks, and I didn't think they'd all decided on San Francisco for a vacation. At the head of the table was Red

Dust, a genial chiseller who was a dead ringer for the Kaiser. By his side was Sad-Eyed Melba, who packed more danger in her five-foot, 100-pound frame than a basketful of cobras. Their usual stamping ground was Detroit, and their table companions included Eddie the Torch from Chicago, Rugs Richmond and Glad-Hand Garrity from Boston, Pinkie Paul and Edge Steinwold from Cleveland, and a big delegation from Philadelphia—Elmo Fingers, Elsie Cowl, the Screwdriver Kid, Gunner Sells, and Gooseberry Lane.

I edged my way to the pay phone, trying to keep my bulky frame in the shadows. I dialled headquarters of the Transcendental Detective Agency and asked for the Old Man.

"Yeah?" he coughed.

"This is going to be big. Real big. Every crook in America seems to be in town. Glad-Hand Garrity, Eddie the Torch, Pinkie Paul, Red Dust, the Screwdriver Kid, Gunner Sells—"

"All after the mud bunny?"

"Naw, it's worth $106,000, but I don't see all these hoods showing up to steal one clay statue. How would they split the take? No, it's bigger than that."

"Our concern at the moment is the mud bunny. Is it safe?"

"Yeah, sure, right in my coat pocket. But look, that's just the line-up at Gory Joe's. I saw Axman Cassidy at Oakland Annie's place having a steak with Sausage Sam Smith, Willie the Wasp, Hospital Hawkins, Peter Collinson, and Berkeley Butch. Their molls were with them too—Marin Maggie, Typhoon Mary, Roxy the Rockette."

"Just hang on to the mud bunny. It may just be a clay rabbit to you, but it's a member of the family to its owner and a meal ticket to the Transcendental. If those jaspers are spoiling for a shootout, the Transcendental's got other ops without $106,000-worth of business in their pockets. And the last I heard, San Francisco still has a police force. Get me?"

"Yeah," I said and hung up. I got out of there and down Powell to Geary, up Geary to Ev Millweedy's speak, and the story was the same. Louis the Louse sampling the local hospitality of Sausalito Slim, Palo Alto Pete, and Mendocino Minnie. They weren't alone. There was Gordy the Gat, in from New York, and Two-Fingered Claude, Denver Doris, Harry the Hoop, and the Alcatraz Kid.

Out of there and up Geary to Polk I sped, almost at a run though I didn't know why, the $106,000 mud bunny in my pocket bouncing heavily and slowing me down. As I slipped into Billy Grabber's place, I looked around me and saw more of the same. There was Con Crete of Cicero, Illinois, and his pal Machine-Gun Morrissy. South Bend Sid was there, with his regular gal Greta Noter—I knew it spelled trouble whenever the Noter dame turned up, because her eyes would turn a guy to melted butter, even certain ops of the Transcendental, though guys who can see through eyes can see through Greta. The host this time was Stockton Stanley, and Ollie the Necktie was there, with Rubout Richie and Ballast Bob.

Coming out of Billy Grabber's, I saw an operative named George Grover coming up Polk. I nudged him and motioned him into the alley.

"Still got the mud bunny?" he asked me.

"Yeah, sure," I said, patting my pocket.

"Good. I been to Madame Glory's place. New talent there, in from the East coast. Montana Pearl and Pekin Annie. Alice Cream and Madcap Nora in from Chi. What's it mean?"

"Something big. Real big. Red Dust's in town."

"Red Dust?"

"Yeah. And Edge Steinwold, the Screwdriver Kid, Glad-Hand Garrity, Rugs Richmond, Axman Cassidy, Gordy the Gat, Two-Fingered Claude, Ollie the Necktie, Sad-Eyed Melba, Harry the Hoop, Gooseberry Lane, Gunner Sells, Pinkie Paul, Axman Cassidy—"

"You said him already."

"Typhoon Mary, Con Crete, Ballast Bob, Machine-Gun Morrissy."

"This *is* big. Watch the mud bunny. The millionaire owner's paying the Transcendental some big change to guard it."

"I know, I know. But this is bigger than the mud bunny. The mud bunny's small change to these hoods. More likely they plan to knock over every bank in San Francisco at high noon tomorrow, and a lot of those banks are Transcendental customers."

"You ain't the only Transcendental op. Be wise. Lay low. I can handle this."

George took one step into Billy Grabber's. A loud noise of fire came fast and he reeled out backward, full of holes. The war was on.

I stormed in, rod drawn and ready. They looked surprised, and for a second it was like a still picture. Red Dust and Axman Cassidy had joined Ollie the Necktie and Ballast Bob for a powwow, and the real bigshot of the bay had joined in—Alameda Elmer. This was where the big play would be made.

Guns blazed and the smoke rose like a fog on the bay. With one shot I took out Con Crete. I got Ollie in his now red necktie, and the same shot went right through him to get Axman Cassidy. Rubout Richie and Stockton Stanley fell together like bookends, and shortly Ballast Bob and Alameda Elmer breathed their last. Greta Noter put those lamps on me and my gun hand almost wavered, but I put a bullet right between them a second later.

The rest scattered, all the big boys dead save one. I had some lead in me, but it was all embedded safely in fat.

I staggered out on to Polk for a breath of air untainted by gunpowder. Then I saw Red Dust running up the street. My rod was fresh out of fishhooks. I reached in my coat and pulled out the mud bunny. I aimed it right at Red's fleeing head and soon made it redder with a throw Walter Johnson would have been proud of. The mud bunny was in a million pieces, but by me it was worth it.

184

Next day the Transcendental gave me my walking papers. A few weeks later they were out of business, the millionaire owner of the mud bunny having put out the word. Now the hoods can run wild, so I guess the mud bunny was what the crooks were gunning for after all.

A lot of sleuths are out of work these days. I may take up writing.

JON L. BREEN

FELICIA HEMANS
1794–1835

A FRAGMENT

The boy stood on the burning deck,
   His feet were covered with blisters.
He had no trousers of his own
   And so he wore his sister's. . . .

ANON

THE STATELY HOMES OF ENGLAND

The Stately Homes of England,
How beautiful they stand,—
To prove the upper classes
Have still the upper hand;
Tho' the fact that they have to be rebuilt
And frequently mortgag'd to the hilt

Is inclin'd to take the gilt
Off the gingerbread,
And certainly damps the fun
Of the eldest son—
But still we won't be beaten,
We'll scrimp and screw and save,—
The playing fields of Eton
Have made us frightfully brave—
And tho' if the Van Dycks have to go
And we pawn the Bechstein Grand,
We'll stand by the Stately Homes of England!

NOËL COWARD

ERNEST HEMINGWAY
1898–1961

BEER IN THE SERGEANT-MAJOR'S HAT
(OR THE SUN ALSO SNEEZES)

Hank went into the bathroom to brush his teeth.

"The hell with it," he said. "She shouldn't have done it."

It was a good bathroom. It was small and the green enamel was peeling off the walls. But the hell with that, as Napoleon said when they told him Josephine waited without. The bathroom had a wide window through which Hank looked at the pines and larches. They dripped with a faint rain. They looked smooth and comfortable.

"The hell with it," Hank said. "She shouldn't have done it."

He opened the cabinet over the washbasin and took out his toothpaste. He looked at his teeth in the mirror. They were large yellow teeth, but sound. Hank could still bite his way for a while.

Hank unscrewed the top of the toothpaste tube, thinking of the day when he had unscrewed the lid of the coffee jar, down on the Pukayuk River, when he was trout fishing. There had been larches there too. It was a damn good river, and the trout had been damn good trout. They liked being hooked. Everything had been good except the coffee, which had been lousy. He had made it Watson's way, boiling it for two hours and a half in his knapsack. It had tasted like hell. It had tasted like the socks of the Forgotten Man.

"She shouldn't have done it," Hank said out loud. Then he was silent.

Hank put the toothpaste down and looked around. There was a bottle of alcohol on top of the built-in drawers where the towels were kept. It was grain alcohol. Velma hated rubbing alcohol with its harsh irritants. Her skin was sensitive. She hated almost everything. That was because she was sensitive. Hank picked up the bottle of alcohol, pulled the cork out, and smelled it. It had a damn good smell. He poured some alcohol into his tooth glass and added some water. Then the alcohol was all misty, with little moving lines in it, like tiny ripples coming to the surface. Only they didn't come to the surface. They just stayed in the alcohol, like goldfish in a bowl.

Hank drank the alcohol and water. It had a warm sweetish taste. It was warm all the way down. It was warm as hell. It was warmer than whiskey. It was warmer than that Asti Spumante they had that time in Capozzo when Hank was with the Arditi. They had been carp fishing with landing nets. It had been a good day. After the fourth bottle of Asti Spumante Hank fell into the river and came out with his hair full of carp. Old Peguzzi laughed until his boots rattled on the hard gray rock. And afterward Peguzzi got gonorrhoea on the Piave. It was a hell of a war.

Hank poured more alcohol into the glass and added less water. He drank solemnly, liking his face in the mirror. It was warm and a bit shiny. His eyes had a kind of fat glitter. They were large pale blue eyes, except when he was mad. Then they were dark blue. When he had a good edge on they were almost gray. They were damn good eyes.

"The hell with it," he said. "She shouldn't have done it."

He poured more alcohol into the glass and added a little water—very little. He raised the glass in a toast to his face in the mirror.

"Gentlemen, I give you alcohol. Not, gentlemen, because I cannot give you wine or whiskey, but because I desire to cultivate in you the fundamental art of intoxication. The alcohol drinker, gentlemen, is the hair-shirt drinker. He likes his penance strong."

Hank drained the glass and refilled it. The bottle was nearly empty now, but there was more alcohol in the cellar. It was a good cellar, and there was plenty of alcohol in it.

"Gentlemen," Hank said, "when I was with Napoleon at Solferino we drank cognac. When I was with Moore at Coruña we drank port with a dash of brandy. It was damn good port, and Moore was a damn good drinker. When I was with Kitchener at Khartoum we drank the stale of horses. With Kuroki on the Yalu I drank saki, and with Byng at Arras I drank Scotch. These, gentlemen, were drinks of diverse charms. Now that I am with you, gentlemen, we shall drink alcohol, because alcohol is the Holy Mother of all drinking."

Hank's face in the mirror wavered like a face behind thin smoke. It was a face drawn on gray silk by unscrupulous shadows. It was not a face at all. Hank scowled at it. The reflected scowl was as merciless as an earthquake.

"The hell with it," he said. "She shouldn't have done it."

He leaned against the washbowl and squeezed some toothpaste on his toothbrush. It was a long toothbrush, about six feet long. It was springy, like a trout rod. Hank brought

188

his elbow around with a sweep and spread some toothpaste on his upper lip. He supported himself with both hands and squinted at his reflection.

"The white moustache, gentlemen," he burbled. "The mark of a goddamn ambassador."

Hank drank the rest of the alcohol straight. For a moment his stomach came up between his ears. But that passed and he only felt as if he had been bitten in the back of the neck by a tiger.

"Not by a damn sight she shouldn't," he said.

With large gestures he applied toothpaste to his eyebrows and temples.

"Not a complete work, gentlemen," he yelled. "Just an indication of what can be done. And now for a brief moment I leave you. While I am gone let your conversation be clean."

Hank stumbled down to the living-room. It seemed a long way to the cellar where the alcohol was. There were steps to go down. The hell with the steps.

The cat was sleeping in a tight curve on the carpet.

"Jeeze Christ," Hank said. "'At's a hell of a fine cat."

It was a large black cat with long fur. It was a cat a guy could get on with. Jeeze Christ, yes. Hank lay down on the floor and put his head on the cat. The cat licked at the toothpaste on Hank's eyebrow. Then it sneezed and bit his ear.

"Jeeze Christ," Hank said. "The hell with it. She shouldn't have done it."

He slept.

RAYMOND CHANDLER

JACK SPRAT

"Come in, Jack."

"I d'wanta come in."

"D'wanta come in, hell. Come in bright boy."

They went in.

"I'll have eats now," she said. She was fat and red.

"I d' want nothing," Jack said. He was thin and pale.

"D'want nothin' hell. You have eats now, bright boy."

She called the waiter. "Bud," she said, "gimme bacon and beans—twice."

Bud brought the bacon and beans.

"I d'want bacon. It's too fat," said Jack.

"D'want bacon, hell. I'll eat the fat. You eat the lean. OK big boy?"

"OK," Jack said.

They had eats.

"Now lick the plate clean," she said.

"Aw, honey," said Jack. "I ain't gotta, do I?"

"Yup," she said. "You gotta."

They both licked their plates clean.

HENRY HETHERINGTON

ROBERT HERRICK
1591–1674

TO JULIA UNDER LOCK AND KEY

When like a bud my Julia blows
In lattice-work of silken hose,
Pleasant I deem it is to note
How, 'neath the nimble petticoat,
Above her fairy shoe is set
The circumvolving zonulet.
And soothly for the lover's ear
A perfect bliss it is to hear
About her limb so lithe and lank
My Julia's ankle-bangle clank.
Not rudely tight, for 'twere a sin
To corrugate her dainty skin;
Nor yet so large that it might fare
Over her foot at unaware;
But fashioned nicely with a view
To let her airy stocking through:
So as, when Julia goes to bed,
Of all her gear disburdenèd,
This ring at least she shall not doff
Because she cannot take it off.
And since thereof I hold the key,
She may not taste of liberty,
Not though she suffer from the gout,
Unless I choose to let her out.

SIR OWEN SEAMAN

ELECTION TIME

Gather ye bank-notes while ye may;
  The happy time is flitting;
The Member canvassing today
  Tomorrow will be sitting.

That glorious crib, the *Rising Sun*,
  Where patriots are glowing,
Too soon its brilliant course is run,
  Its beer will soon stop flowing.

ANON

THOMAS HOOD
1799–1845

ELEGY ON THOMAS HOOD

O spare a tear for poor Tom Hood,
Who, dazed by death, here lies;
His days abridged, he sighs across
The Bridge of Utmost Size.

His *penchant* was for punning rhymes
(Some lengthy, others—shorties);
But though his *forte* was his life,
He died within his forties.

The Muses cried: "To you we give
The crown of rhymester's bay, Thos."
Thos mused and thought that it might pay
To ladle out the pay-thos.

He spun the gold yet tangled yarn
Of sad Miss Kilmansegg;
And told how destiny contrived
To take her down a peg.

But now the weary toils of death
Have closed his rhyming toil,
And charged this very vital spark
To jump his mortal coil.

MARTIN FAGG

GERARD MANLEY HOPKINS
1844–89

BREAKFAST WITH GERARD MANLEY HOPKINS

*Delicious heart-of-the corn, fresh-from-the-oven flakes are sparkled
and spangled with sugar for a can't-be-resisted flavour.*

Legend on a packet of breakfast cereal

Serious over my cereals I broke one breakfast my fast
   With something-to-read-searching retinas retained by
      print on a packet;
Sprung rhythm sprang, and I found (the mind fact-mining
      at last)
   An influence Father-Hopkins-fathered on the copy-
      writing racket.

Parenthesis-proud, bracket-bold, happiest with hyphens,
  The writers stagger intoxicated by terms, adjective-
    unsteadied—
Describing in graceless phrases fizzling like soda siphons
  All things crisp, crunchy, malted, tangy, sugared and
    shredded.
Far too, yes, too early we are urged to be purged, to
    savour
  Salt, malt and phosphates in English twisted and torn,
As, sparkled and spangled with sugar for a can't-be-
    resisted flavour,
  Come fresh-from-the-oven flakes direct from the heart
    of the corn.

ANTHONY BRODE

A. E. HOUSMAN
1859–1936

A POEM, AFTER A. E. HOUSMAN

What, still alive at twenty-two,
A clean upstanding chap like you?
Sure, if your throat 'tis hard to slit,
Slit your girl's, and swing for it.

Like enough, you won't be glad,
When they come to hang you, lad:
But bacon's not the only thing
That's cured by hanging from a string.

So, when the spilt ink of the night
Spreads o'er the blotting pad of light,
Lads whose job is still to do
Shall whet their knives, and think of you.

HUGH KINGSMILL

MR HOUSMAN'S MESSAGE

O woe, woe,
People are born and die,
We also shall be dead pretty soon
Therefore let us act as if we were dead already.

The bird sits on the hawthorn tree
But he dies also, presently.
Some lads get hung, and some get shot.
Woeful is this human lot.
     Woe! woe, etcetera. . . .

London is a woeful place,
Shropshire is much pleasanter.
Then let us smile a little space
Upon fond nature's morbid grace.
     Oh, Woe, woe, woe, etcetera. . . .

EZRA POUND

TED HUGHES
1930–

CROW RESTING

I sit at the top of the tree,
My mouth closed. I have been sitting here
Since the beginning of Time.
I am going to carry on sitting here
And if anybody tries to stop me sitting here
I will remove his head;
A single-mind-sized bite will do it.
I will eat his head and with a stab, a jerk
A bounce I'll have his bowels, balls,
Big toes, his colon and his semi-colon.
I will drink his blood from the goblet
Of his skull, his thin giblets
From the platter of his pelvic bone. And
I will spread his shit with generosity.
In other words forget it.
I was here first, I was here long ago.
I was here before you. And I will be here
Long after you have gone. What Superbard says
Goes. I am going to keep things like this.

EDWARD PYGGE

BUDGIE FINDS HIS VOICE

from "The Life and Songs of the Budgie"
by Jake Strugnell

God decided he was tired
Of his spinning toys.
They wobbled and grew still.

When the sun was lifted away
Like an orange lifted from a fruit-bowl

And darkness, blacker
Than an oil-slick
Covered everything forever

And the last ear left on earth
Lay on the beach,
Deaf as a shell

And the land froze
And the seas froze

"Who's a pretty boy then?" Budgie cried.
WENDY COPE

ALDOUS HUXLEY
1894–1963

TOLD IN GATH

Vulgarity is the garlic in the salad of charm.
St Bumpus

It was to be a long week-end, thought Giles Pentateuch apprehensively, as the menial staggered up the turret stairs with his luggage—staggered all the more consciously for the knowledge that he was under observation, just as, back in Lexham Gardens, his own tyrannical Amy would snort and groan outside the door to show how steep the back-stairs were, before entering with his simple vegetarian breakfast of stinkwort and boiled pond-weed. A long week-end; but a week-end at Groyne! And he realized, with his instinct for merciless analysis that amounted almost to torture, that in spite, yes, above all, in spite of the apprehension, because of it even, he would enjoy all the more saying afterwards, to his friend Luke Snarthes perhaps, or to little Reggie Ringworm, "Yes, I was at Groyne last week-end," or "Yes, I was there when the whole thing started, down at Groyne."

The menial had paused and was regarding him. To tip or not to tip? How many times had he not been paralysed by that problem? To tip was to give in, yes, selfishly to give in to his hatred of human contacts, to contribute half a crown as hush-money, to obtain "protection", protection from other people, so that for a little he could go on with the luxury of being Giles Pentateuch, "scatologist and eschatologist", as he dubbed himself. Whereas not to tip. . . .

For a moment he hesitated. What would Luke Snarthes have done? Stayed at home, with that splayed ascetic face of his, or consulted his guru, Chandra Nandra? No—no tip!

The menial slunk away. He looked round the room. It was comfortable, he had to admit; a few small Longhis round the walls, a Lupanar by Guido Guidi, and over the bed an outsize Stuprum Sabinarum, by Rubens—civilized people, his hosts, evidently.

He glanced at the books on the little table—the *Odes of Horace, Rome 23* BC, apparently a first edition, the *Elegancies of Meursius* (Rochester's copy), *The Piccadilly Ambulator, The Sufferings of Saint Rose of Lima, Nostradamus* (the Lérins Press), *Swedenborg, The Old Man's Gita.* "And cultivated," he murmured, "too." The bathroom, with its sun-lamp and Plombières apparatus, was such as might be found in any sensible therapeutic home. He went down to tea considerably refreshed by his lavage.

The butler announced that Lady Rhomboid was "serving" on the small west lawn, and he made his way over the secular turf with genuine pleasure. For Minnie Rhomboid was a remarkable woman.

"How splendid of you to come," she croaked, for she had lost her voice in the old suffragette days. "You know my daughter, Ursula Groyne."

"Only too well," laughed Giles, for they had been what his set at Balliol used to call "lovers"

"And Mrs Amp, of course?"

"Of course!"

"And Mary Pippin?"

"Decidedly," he grimaced.

"And the men," she went on. "Giles Pentateuch—this is Luke Snarthes and Reggie Ringworm and Mr Encolpius and Roland Narthex. Pentateuch writes—let me see?—like a boot, isn't it?" (Her voice was a husky roar.) "Yes, a boot with a mission! Oh, but I forgot"—and she laughed delightedly—"you're all writers!"

"Encantado, I'm sure!" responded Giles. "But we've all met before. I see you have the whole Almanach de Golgotha in fact," he added.

Mary Pippin, whose arm had been eaten away by termites in Tehuantepec, was pouring out with her free hand. "Orange Pekoe or *Chandu*, Giles?" she burbled in her delicious little voice. Like a carrier pigeon's, he thought.

"*Chandu*, please." And she filled him a pipe of the consoling poppy, so that in a short while he was smoking away like all the others.

"Yes, yes," continued Mr Encolpius, in his oily voice which rose and fell beneath the gently moving tip of his nose, "Man axalotl here below but I ask very little. Some fragments of Pamphylides, a Choctaw blood-mask, the prose of Scaliger the Elder, a painting by Fuseli, an occasional visit to the all-in wrestling, or to my meretrix; a cook who can produce a passable 'poulet à la Khmer', a Pong vase. Simple tastes, you will agree, and it is my simple habit to indulge them!"

Giles regarded him with fascination. That nose, it was, yes, it was definitely a proboscis. . . .

"But how can you, how can you?" It was Ursula Groyne. "How *can* you when there are two million unemployed, when Russia has reintroduced anti-abortionary legislation, when Iceland has banned *Time and Tide*, when the Sedition Bill hangs over us all like a rubber truncheon?"

Mary Pippin cooed delightedly; this was intellectual life with a vengeance—definitely haybrow—only it was so difficult to know who was right. Giles, at that moment, found her infinitely desirable.

"Yes, and worse than that." It was Luke Snarthes, whose strained voice emerged from his tortured face like a cobra from the snake-charmer's basket. "Oh, decidedly, appallingly worse. The natives of Ceylon take the slender Loris and hold it over the fire till its eyes pop, to release the magic juices. Indicible things are done to geese that you may eat your runions with a sauce of *foie gras*. Caviare is ripped from the living sturgeon, karakul fur torn from the baby lamb inside its mother. The creaking plates of the live dismembered lobster scream to you from the *Homard Newburg*, the oyster winces under the lemon. How would *you* like, Mr Encolpius, to be torn from your bed, embarrelled, prised open with a knife, seasoned with a few drips of vitriol, shall we say, and sprayed with a tabasco as strong as mustard-gas to give you flavour; then to be swallowed alive and handed over to a giant's digestive juices?"

"I shouldn't like it at all!" said Mr Encolpius, "just as I shouldn't, for that matter, like living in the bottom of the sea and changing my sex every three years. Not that it might not"—and he twitched his nose at Mary Pippin—"have its compensations."

"S-s-s-s-s-s-s-s-s-s-s-s-s-s-s-s-s-s-s-s-s-s-suppose," said Reggie Ringworm, who stammered, etc., "vat ve thilly oythter is weally weady and villing to be ab-s-s-s-orbed, I mean ab-th-th-th-th-th-thorbed, by our fwend, vat vat is in f-f-f-fact exactly ve end for which it has been cweated. Vat th-then?"

"What are we to think then," snarled Snarthes savagely, "of the Person or Purpose who created creatures for such an end? Awful!" And he took out his notebook and wrote rapidly, "The end justifies the means! But the end *is* the means! And how rarely, how confoundedly rarely, can we even say the end justifies the end! Like Oxenstierna, like Ximenes, like Waldorf, we must be men of means"—he closed the book with a snap—"men of golden means."

"I know what you mean," cried Mary Pippin from her dovecot. "That if Cleopatra's nose had been half an inch longer Menelaus would never have run away with her!"

Luke's face softened, and he spread out his splayed fingers almost tenderly. "And I don't mind wagering, if we can believe Diodorus Siculus, that, the nose unaltered, she bore a remarkable likeness, Mary, to you!"

"Ah, but can we believe Old Siculus?" The other nose quested speculative. "Any more than we can believe old Paterculus, old Appian, Arrian, Ossian, and Orrian? Now a Bolivar Corona or a nicely chambered glass of sparkling

201

Douro—even a pretty tea-gown by Madame Groult, I opine"—and he bowed to Mary—"these convince me. They have a way with one. Oh, yes, a way, decidedly! And just because they have that way it is necessary for me to combine them, how often, how distressingly often, with my lamentable visits to the Ring at Blackfriars, or to my meretrix in Holland Park. Why is it that we needs must see the highest though we loathe it? That happy in my mud—my hedonistic, radio-active, but never-the-less quite genuine nostalgic *boue*, I should be reminded of the stars, of you, Miss Pippin, and of Cleopatra?" And he snuffled serio-comically, "Why can't you let hell alone?"

A gong rang discreetly. The butler removed the pipes and Mrs Amp and Roland Narthex, who were still in a state of kif, while the others went away to dress. Giles, who found something stimulating in Mr Encolpius' nose, took out his notebook and wrote:

"Platitudes are eternally fresh, and even the most paradoxical are true; even when we say the days draw in we are literally right—for science has now come largely to the rescue of folklore; after the summer and still more after the equinoctial solstice the hours do definitely get shorter. It is this shortness of our northern day that has occasioned the luxuriance of our literature. Retractile weather—erectile poetry. No one has idealized, in our cold climate, more typically than Shakespeare and Dryden the subtropical conditioning. But we can consider Antony and Cleopatra to have been very different from their counterparts in the Elizabethan imagination, for on the Mediterranean they understand summer better and, with summer, sex.

"What were they really like, those prototypes of Aryan passion, of brachycephalic amour? Were Cleopatra's breasts such as 'bore through men's eyes' and tormented those early sensualists, Milton, Dante, Coventry Patmore, and St John of the Cross? We shall never know.

"Professor Pavlov has shown that when salivation has been

artificially induced in dogs by the ringing of a dinner bell, if you fire simultaneously into them a few rounds of small shot they exhibit an almost comical bewilderment. Human beings have developed very little. Like dogs we are not capable of absorbing conflicting stimuli; we cannot continue to love Cleopatra after communism and the electro-magnetic field have played Old Harry with our romantic mythology. That characteristic modern thinker, Drage Everyman, remarks, 'Destroy the illusion of love and you destroy love itself', and that is exactly what the machine age, through attempting to foster it through cinemas and gin-palaces, deodorants and depilatories, has succeeded in doing. Glory, glory halitosis! No wonder we are happier in the present! If we think of the 'Eastern Star', in fact, it is as advertising something. And when we would reconstruct those breasts of hers, again we are faced with the diversity of modern knowledge. What were they like? To a poet twin roes, delectable mountains; to a philanderer like Malthus festering cancers; to a pneu-matogogue simply a compound of lacticity and hetero-geneous pyrites; to a biologist a sump and a pump. Oh, sweet are the uses, or rather the abuses, of splanchnology! No, for details of the pathological appeal of these forgotten beauties we must consult the poets. The ancients were aware of a good thing when they saw it, and Horace knew, for instance, with almost scatological percipience, exactly what was what.

"There are altitudes, as well as climates, of the mind. Many prefer the water-meadows, but some of us, like Kant and Beethoven, are at home on the heights. There we thermo-statically control the rarefied atmosphere and breathe, per-force, the appropriate mental air."

In another room Luke Snarthes was doing his exercises. Seated in the lotus position, he exhaled deeply till his stomach came against his backbone with a smart crack. After a little he relaxed and breathed carefully up one nostril and down the other and then reversed the process. He took a nail out of the calf of his leg, and after he had reinserted it, it was time to put the studs into his evening shirt. "I was there," he murmured, "when it started, down at Groyne."

When he had dressed he unlocked his despatch-case and took out a sealed tube. It was marked, "Anthrax—non-filterable virus, only to be opened by a qualified literary scientist." "Jolly little beggars," he thought, and the hard lines on his face softened. "I'll take them down to amuse Miss Pippin. She looked the kind of person who'd *understand*."

"Snuff, peotl buds, hashish, or Indian hemp, sir?" said the butler. Dinner was drawing to an end. It had been an interesting meal. For Giles and Luke (on the "regime"), grass soup and groundsel omelette, washed down with a bottle of "pulque"; for Mrs Amp, whose huge wen, like Saint-Evremond's, made her look more than ever like some heavily wattled turkey, a chicken gumbo; for the rest Risi-bisi Mabel Dodge, bêche de mer, bear steak, and Capri pie.

"There's some *bhang* on the mantelpiece," said Minnie Rhomboid, "in poor Rhomboid's college tobacco jar."

"Delicious." It was Mr Encolpius. "Common are to either sex artifex and opifex," he continued. "But, golly, how rare to find them contained in the same person—qualis opifex, Lady Rhomboid! I congratulate you—and this *barask*—perfection!" And he poured himself some more, while the snout wiggled delightedly.

"And you can drink that when Hungary is deliberately making a propaganda war for the recovery and re-enslavement of a hundred thousand at last sophisticated Slovakians!" It was Ursula Groyne.

Poor Ursula, thought Giles, she carries her separate hell about with her like a snail its carapace! Not all the lost causes, all the lame dogs in the world could console her for the loss of her three husbands, and now she was condemned to the Hades of promiscuity—every three or four years a new lover. Poor Ursula!

"And if you knew how the stuff was made!" The phrase was wrung from Luke Snarthes on his tortured calvary. "The apricots are trodden by the naked feet of bromidrosis-ridden Kutzo-Vlachs who have for centuries lived in conditions far below the poverty line! The very glass-blowers who spun that Venetian balloon for you are condemned to the agonies of alembic poisoning."

"Doubtless," answered Mr Encolpius urbanely, "that is why it tastes so good. It all boils down to a question of proteins. You, my dear Ursula, are allergic to human misery; the sufferings of Slovaks and Slovenes affect you as pollen the hay-fever victim, or me (no offence, Minnie) a cat in the room. To ethics, mere questions of good and evil, I am happily immune, like my cara doncella here—am I right, Mary? Let Austin have his swink to him reserved, especially when it is a swink of the Rhomboid order. Go to the slug, thou ant-herd! If you could make up to kings (you remember what Aristippus said to Diogenes, Snarthes), you would not have to live on grass!"

"B-b-b-b-b-b-b-b-b-b-b-b-b-b-b-b-b-but all flesh is gwath, so ve pwoblem is only sh-shelved." It was Reggie Ringworm!

"Sit down, everybody, it's time for the seance," commanded Lady Rhomboid. "We have persuaded Madame Yoni."

In darkness they took their seats, Mr Encolpius and Giles on each side of Mary Pippin, while Snarthes elevated himself to a position of trans-Khyber ecstasy suspended between the table and the laquearia. The *bhang*-sodden bodies of Mrs Amp and Roland Narthex they left where they were.

The darkness was abysmal, pre-lapsarian. Time flowed stanchlessly, remorselessly, from a wound inenarrable, as with catenary purpose. Madame Yoni moved restlessly, like Bethesda.

In her private dovecot Mary Pippin abandoned herself to the eery. What a thrill, to be here at Groyne, and for a seance!

There had been nothing like it since she had joined the Anglican Church, to the consternation of her governess, Miss Heard, because of the deep mythical significance (as of some splendid sinner repenting on the ashes of lust) of the words, "for Ember Days". All the same, she was not quite sure if she liked Mr Encolpius. But what was this?—another thrill, but positive, physical. With moth-like caresses something was running up and down her arm—1, 2, 3, 4, 5,—spirit fingers, perhaps: the tremulous titivation continued, the moths were relentless, inexorable, 86, 87, 88. Then on her other side, along her cheek, she felt a new set of moth antennae playing. From the chandelier above came the faintest ghostly antici-patory tinkle—someone was on the move as well, up there! 98, 99. . . . Suddenly Madame Yoni screamed—there was a crash, as of three heads bumping together, and the lights went up to reveal Pentateuch and Mr Encolpius momentarily stunned by the Ixionic impact of the fallen Snarthes. His power had failed him.

"W-w-w-w-w-w-w—" stammered Reggie Ringworm, but he was interrupted by a shout from Luke. "My God—the anthrax! He took from his pocket the fragments of the broken tube. "At the rate of multiplication of these bacilli"—he made a rapid calculation—"we shall all be by morning, Lady Rhomboid, dead souls." His splayed face had at last found its justification.

"Death!" said Mr Encolpius, "the distinguished visitor! One bids good-bye, one hopes gracefully, to one's hostess, and then, why then I think one degusts the Cannabis Indica. Well, cheerio, kif-kif!" And he picked up the Brasenose jar.

Imperturbable, schizophrene, the portraits of Groynes and Rhomboids by Laurencin and the excise-man Rousseau looked down from the walls. So Miss Heard had been right, thought Mary. The wicked *do* perish. Than this there could have been no other conceivable termination to a week-end of pleasure!

206

> They say of old in Babylon
> That Harlequin and Pantalon
> Seized that old topiary, Truth,
> And held him by Time's Azimuth. . . .

Why had the nursery jingle recurred to her?

Luke removed a nail or two disconsolately. They would be of little use now. He tried to reassure Minnie Rhomboid. "After all, what is anthrax? What, for that matter, are yaws, beri-beri, dengue or the Bagdad Boil, but fascinating bio-chemical changes in the cellular constitution of our bodies, a re-casting of their components to play their new cadaverous roles? Believe me, Lady Rhomboid," he concluded, "there are more things in heaven and earth than are dreamt of in the British Pharmacopoeia!"

Giles took out his note-book. "*La Muerte, Der Tod, Thanatos*," he wrote.

"Your C-c-c-Collins perhaps?" stammered Reggie.

Giles began again: "It was at Groyne, during one of Minnie Rhomboid's most succulent week-ends, that it all happened, happened because it had to happen, because it was in the very nature of Luke Snarthes and Mary Pippin that exactly such things should happen, just as it was character not destiny, character that *was* destiny, that caused Napoleon. . . ." He paused and looked up. The menial was regarding him reproachfully.

CYRIL CONNOLLY

JEAN INGELOW
1820–97

LOVERS, AND A REFLECTION

In moss-prankt dells which the sunbeams flatter
   (And heaven it knoweth what that may mean;
Meaning, however, is no great matter)
    Where woods are a-tremble, with rifts atween;

Thro' God's own heather we wonn'd together,
   I and my Willie (O love my love):
I need hardly remark it was glorious weather,
    And flitterbats waver'd alow, above:

Boats were curtseying, rising, bowing,
   (Boats in that climate are so polite),
And sands were a ribbon of green endowing,
    And O the sundazzle on bark and bight!

Thro' the rare red heather we danced together,
   (O love my Willie!) and smelt for flowers:
I must mention again it was gorgeous weather,
    Rhymes are so scarce in this world of ours:—

By rises that flush'd with their purple favours,
   Thro' becks that brattled o'er grasses sheen,
We walked and waded, we two young shavers,
    Thanking our stars we were both so green.

We journeyed in parallels, I and Willie,
   In fortunate parallels! Butterflies,
Hid in weltering shadows of daffodilly
    Or marjoram, kept making peacock eyes:

Songbirds darted about, some inky
   As coal, some snowy (I ween) as curds;
Or rosy as pinks, or as roses pinky—
   They reck of no eerie To-come, those birds!

But they skim over bents which the millstream washes,
   Or hang in the lift 'neath a white cloud's hem;
They need no parasols, no goloshes;
   And good Mrs Trimmer she feedeth them.

Then we thrid God's cowslips (as erst His heather)
   That endowed the wan grass with their golden blooms;
And snapt—(it was perfectly charming weather)—
   Our fingers at Fate and her goddess-glooms:

And Willie 'gan sing (O, his notes were fluty;
   Wafts fluttered them out to the white-wing'd sea)—
Something made up of rhymes that have done much duty,
   Rhymes (better to put it) of "ancientry":

Bowers of flowers encounter'd showers
   In William's carol—(O love my Willie!)
Then he bade sorrow from blithe tomorrow
   I quite forgot what—say a daffodily:

A nest in a hollow, "with buds to follow",
   I think occurred next in his nimble strain;
And clay that was "kneaden" of course in Eden—
   A rhyme most novel, I do maintain:

Mists, bones, the singer himself, love-stories,
   And all least furlable things got "furled";
Not with any design to conceal their "glories".
   But simply and solely to rhyme with "world".

* * *

O if billows and pillows and hours and flowers,
  And all the brave rhymes of an elder day,
Could be furled together, this genial weather,
  And carted, or carried on "wafts" away,
Nor ever again trotted out—ah me!
How much fewer volumes of verse there'd be!

C. S. CALVERLEY

CLIVE JAMES
1939–

LETTER TO MYSELF

Dear *Clive*, I've meant to scribble you a letter
For some time now. I know you like to get a
Brown-noser now and then, and—well—who better

To do the honours than yours truly, *Clive*?
Over the past few years I think that I've
Proven myself the handiest hack alive

(Or even dead) at pumping up the egos
Of my illustrious *Grub Street amigos*.
It's sometimes said of me, "Too bad that he goes

Over the top so often. Are his pals
Really the *Goethes, Mozarts, Juvenals,
Einsteins, Nijinskys, Chaplins, Bluff King Hals*,

Elijahs, Pee Wee Russells, Leonardos,
Jane Austens, Churchills, Platos, Giottos, Bardots—
This list could grow as long as a *Mikado's*

Great fingernail, if I don't stop it pronto—
Et cetera, of his peer-group? I don't want to
Malign the poor sap, but he sounds like *Tonto*

At times, whose quaint devotion to the *Ranger*
I never understood. He runs the danger
Of taking every passing *Percy Grainger*

For *Beethoven*; or seeing *Botticelli*'s
Mind-boggling artistry (or, say, *Crivelli*'s)
In some chum's doodle on a *Bertorelli*'s

Table-napkin. Good *God*, where will it end?
I like a fellow who sticks by his friend,
But *Clive*'s like *Don Quixote*, round the bend!"

I've heard this stuff a zillion times before.
Every great poet meets the kind of bore,
Straight from the *Dunciad*, who feels as sore

As *Grendel* and *Beowulf*, because
He's not in on the act. As if I was
A sort of literary *Wiz of Oz*,

Holding my court, but waiting to be rumbled
By *Judy Garland*'s pooch! I bet they grumbled
When *Pope* flashed *Dryden*'s name, or *Piero* mumbled

Something about *Veneziano*. Blimey!
These runty characters were sent to try me,
But I'm not *Gulliver* and they can't tie me

Down, sport. I'll lay off writing to my chinas
For now—those *Schopenhauers*, *Kafkas*, *Heines*—
And magic up some several-hundred-liners

About myself. The prospect's fairly heady!
Make sure the old adrenal pump is steady:
Not too much juice. Ready when you are . . . Ready!

Actually, *Clive*, I must admit I'm nervous.
I've never had to face the champion servers—
Toe-amputators, any-which-way swervers—

But now I feel the terror of some boy
Alone before the *Wimbledon polloi*,
Waiting for *Hoad* or *Laver* to destroy

Him smash by smash. Will some allusion ace
Me, as I flail about, *gauche*, in disgrace?
Will metaphors bounce up and dent my face?

Or will . . .? But wait a tick; don't let's forget
That's me as well the far side of the net.
Christ, what a bummeroo! I'd better let

This metaphor drop like a hot potato
And settle down to something a bit straighter,
More in the style of *Horace*, *le grand Maître*.

Clive, you're the greatest poet in the business!
To contemplate your talents brings on dizziness.
Just as a *Bollinger* is full of fizziness—

The mark, I'm told, of any good champagne—
Ideas appear to bubble in your brain.
I'm baffled that your head can take the strain.

Tchaikovsky thought his bonce might topple off.
I don't think his mate *Rimsky-Korsakov*
Suffered the same delusion, but some prof

Might put us right on that one. Anyhow,
I like the splendid eminence of your brow
(*Hokusai's Fuji*, *Mallory's Jungfrau*

Seem the right names to drop in this connection).
I like your well-used cricket-ball complexion.
I like—and let's waive *Jamesian* circumspection

(I'm talking about me, not *Uncle Harry*)—
I like the whole caboodle. Yes, I'd marry
Me if I could. On honeymoon in *Paris*,

In any other *chic*, *kulturni* city,
We'd do the local *Hermitage* or *Pitti*
And jot down names of painters for our witty

Verse letters to each other. Life and art?
Both *Proust* and *Aristotle* said some smart,
Quotable things about this, but apart

From them (the *Hobbs* and *Bradman* of their field)
A fair amount remains to be revealed.
Which is where we waltz in. Art has appealed

To us for yonks. We've always nursed a pash
For Russian Lit., Expressionist *gouaches*,
The Blues, *Ming* vases, *Rosewall's* cross-court smash,

Early *Walt Disney*, madrigals, *Kung Fu*,
Homer, French cooking, *Mahler's* no. 2,
Dame Sybil Thorndyke, *Pascal's Pensées*, *Pooh* . . .

The names! The names! They give me such a thrill,
I could run on till Doomsday in this shrill,
Pindaric fashion, and, dear *Clive*, no doubt I will.

CHRISTOPHER REID

HENRY JAMES
1843–1916

THE MOTE IN THE MIDDLE DISTANCE

It was with the sense of a, for him, very memorable something that he peered now into the immediate future, and tried, not without compunction, to take that period up where he had, prospectively, left it. But just where the deuce *had* he left it? The consciousness of dubiety was, for our friend, not, this morning, quite yet clean-cut enough to outline the figures on what she had called his "horizon", between which and himself the twilight was indeed of a quality somewhat intimidating. He had run up, in the course of time, against a good number of "teasers"; and the function of teasing them back—of, as it were, giving them, every now and then, "what for"—was in him so much a habit that he would have been at a loss had there been, on the face of it, nothing to lose. Oh, he always had offered rewards, of course—had ever so liberally pasted the windows of his soul with staring appeals, minute descriptions, promises that knew no bounds. But the actual recovery of the article—the business of drawing and crossing the cheque, blotched though this were with tears of joy—had blankly appeared to him rather in the light of a sacrilege, casting, he sometimes felt, a palpable chill on the fervour of the next quest. It was just this fervour that was threatened as, raising himself on his elbow, he stared at the foot of his bed. That his eyes refused to rest there for more than the fraction of an instant, may be taken—*was*, even then, taken by Keith Tantalus—as a hint of his recollection that after all the phenomenon wasn't to be singular. Thus the exact repetition, at the foot of Eva's bed, of the shape pendulous at the foot of *his* was hardly enough to account for the fixity with which he envisaged it, and for which he was to find, some years later, a motive in the (as it turned out) hardly generous fear that Eva had already made the great investigation "on her own". Her very regular breathing presently reassured him that, if she *had* peeped into "her" stocking, she must have done so in sleep. Whether he should wake her now, or wait for their nurse to wake them both in due course, was a problem presently solved by a new development. It was plain that his sister was now watching him between her eyelashes. He had half expected that. She really was— he had often told her that she really was—magnificent; and her magnificence was never more obvious than in the pause that elapsed before she all of a sudden remarked, "They so very indubitably *are*, you know!"

It occurred to him as befitting Eva's remoteness, which was part of Eva's magnificence, that her voice emerged somewhat muffled by the bedclothes. She was ever, indeed, the most telephonic of her sex. In talking to Eva you always had, as it were, your lips to the receiver. If you didn't try to meet her fine eyes, it was that you simply couldn't hope to: there were too many dark, too many buzzing and bewildering and all frankly not negotiable leagues in between. Snatches of other voices seemed often to intertrude themselves in the parley; and your loyal effort not to overhear these was complicated by your fear of missing what Eva might be twittering. "Oh, you certainly haven't, my dear, the trick of propinquity!" was a thrust she had once parried by saying that, in that case, *he* hadn't—to which his unspoken rejoiner that she had caught in her tone from the peevish young women at the Central seemed to him (if not perhaps in the last, certainly in the last

215

but one, analysis) to lack finality. With Eva, he had found, it was always safest to "ring off". It was with a certain sense of his rashness in the matter, therefore, that he now, with an air of feverish "holding the line", said "Oh, as to that!"

Had *she*, he presently asked himself, "rung off"? It was characteristic of our friend—was indeed "him all over"—that his fear of what she was going to say was as nothing to his fear of what she might be going to leave unsaid. He had, in his converse with her, been never so conscious as now of the intervening leagues; they had never so insistently beaten the drum of his ear; and he caught himself in the act of awfully computing, with a certain statistical passion, the distance between Rome and Boston. He has never been able to decide which of these points he was physically the nearer to at the moment when Eva, replying "Well, one does, anyhow, leave a margin for the pretext, you know!" made him, for the first time in his life, wonder whether she were not more magnificent than even he had ever given her credit for being. Perhaps it was to test this theory, or perhaps merely to gain time, that he now raised himself to his knees, and, leaning with outstretched arm towards the foot of his bed, made as though to touch the stocking which Santa Claus had, overnight, left dangling there. His posture, as he stared obliquely at Eva, with a sort of beaming defiance, recalled to him something seen in an "illustration". This reminiscence, however—if such it was, save in the scarred, the poor dear old woebegone and so very beguilingly *not* refractive mirror of the moment—took a peculiar twist from Eva's behaviour. She had, with startling suddenness, sat bolt upright, and looked to him as if she were overhearing some tragedy at the other end of the wire, where, in the nature of things, she was unable to arrest it. The gaze she fixed on her extravagant kinsman was of a kind to make him wonder how he contrived to remain, as he beautifully did, rigid. His prop was possibly the reflection that flashed on him that, if *she* abounded in attenuations, well, hang it all, so did *he*! It was simply a

216

difference of plane. Readjust the "values", as painters say, and there you were! He was to feel that he was only too crudely "there" when, leaning further forward, he laid a chubby forefinger on the stocking, causing that receptacle to rock ponderously to and fro. This effect was more expected than the tears which started to Eva's eyes, and the intensity with which "Don't you", she exclaimed, "see?"

"The mote in the middle distance?" he asked. "Did you ever, my dear, know me to see anything else? I tell you it blocks out everything. It's a cathedral, it's a herd of elephants, it's the whole habitable globe. Oh, it's, believe me, of an obsessiveness!" But his sense of the one thing it *didn't* block out from his purview enabled him to launch at Eva a speculation as to just how far Santa Claus had, for the particular occasion, gone. The gauge, for both of them, of this seasonable distance seemed almost blatantly suspended in the silhouettes of the two stockings. Over and above the basis of (presumably) sweetmeats in the toes and heels, certain extrusions stood for a very plenary fulfilment of desire. And, since Eva *had* set her heart on a doll of ample proportions and practicable eyelids—had asked that most admirable of her sex, their mother, for it with no less directness than he himself had put into his demand for a sword and helmet—her coyness now struck Keith, as lying near to, at indeed a hardly measurable distance from, the border-line of his patience. If she didn't *want* the doll, why the deuce had she made such a point of getting it? He was perhaps on the verge of putting this question to her, when, waving her hand to include both stockings, she said "Of course, my dear, you *do* see. There they are, and you know I know you know we wouldn't, either of us, dip a finger into them." With a vibrancy of tone that seemed to bring her voice quite close to him, "One doesn't," she added, "violate the shrine—pick the pearl from the shell!"

Even had the answering question "Doesn't one just?" which for an instant hovered on the tip of his tongue, been uttered, it could not have obscured for Keith the change which her magnificence had wrought in him. Something, perhaps, of the bigotry of the convert was already discernible in the way that, averting his eyes, he said "One doesn't even peer." As to whether, in the years that have elapsed since he said this either of our friends (now adult) has, in fact, "peered", is a question which, whenever I call at the house, I am tempted to put to one or other of them. But any regret I may feel in my invariable failure to "come up to the scratch" of yielding to this temptation is balanced, for me, by my impression—my sometimes all but throned and anointed certainty—that the answer, if vouchsafed, would be in the negative.

MAX BEERBOHM

THE BETTER END

The scene is a gentleman's library. A small company, select, is assembled. One gentleman, somewhat elderly, stands bending near the fire, his head parallel to his knees. Another gentleman, younger, stands behind him, unbent. The trousers of both gentlemen lie gathered about their ankles.

It was, the advance to that target, heralded by a preamble somewhat more deferring than he, the bender, would, we might suppose, himself have chosen, though he was not— most indubitably he was not—one to be, on any occasion even remotely imaginable, figured as betraying an eagerness that could emerge, in the least discernibly, as "vulgar". He reflected, indeed, how fine, after a manner, this choice of method—of style and mode—was; and how engaging—how really and perfectly, one might even call it, whimsical—was the way of his friend to rearward, who, while he so bristled, stiffly enough, he safely trusted, to satisfy, most admirably, their common great intent, yet with a kind of reluctant—or, it might be, even coy—patience, stretching tangents, he conceived, unexpectedly this way and unexpectedly that, held so strangely aloof, in the very aloofness none the less conveying the sense of an, at any rate not far from, almost vertiginous precipitancy. Ray Lester had, as the phrase is, the horn; but it strained, this nervous pointer, for him, under what was, in a fashion, an intellectual—could it be?—subjugation; those alert anticipatory fibres, with the quite visible quiver that they had—or indeed, if one were brought to the point of admitting it, the swelling and throbbing—hinted, and more than hinted, at some subtle variation, hardly definable, of a tragic mental tensity; while they submitted none the less—indeed, all the more—to the nicest conditions of some remoter and blander—in a way—influence: or perhaps we may conceive of them, in a more romantic view, enskied, as it were, in some far blue extraordinary recess, where vapours curl thinly, too tenuous—hardly that, though—but quite exquisitely communicative their slender— should we say?— smoke-coils and delicate film of mist. This tensity, then, held, under a certain exterior grossness of mere appearance, a quality definable, after all, as frail; something, indeed, quite undeniably shy and sweet, while with a felicity—how rare this was!—it interrelated aether with lowly matter, and revealed—almost you might believe—the secrets—some at least—of such an interrelation, so magically penetrative, and more than a little likely—in fact, "not half" as they say, "bloody likely"—to pass beyond the reach of any interpreting that one could, in the usual "set terms", express. The older man sustained his posture, cherished his—ah!— anticipations; nor did even the indifferent warmth of that slowly dying fire prove, so far as any of the little party assembled could opine, an affliction to the forbearance that he, so incomparably, guarded.

219

The, as some might have supposed it, dilatoriness of Ray Lester was, rather, a test to him, to the bender, of the fine endurance, the supremely extensive restraint, that he was able—how magnificently well!—to summon and to stand—how beautifully completely!—by; and it brought about, into the, so to speak, bargain, a superlative emergence, unexpected—oh, "a bit!"—of hidden values, the patency of which was quite blithely vivifying, and therefore welcome utterly, at all tangible points, for the assurance that it, so luminous an enlightenment, conveyed.

Nor did the fact that, in the end, little would seem to have come of it all, break the real, the unquestioned—unquestionable, even—beauty of this "preparedness" that they had had between them, this perfectly outlined preoccupation, either for Lester or for—more strangely, perhaps? or less?—the other. It could not, this especial situation, this lovely little particular phase of theirs, go on, they knew, for ever; and if that devolvulent blanching stain now perceivable upon the space of carpet dividing, yet, the two—Lester had "come", as they say, "off"—may have furnished a consummation that they could not too enthusiastically greet as the most appropriate and, wholly, satisfying that might have been looked for, at least they could recognize it as one worthy—and why not?—of their acceptance; one, indeed, to be—you understand?—bowed to.

"Ah, well, my dear," said the elder, turning and straightening, a little, and glancing forth, as he spoke, the most incalculable of comprehending eye-beams towards his— could one say "companion?"—"ah, well, my dear, so there, you see, we are!"

LOUIS WILKINSON

SAMUEL JOHNSON
1709–84

from JOHNSON'S GHOST

Ghost of DR JOHNSON *rises from trap-door P.S., and Ghost of* BOSWELL *from trap-door O.P. The latter bows respectfully to the House, and obsequiously to the Doctor's Ghost, and retires.* DOCTOR'S GHOST *loquitur:*

That which was organized by the moral ability of one has been executed by the physical efforts of many, and Drury Lane Theatre is now complete. Of that part behind the curtain, which has not yet been destined to glow beneath the brush of the varnisher, or vibrate to the hammer of the carpenter, little is thought by the public, and little need be said by the committee. Truth, however, is not to be sacrificed for the accommodation of either; and he who should pronounce that our edifice has received its final embellishment would be disseminating falsehood without incurring favour, and risking the disgrace of detection without participating the advantage of success.

Professions lavishly effused and parsimoniously verified are alike inconsistent with the precepts of innate rectitude and the practice of external policy: let it not then be conjectured, that because we are unassuming, we are imbecile; that forbearance is any indication of despondency, or humility of demerit. He that is the most assured of success will make the fewest appeals to favour, and where nothing is claimed that is undue, nothing that is due will be withheld. A swelling opening is too often succeeded by an insignificant conclusion. Parturient mountains have ere now produced muscipular abortions; and the auditor who compares incipient grandeur with final vulgarity is reminded of the pious hawkers of

Constantinople, who solemnly perambulate her streets, exclaiming, "In the name of the Prophet—figs!"

Of many who think themselves wise, and of some who are thought wise by others, the exertions are directed to the revival of mouldering and obscure dramas; to endeavours to exalt that which is now rare only because it was always worthless, and whose deterioration, while it condemned it to living obscurity, by a strange obliquity of moral perception constitutes its title to posthumous renown. To embody the flying colours of folly, to arrest evanescence, to give to bubbles the globular consistency as well as form, to exhibit on the stage the piebald denizen of the stable, and the half reasoning parent of combs, to display the brisk locomotion of Columbine, or the tortuous attitudinizing of Punch;—these are the occupations of others, whose ambition, limited to the applause of unintellectual fatuity, is too innocuous for the application of satire, and too humble for the incitement of jealousy.

HORACE SMITH

JAMES JOYCE
1882–1941

PLEASUREBUBBLE HUBBYHOUSE

Cobblears, I queek, con naught con all. This is a misbegoblin effart from swive of wive to brickfist type and four pines ninetofive in any buddy's monure. Where's your woollen tears, I asp yo, to be token by're lurke-wake root sexhundread pagan laing (in your Fibre papalbag) back to Head Case Engineering, wench we came. (No anchor was the stern reply.)

222

Finagles Waste, bejamers joist, cannondrum in excresis, insproats a crumplicadent nexicon of dumpstincts within yr fightful reportwire. He sews seemseeds in the earshell (moultigreyed). Echo homo, littlesurs! Yet in the upperroof of our puerole Humptyhead, alass, wee stans a ghost. All tug Heather now, Here Comes Excess! (Nutting degrees like digress, my old donski use to shay, God press his iddle-gotten saul.) Well a big fat darty booker it is to be Shaw, and I wouldn't have the spiers to be waterlogging all the arks and chunderment of openprism reduxdiceased betwee these greeny backs, so geld me Hobson. Suffixit touche, o gintill redrum, it's oh, allerline schoolerschrift filluphaben in a therasputin donghell incarnabine. (Otis lifteywater I must dyke for it, Father, plash me for I have skimmed. Or shuteye see, flush me, Farber, for I am skint? Hamsters on a boastcart, please.)

I'll not abound to say you won't fine yourself tungling over the odd tibs and bogs that hueffer to the kyries mine pleasurebubble sensehavens of interlarkin dizzypin. Not at Hall, the very tort of it is anaspirin for Deloittes of me. Old Joys is low-undo-himself. (And don't wee all.) Notwith-shandy he guts no eyes with ewers drooling. And why should he, Gott safes the Mark, we cannot all be Hainault Hobcecils scrimbling lists of the midevil sainsburys, we'd all go roust the twins.

But, you interplate (those of you in whom the shap of egremont is heather rising, gold blast you sirs, would you heave the price of a Riles-Royals about yez?) this is no rumtomb teararts billyphant from the Dully Bullygraft! This is Highly Charged Engrishe or I'm a touchmum! How ripe you are, penine interlexapples, I bough to your supearier fudgement. But are you shaun, are you dolgelly convicted we are dwelling with a Wort of Ark and not a Pickforth's vain of finto seems belunging to a literarty hen's teeth diva? Hom? You mistumblestand the jeskin? Swerve you right, you anchor! (Part my fringe.)

In the embolism comes it doubt to this: Filigrees Whelk, bejams juice is a bleeding grant for pores, a hubbyhouse for the aldebarans of the acadome, och it's an obsolate condgeree of your hockmugrandiose christable prankhearse, and all the finn in it is in the parting together (on Joisus' path) and biggerole in the pollen-asonder by ourshelf, misteral stingers that we bee. Sore knackers to Sham and Shawn! Annie Luvya Liverpool a la long term! Abbasso profungus in arsepick! Flaherty-o for the Missus! (The remarque is out of plays. I withdrawl it entimely with sunblest apollogrease.)

Now *Boatrace of the Hearties as a Ying Yang*, on the upperham, I meal your *Potroast of the Hartebeeste as a York Ham*, ah yer *Prostitute of the Alldust as our Yom Mahon*, well that's a dufferin Cathal O'Fish altargodder. Innis?

RUSSELL DAVIES

from TRAVESTIES

JOYCE: (*Dictating to* GWEN) Deshill holles eamus . . .

GWEN: (*Writing*) Deshill holles eamus . . .

JOYCE: Thrice.

GWEN: Uh-hum.

JOYCE: Send us bright one, light one, Horhorn, quickening and wombfruit.

GWEN: Send us bright one, light one, Horhorn, quickening and wombfruit.

JOYCE: Thrice.

GWEN: Uh-hum.

JOYCE: Hoopsa, boyaboy, hoopsa!

GWEN: Hoopsa, boyaboy, hoopsa!

JOYCE: Hoopsa, boyaboy, hoopsa!

GWEN: Likewise thrice?

JOYCE: Uh-hum.

TOM STOPPARD

JOHN KEATS
1795–1821

ODE TO A JAR OF PICKLES

A sweet, acidulous, dawn-reaching thrill
   Pervades my sense: I seem to see or hear
The lushy garden-grounds of Greenwich Hill
   In autumn, when the crispy leaves are sere:
And odours haunt me of remotest spice
   From the Levant or musky-aired Cathay,
Or from the saffron-fields of Jerico,
      Where everything is nice:
   The more I sniff, the more I swoon away,
And what else mortal palate craves, forego.

Odours unsmelled are keen, but those I smell
   Are keener; wherefore let me sniff again!
Enticing walnuts, I have known ye well
   In youth, when pickles were a passing pain;
Unwitting youth, that craves the candy stem,
   And sugar-plums to olives doth prefer.
And even licks the pots of marmalade
      When sweetness clings to them:
   But now I dream of ambergris and myrrh,
Tasting these walnuts in the poplar shade.

Lo! hoarded coolness in the heart of noon,
   Plucked with its dew, the cucumber is here,
As to the Dryad's parching lips a boon,
   And crescent, bean-pods, unto Bacchus dear;
And, last of all, the pepper's pungent globe,
   The scarlet dwelling of the sylph of fire,
Provoking purple draughts; and, surfeited,
      I cast my trailing robe

O'er my pale feet, touch up my tuneless lyre,
And twist the Delphic wreath to suit my head.

Here shall my tongue in other wise be soured
  Than fretful men's in parched and palsied days;
And, by the mid–May's dusky leaves embowered,
  Forget the fruitful blame, the scanty praise.
No sweets to them who sweet themselves were born,
  Whose natures ooze with lucent saccharine;
Who, with sad repetition soothly cloyed,
    The lemon-tinted morn
  Enjoy, and find acetic twilight fine:
Wake I, or sleep? The pickle-jar is void.

BAYARD TAYLOR

FRANCIS SCOTT KEY
1780–1843

FINAL CURTAIN

Tune: "The Star-Spangled Banner"

Just say this is a comedy of errors.
President Nixon on a White House tape

Oh, say you can hear
On the Watergate tapes
That I gave to the Judge
How I lied like a trooper?
When the chips are all down
I guess no one escapes;

I've a date at high noon,
And I'm no Gary Cooper.
If they're going to impeach
There's no gun I can reach,
So I may as well quit
With a heart–rending speech.
Oh, say does that flag
That I've dirtied still wave?
If I play my cards right,
There's some loot I can save.

Oh, this is the crunch,
I may have to resign,
But those bums are dead wrong
If they think I'm defeated.
When they pension me off
At the end of the line
And my taxes are paid,
They can (passage deleted).
I'm not out of the woods,
But I've still got the goods,
Though I may go to jail
With the rest of the hoods.
George Washington's dead,
Like the pledge that I gave,
But if he were alive
He would turn in his grave.

ROGER WODDIS

RUDYARD KIPLING
1865–1936

TO R. K.

As long as I dwell on some stupendous
And tremendous (Heaven defend us!)
Monstr'-inform'-ingens-horrendous
Demoniaco-seraphic
Penman's latest piece of graphic.

      Browning

Will there never come a season
Which shall rid us from the curse
Of a prose which knows no reason
And an unmelodious verse:
When the world shall cease to wonder
At the genius of an Ass,
And a boy's eccentric blunder
Shall not bring success to pass:
When mankind shall be delivered
From the clash of magazines,
And the inkstand shall be shivered
Into countless smithereens:
When there stands a muzzled stripling,
Mute, beside a muzzled bore:
When the Rudyards cease from Kipling
And the Haggards Ride no more.

      J. K. STEPHEN

JACK AND JILL

Here is the tale—and you must make the most of it!
 Here is the rhyme—ah, listen and attend;
Backwards—forwards—read it all and boast of it
 If you are anything wiser at the end!

Now Jack looked up—it was time to sup, and the bucket
 was yet to fill,
And Jack looked round for a space and frowned, then
 beckoned his sister Jill,
And twice he pulled his sister's hair, and thrice he smote
 her side;
"Ha' done, ha' done with your impudent fun—ha' done
 with your games!" she cried;
"You have made mud-pies of a marvellous size—finger
 and face are black,
You have trodden the way of Mire and Clay—now up and
 wash you, Jack!
Or else, or ever we reach our home, there waiteth an angry
 dame—
Well you know the weight of her blow—the supperless
 open shame!
Wash, if you will, on yonder hill—wash, if you will, at
 the spring,—
Or keep your dirt, to your certain hurt, and an imminent
 walloping!"
"You must wash—you must scrub—you must scrape!"
 growled Jack, "you must traffic with cans and pails,
Nor keep the spoil of good brown soil in the rim of your
 fingernails!
The morning path you must tread to your bath—you must
 wash ere the night descends,
And all for the cause of conventional laws and the
 soapmakers' dividends!

229

But if 'tis sooth that our meal in truth depends on our
                                                    washing, Jill,
By the sacred right of our appetite—haste—haste to the
                                                    top of the hill!"

They have trodden the Way of the Mire and Clay, they
                                                    have toiled and travelled far,
They have climbed to the brow of the hill-top now, where
                                                    the bubbling fountains are,
They have taken the bucket and filled it up—yea, filled it
                                                    up to the brim;
But Jack sneered at his sister Jill, and Jill she jeered at him:
"What, blown already!" Jack cried out (and his was a
                                                    biting mirth!)
"You boast indeed of your wonderful speed—but what is
                                                    the boasting worth?
Now, if you can run as the antelope runs, and if you can
                                                    turn like a hare,
Come, race me, Jill, to the foot of the hill—and prove
                                                    your boasting fair!"
"Race? What is a race" (and a mocking face had Jill as she
                                                    spake the word)
"Unless for a prize the runner tries? The truth indeed ye
                                                    heard,
For I can run as the antelope runs, and I can turn like a
                                                    hare:—
The first one down wins half-a-crown—and I will race
                                                    you there!"
"Yea, if for the lesson that you will learn (the lesson of
                                                    humbled pride)
The price you fix at two-and-six, it shall not be denied;
Come, take your stand at my right hand, for here is the
                                                    mark we toe:
Now, are you ready, and are you steady? Gird up your
                                                    petticoats! Go!"

And Jill she ran like a winging bolt, a bolt from the bow
                                                released,
But Jack like a stream of the lightning gleam, with its
                                        pathway duly greased;
He ran downhill in front of Jill like a summer lightning
                                                    flash—
Till he suddenly tripped on a stone, or slipped, and fell
                                        to earth with a crash.
Then straight did rise on his wondering eyes the
                                        constellations fair,
Arcturus and Pleiades, the Greater and Lesser Bear,
The swirling rain of a comet's train he saw, as he swiftly
                                                    fell—
And Jill came tumbling after him with a loud triumphant
                                                    yell:
"You have won, you have won, the race is done! And as
                                    for the wager laid—
You have fallen down with a broken crown—the half-
                                    crown debt is paid!"

They have taken Jack to the room at the back where the
                                    family medicines are,
And he lies in bed with a broken head in a halo of vinegar;
While, in that Jill had laughed her fill as her brother fell
                                                to earth,
She hath felt the sting of a walloping—she hath paid the
                                        price of her mirth!

Here is the tale—and now you have the whole of it,
  Here is the story—well and wisely planned,
Beauty—Duty—these make up the soul of it—
  But, ah, my little readers, will you mark and understand?
                                        ANTHONY C. DEANE

IF NOT

*Kipling's "If" rewritten to conform
with the spirit of the times*

If you can't trim your sails to suit the weather,
If you can't take your chance to pass the buck,
If you can't offer cardboard goods as leather
And then persuade the mugs to buy the muck;
If you can't work a profitable fiddle
Or cheat the Customs when you've been abroad,
If you can't wangle your returns, and diddle
The Income Tax, yet not be charged with fraud;

If you can't learn the craft of social climbing
And damn the eyes of those who're underneath;
If you can't kid your friend you're not two-timing,
Then, when it suits you, kick him in the teeth;
If you can't run a car on public money,
Or have your lunch each day at the Savoy,
You're going to find that life's not at all funny,
For, take my tip, you'll miss the bus, old boy.

H. A. C. EVANS

Then it's collar 'im tight,
  In the name o' the Lawd!
'Ustle 'im, shake 'im till 'e's sick!
  Wot, 'e would, would 'e? Well,
  Then yer've got ter give 'im 'Ell,
An' it's trunch, trunch, truncheon does the trick!
                              Police Station Ditties

I had spent Christmas Eve at the Club listening to a grand pow-pow between certain of the choicer sons of Adam. Then Slushby had cut in. Slushby is one who writes to newspapers and is theirs obediently "HUMANITARIAN". When Slushby cuts in, men remember they have to be up early next morning.

Sharp round a corner on the way home, I collided with something firmer than the regulation pillar-box. I righted myself after the recoil and saw some stars that were very pretty indeed. Then I perceived the nature of the obstruction.

"Evening, Judlip," I said sweetly, when I had collected my hat from the gutter. "Have I broken the law, Judlip? If so, I'll go quiet."

"Time yer was in bed," grunted X, 36. "Yer Ma'll be lookin' out for yer."

This from the friend of my bosom! It hurt. Many were the night-beats I had been privileged to walk with Judlip, imbibing curious lore that made glad the civilian heart of me. Seven whole 8 x 5 inch notebooks had I pitmanized to the brim with Judlip. And now to be repulsed as one of the uninitiated! It hurt horrid.

There is a thing called Dignity. Small boys sometimes stand on it. Then they have to be kicked. Then they get down, weeping. I don't stand on Dignity.

"What's wrong, Judlip?" I asked, more sweetly than ever. "Drawn a blank tonight?"

"Yuss. Drawn a blank blank blank. 'Avent 'ad so much as a

kick at a lorst dorg. Christmas Eve ain't wot it was." I felt for my notebook. "Lawd! I remembers the time when the drunks and disorderlies down this street was as thick as flies on a fly-paper. One just picked 'em orf with one's finger and thumb. A bloomin' battew, that's wot it wos."

"The night's yet young, Judlip," I insinuated with a jerk of my thumb at the flaring windows of the Rat and Blood Hound. At that moment the saloon door swung open, emitting a man and woman who walked with linked arms and exceeding great care.

Judlip eyed them longingly as they tacked up the street. Then he sighed. Now, when Judlip sighs that sound is like unto that which issues from the vent of a Crosby boiler when the cog-gauges are at 260°F.

"Come, Judlip," I said. "Possess your soul in patience. You'll soon find someone to make an example of. Mean-while"—I threw back my head and smacked my lips—"the usual, Judlip?"

In another minute I emerged through the swing-door, bearing a furtive glass of that same "usual", and nipped down the mews where my friend was wont to await these little tokens of esteem.

"To the Majesty of the Law, Judlip!"

When he had honoured the toast, I scooted back with the glass, leaving him wiping the beads off his beard-bristles. He was in his philosophic mood when I rejoined him at the corner.

"Wot am I?" he said, as we paced along. "A bloomin' cypher. Wot's the sarjint? 'E's got the Inspector over 'im. Over above the Inspector there's the Sooprintendent. Over above 'im's the old red-tape-masticatin' Yard. Over above that there's the 'Ome Sec. Wot's 'e? A cypher, like me. Why?" Judlip looked up at the stars. "Over above 'im's We Dunno Wot. Somethin' wot issues its horders an' regulations an' divisional injunctions, inscrootable like, but p'remptory; an' we 'as ter see as 'ow they're carried out, not arskin' no questions, but each man goin' about 'is dooty."

" 'Is dooty'," said I, looking up from my notebook. "Yes, I've got that."

"Life ain't a bean-feast. It's a 'arsh reality. An' them as makes it a bean-feast 'as got to be 'arshly dealt with accordin'. That's wot the Force is put 'ere for from Above. Not as 'ow we ain't fallible. We makes our mistakes. An' when we makes 'em we sticks to 'em. For the honour o' the Force. Which same is the jool Britannia wears on 'er bosom as a charm against hanarchy. That's wot the brarsted old Beaks don't understand. Yer remember Smithers of our Div?"

I remembered Smithers—well. As fine, upstanding, square-toed, bullet-headed, clean-living a son of a gun as ever perjured himself in the box. There was nothing of the softy about Smithers. I took off my billicock to Smithers' memory.

"Sacrificed to public opinion? Yuss," said Judlip, pausing at a front door and flashing his 45 c.p. down the slot of a two-grade Yale. "Sacrificed to a parcel of screamin' old women wot ort ter 'ave gorn down on their knees an' thanked Gawd for such a protector. 'E'll be out in another 'alf year. Wot'll 'e do then, pore devil? Go a bust on 'is conduc' money an' throw in 'is lot with them same hexperts wot 'ad a 'oly terror of 'im." Then Judlip swore gently.

"What should you do, O Great One, if ever it were your duty to apprehend him?"

"Do? Why, yer blessed innocent, yer don't think I'd shirk a fair clean cop? Same time, I don't say as 'ow I wouldn't 'andle 'im tender like, for sake o' wot 'e wos. Likewise cos 'e'd be a stiff customer to tackle. Likewise 'cos—"

He had broken off, and was peering fixedly upwards at an angle of 85° across the moonlit street. "Ullo!" he said in a hoarse whisper.

Striking an average between the direction of his eyes—for Judlip, when on the job, has a soul-stirring squint—I perceived someone in the act of emerging from a chimney-pot.

Judlip's voice clove the silence. "Wot are yer doin' hup there?"

The person addressed came to the edge of the parapet. I saw then that he had a hoary white beard, a red ulster with the hood up, and what looked like a sack over his shoulder. He said something or other in a voice like a concertina that has been left out in the rain.

"I dessay," answered my friend. "Just you come down, an' we'll see about that."

The old man nodded and smiled. Then—as I hope to be saved—he came floating gently down through the moon-light, with the sack over his shoulder and a young fir-tree clasped to his chest. He alighted in a friendly manner on the curb beside us.

Judlip was the first to recover himself. Out went his right arm, and the airman was slung round by the scruff of the neck, spilling his sack in the road. I made a bee-line for his shoulder blades. Burglar or no burglar, he was the best airman out, and I was muchly desirous to know the precise nature of the apparatus under his ulster. A backhander from Judlip's left caused me to hop quickly aside. The prisoner was squealing and whimpering. He didn't like the feel of Judlip's knuckles at his cervical vertebrae.

"Wot wos yer doin' hup there?" asked Judlip, tightening his grip.

"I'm S-Santa Claus, Sir. P-please, Sir, let me g-go."

"Hold him," I shouted. "He's a German."

"It's my dooty ter caution yer that wotever yer say now may be used in hevidence against yer, yer old sinner. Pick up that there sack, an' come along o' me."

The captive snivelled something about peace on earth, good will toward men.

"Yuss," said Judlip. "That's in the Noo Testament, ain't it? The Noo Testament contains some uncommon nice readin' for old gents an' young ladies. But it ain't included in the librery o' the Force. We confine ourselves to the Old

236

Testament—O.T., 'ot. An' 'ot you'll get it. Hup with that sack, an' quick march!"

I have seen worse attempts at a neck-wrench, but it was just not slippery enough for Judlip. And the kick that Judlip then let fly was a thing of beauty and a joy for ever.

"Frog's-march him!" I shrieked, dancing. "For the love of heaven, frog's-march him!"

Trotting by Judlip's side to the Station, I reckoned it out that if Slushby had not been at the Club I should not have been here to see. Which shows that even Slushbys are put into this world for a purpose.

MAX BEERBOHM

PHILIP LARKIN
1922–

MR STRUGNELL

"This was Mr Strugnell's room," she'll say—
And look down at the lumpy, single bed.
"He stayed here up until he went away
And kept his bicycle out in that shed.

"He had a job at Norwood library—
He was a quiet sort who liked to read—
Dick Francis mostly, and some poetry—
He liked John Betjeman very much indeed

"But not Pam Ayres or even Patience Strong—
He'd change the subject if I mentioned them.
Or say, 'It's time for me to run along—
Your taste's too highbrow for me, Mrs M.'

"And up he'd go and listen to that jazz.
I don't mind telling you—it was a bore:
Few things in this house have been tiresome as
The sound of his foot tapping on the floor.

"He didn't seem the type for being free
With girls, or going out and having fun.
He had a funny turn in 'sixty-three
And ran around shouting 'Yippee! It's begun!'

"I don't know what he meant, but after that
He had a different look, much more relaxed.
Some nights he'd come in late, too tired to chat,
As if he had been somewhat overtaxed.

"And now he's gone. He said he found Tulse Hill
Too stimulating—wanted somewhere dull,
At last he's found a place that fits the bill—
Enjoying perfect boredom up in Hull."

WENDY COPE

D. H. LAWRENCE
1885–1930

SONS AND AZTECS

She lay, motionless, in the burning heat. She gave herself to
the sun in an act of supreme worship. Her body was the
sacrament.

He watched and was thrilled to the soul. A dark primeval
shout resounded through his whole being. To him, she was

the true female spirituality. Not the whimpering, cloying, tendrilled feminine grasp of demand and duty, not the empty ache of sentiment, but the pure lambent flame of passion. He warmed to her flame. She basked in his primitive mooncold light. She was the sun, and he the moon.

He lay down beside her. Then he climbed on top of her, and did it to her.

RICHARD CURTIS

F. R. LEAVIS
1895–1978

from ANOTHER BOOK TO CROSS OFF YOUR LIST

by
Simon Lacerous[1]

The great English novels are *Sons and Lovers*, *Lady Chatterley's Lover* and *Women in Love*. Some malicious persons, who have had the cheek to call me narrow-minded in the past, will doubtless welcome this statement as proof of their views. I don't care; I let it stick. There will always be literary scum to laugh at every honest effort to make tasteful discriminations, and we are now in greater need than ever before of critics—or shall I say, of *a* critic—who will stand up as a moral and aesthetic guide, leading the culture-hungry masses to the finest and purest literature and keeping the rest in outer darkness. If destiny must choose me as its messenger, I do not shirk from the call, but cry out in all directions: Beware, you complacent dolts who are still wallowing in Victorian trash! Beware, you academic leeches who will praise any dull sonnet you can find that has not already been worked over by your brethren! A judgement day is at hand! You are going to have to submit your crackpot notions and juvenile tastes to the severe gaze of common sense, intelligence, and Life!

D. H. Lawrence is the only English novelist worth reading. Now, I know that some of you—the sort that creep around in libraries looking for inconsistencies in a man's work—will say that my position has changed since last year, when I said the great English novelists were Richardson, Fanny Burney, Disraeli, and Lawrence. What you don't seem to realize is that in the meantime another book on the English novel has appeared, by Lord Wendell Dovetail. Now, Lord Wendell Dovetail is a fine person, I suppose; at least he has many friends in his circle, so I am told by some friends of mine who have some contacts in his circle (that kind of counterspy work is not for me, by the bye). I have nothing against Lord Wendell Dovetail personally. But really, I cannot be expected to keep my temper when he publishes a book saying that the great English novelists are Richardson, Fanny Burney, and Disraeli! I went out at once and reread these people, and so did Trixie, and we agreed that they were no good at all.

Now that I have gotten down to Lawrence alone, the number of English novelists on my Index is greater than ever, and this I take to be a sign that things may be improving at last on the literary scene. Perhaps readers are finally beginning to learn that their reading time is precious and very limited, and mustn't be wasted on third-raters like Fielding and Joyce.[2] There was an undergraduate just last week asking me which of Shakespeare's plays he should start with, to work up Shakespeare for his examinations. "Shakespeare!" I said. "Why, man, you haven't even read *The Rainbow* yet! Don't talk to me of Shakespeare until you've gone through Lawrence twice and made a list of everything he has to say against the Establishment." He took it rather hard, but the point is, he took it. Another soul saved from dilettantism, if I may put it thus. . . .

240

[1]Simon Lacerous is perhaps the most feared and respected critic in England. An implacable foe of sentimentality, flabby aestheticism, and inflated reputations, he has made English authors tremble since the publication of his first volume, *Assassinations*, thirty years ago. Though he is a Fellow of Magdalen College, Oxford, he despises the entire English university system. Of his fellow Fellows he has said: "They can all go to hell. Of course, some should go before others. One has a responsibility to make discriminations." He and his wife, Trixie, were the guiding spirits behind the now defunct but extremely influential quarterly, *Thumbscrew*. Several of the younger critics who have taken up the battle against sentimentality, flabby aestheticism, and inflated reputations owe their start and their moral guidance to Dr Lacerous.

[2]Naturally, there are still persons willing to read into *Tom Jones* a few pages and then pretend to have devoured all of Fielding with hearty pleasure. The fact is, that when I get such people into my chambers, give them a straight look, and *demand* the *truth*, they admit to having aped the taste of several critics who bear me particular ill will. As for Joyce, he is a nasty trifler and, what is worse, an Irishman.

FREDERICK C. CREWS

JOHN LE CARRÉ
1931–

from THE DOG IT WAS THAT DIED

PURVIS: I'm going back thirty-five years now, when I was still being run by Gell, or Rashnikov. Now Gell is dead and Rashnikov is probably dead too. They set me going between them like one of those canisters in a department store, and they disappeared leaving me to go back and forth, back and forth, a canister between us and you, or us and them.

BLAIR: I didn't quite follow that last bit.

PURVIS: I remember some of it, no problem. I remember striking up a conversation with Rashnikov in one of the stacks in the Westminster library—political economy. Or perhaps he struck up a conversation with me. I remember having a few dinners with him, meeting some of his friends, arguing long into the night about politics, and I remember finally being asked to look something up for him in our back-numbers room in Whitehall . . . You remember that basement we used to have before we had microfilm? The thing he wanted was perfectly innocuous, but by that time, of course, I knew he was supposedly on the staff of the Soviet Commercial Attaché, so the next time he asked me to look something up, something which wasn't quite so innocuous, I of course reported the whole thing to Gell who was my superior.

BLAIR: Of course.

PURVIS: Sure enough, Gell told me to pretend to swallow the bait and to await instructions.

BLAIR: Straightforward enough.

PURVIS: It wasn't. Rashnikov was playing a subtle game. He had told me to tell Gell.

BLAIR: To tell him what?

PURVIS: To tell Gell that I was being recruited by Rashnikov. So that Gell would be fooled into thinking that I was pretending to be Rashnikov's man while I was really Gell's man.

BLAIR: Looking at it from Rashnikov's point of view.

PURVIS: Yes.

BLAIR: And did you tell Gell that this was going on, that Rashnikov had told you to tell Gell?

PURVIS: Yes. I did. But . . .

BLAIR: But . . .?

PURVIS: Well, I'm pretty sure that when I told Gell that all this was going on, I was also acting on Rashnikov's instructions.

(*Pause.*)

BLAIR: But, if that were so, no doubt you told Gell that it *was* so. No doubt you told Gell that Rashnikov had told you to tell Gell that Rashnikov had told you to tell him that you were being offered the bait.

PURVIS: That's what I can't remember. I've forgotten who is my primary employer and who my secondary. For years I've been feeding stuff in both directions, following my instructions from either side, having been instructed to do so by the other, and since each side wanted the other side to believe that I was working for *it*, both sides were often giving me genuine stuff to pass on to the other side . . . so the side I was actually working for became . . . well, a matter of opinion really . . . it got lost.

(*Pause.*)

Blair?

BLAIR: I didn't speak.

PURVIS: Well, I just carried on doing what I was told . . . and one day, not very long ago, I started thinking about my retirement. The sherry party with the Chief. The presentation clock. The London Transport senior citizen's bus pass. The little dacha on the Vistula.

BLAIR: Purvis . . .?

PURVIS: Exactly. Hang on a sec, I thought—hello!—which—? . . .? And blow me, I found I had forgotten.

BLAIR: But you worked for Gell. For *me*.

PURVIS: I worked for Rashnikov too.

BLAIR: Only because we asked you to play along.

PURVIS: *He* asked me to play along.

BLAIR: Let's not get into that again. You're one of us.

PURVIS: Well, I'd have to be, wouldn't I, to be of any use to him?

TOM STOPPARD

243

HENRY WADSWORTH LONGFELLOW
1807–82

THE MODERN HIAWATHA

He killed the noble Mudjokivis.
Of the skin he made him mittens,
Made them with the fur side inside,
Made them with the skin side outside.
He, to get the warm side inside,
Put the inside skin side outside;
He, to get the cold side outside,
Put the warm side fur side inside,
That's why he put the fur side inside,
Why he put the skin side outside,
Why he turned them inside outside.

GEORGE A. STRONG

HIAWATHA'S PHOTOGRAPHING

In an age of imitation, I can claim no sort of merit for this slight attempt at doing what is known to be so easy. Anyone who knows what verse is, with the slightest ear for rhythm, can throw off a composition in the easy running metre of "The Song of Hiawatha". Having, then, distinctly stated that I challenge no attention, in the following little poem, to its merely verbal jingle, I must beg the candid reader to confine his criticism to its treatment of the subject.

From his shoulder Hiawatha
Took the camera of rosewood,
Made of sliding, folding rosewood;
Neatly put it all together.
In its case it lay compactly,
Folded into nearly nothing;
But he opened out the hinges,
Pushed and pulled the joints and hinges,
Till it looked all squares and oblongs,
Like a complicated figure
In the second book of Euclid.

   This he perched upon a tripod,
And the family in order
Sat before him for their pictures.
Mystic, awful was the process.

   First a piece of glass he coated
With Collodion, and plunged it
In a bath of Lunar Caustic
Carefully dissolved in water:
There he left it certain minutes.

   Secondly, my Hiawatha
Made with cunning hand a mixture
Of the acid Pyro-gallic,
And of Glacial Acetic,
And of Alcohol and water:
This developed all the picture.

   Finally, he fixed each picture
With a saturate solution
Of a certain salt of Soda—
Chemists call it Hyposulphite.
(Very difficult the name is
For a metre like the present,
But periphrasis has done it.)

   All the family in order
Sat before him for their pictures.
Each in turn, as he was taken,

Volunteered his own suggestions,
His invaluable suggestions.
　　First the Governor, the Father:
He suggested velvet curtains
Looped about a massy pillar;
And the corner of a table,
Of a rosewood dining-table.
He would hold a scroll of something,
Hold it firmly in his left hand;
He would keep his right hand buried
(Like Napoleon) in his waistcoat;
He would contemplate the distance
With a look of pensive meaning,
As of ducks that die in tempests.
　　Grand, heroic was the notion:
Yet the picture failed entirely:
Failed, because he moved a little,
Moved, because he couldn't help it.
　　Next, his better half took courage;
She would have her picture taken:
She came dressed beyond description,
Dressed in jewels and in satin
Far too gorgeous for an empress.
Gracefully she sat down, sideways,
With a simper scarcely human,
Holding in her hand a nosegay
Rather larger than a cabbage.
All the while that she was taking,
Still the lady chattered, chattered,
Like a monkey in the forest.
"Am I sitting still?" she asked him.
"Is my face enough in profile?
Shall I hold the nosegay higher?
Will it come into the picture?"
And the picture failed completely.
　　Next the Son, the Stunning-Cantab:

246

He suggested curves of beauty,
Curves pervading all his figure,
Which the eye might follow onward,
Till they centred in the breast-pin,
Centred in the golden breast-pin.
He had learnt it all from Ruskin
(Author of "The Stones of Venice",
"Seven Lamps of Architecture",
"Modern Painters", and some others);
And perhaps he had not fully
Understood his author's meaning;
But, whatever was the reason,
All was fruitless, as the picture
Ended in an utter failure.

Next to him the eldest daughter:
She suggested very little;
Only asked if he would take her
With her look of "passive beauty".

Her idea of passive beauty
Was a squinting of the left eye,
Was a drooping of the right eye,
Was a smile that went up sideways
To the corner of the nostrils.

Hiawatha, when she asked him,
Took no notice of the question,
Looked as if he hadn't heard it;
But, when pointedly appealed to,
Smiled in his peculiar manner,
Coughed and said it "didn't matter",
Bit his lip and changed the subject.

Nor in this was he mistaken,
As the picture failed completely.

So in turn the other sisters.
Last, the youngest son was taken:
Very rough and thick his hair was,
Very round and red his face was,

Very dusty was his jacket,
Very fidgety his manner.
And his overbearing sisters
Called him names he disapproved of:
Called him Johnny, "Daddy's Darling",
Called him Jacky, "Scrubby School-boy".
And, so awful was the picture,
In comparison the others
Might be thought to have succeeded,
To have partially succeeded.
    Finally my Hiawatha
Tumbled all the tribe together,
("Grouped" is not the right expression,)
And, as happy chance would have it,
Did at last obtain a picture
Where the faces all succeeded:
Each came out a perfect likeness.
    Then they joined and all abused it,
Unrestrainedly abused it,
As "the worst and ugliest picture
They could possibly have dreamed of.
Giving one such strange expressions!
Sulkiness, conceit, and meanness!
Really any one would take us
(Any one that did not know us)
For the most unpleasant people!"
(Hiawatha seemed to think so,
Seemed to think it not unlikely.)
All together rang their voices,
Angry, loud, discordant voices,
As of dogs that howl in concert,
As of cats that wail in chorus.
    But my Hiawatha's patience,
His politeness and his patience,
Unaccountably had vanished,
And he left that happy party.

Neither did he leave them slowly,
With that calm deliberation,
That intense deliberation
Which photographers aspire to:
But he left them in a hurry,
Left them in a mighty hurry,
Vowing that he would not stand it.
   Hurriedly he packed his boxes,
Hurriedly the porter trundled
On a barrow all his boxes;
Hurriedly he took his ticket,
Hurriedly the train received him:
Thus departed Hiawatha.

LEWIS CARROLL

ED MCBAIN (EVAN HUNTER)
1926–

from THE CROWDED HOURS

The city in these pages is real.
   The characters are drawn directly from life.
   The police procedure is strictly a product of the author's imagination.

The city.
   She.
   They'll all tell you the city's a female. To some she's a laughing girl, to some a full, ripe woman; to some a lady, to some a dame, and to more than a few a bitch. But she's a female to all of them—just as she is to you, whether you grew

249

up in a swank penthouse in Tewart Towers or a slum tenement in downtown Itolja, whether you graduated from the plush country club of Elizabethtown High or survived the hard knocks of North Manual Trades—or even if you met her only as a mature man and felt you'd known her always.

A female, this city, a she, whether she's warm and comforting or cool and exhilarating or hot and making you drip sweat or cold and unfriendly and chilling—she can be any of these, and she'll be all of them at some point to every man, even you who love her. At noon her tall spires implore heaven like arms of shimmering brilliance, gazing with haughty magnificence at the clear waters of her harbour. She exudes exuberant life. The curves of her shoreline, the patterns of her streets and freeways can be graceful or provocative or cute—their charm can obscure the midriff bulge of her slums. She's home to more Swiss than the city of Geneva, more Canadians than Toronto and Vancouver combined.

When you love her—if you love her, and how could one not love her?—her small flaws don't repel you but make you love her all the more, this sweetheart of your youth, this mistress of your best years, this comforting friend of your old age.

She's a female, this city, your female.

And you love her.

But you wish she'd change her deodorant and take a bath, because she's dirty and she stinks. . . .

Steve Berella was bleeding and wondering why.

Not why he was bleeding. He was bleeding because someone had smashed the side of his head in with a bottle. And his belly ached because someone had kicked him there repeatedly.

The feel and taste and smell of blood were easy to explain. So was the aching gut.

But Steve Berella was wondering why he had become a

cop. Was it his job to collect the city's human trash? Was it his duty to clean the stains off her shimmering spires? Was it his job to maintain the Chamber of Commerce's façade of respectability? Was it his job to get bottles smashed over his head and get kicked in the gut? Repeatedly? In his own apartment?

Steve Berella thought about it and decided he was glad he was a cop.

But he wished he could stop bleeding.

On the carpet.

He kept bleeding for a while.

Blood is messy. . . .

JON L. BREEN

GEORGE MACBETH
1932–

from PEREGRINE PRYKKE'S PILGRIMAGE

The blood has soaked the bone which hides the stone
The rat excreted in the telephone.
Fellating stone and bone I taste the blood
Which laps around my pelvis like a flood.
I feel a painful pressure in my groin
On either side of which I have a loin.
My loins are groined, my stone's a bloody bone:
I'll have to learn to leave myself alone.

CLIVE JAMES

CHRISTOPHER MARLOWE
1564–93

THE NYMPH'S REPLY TO THE PASSIONATE SHEPHERD

If all the world and love were young,
And truth in every shepherd's tongue,
These pretty pleasures might me move,
To live with thee, and be thy love.

Time drives the flocks from field to fold
When rivers rage, and rocks grow cold,
And Philomel becometh dumb;
The rest complain of cares to come.

The flowers do fade, and wanton fields
To wayward winter reckoning yields;
A honey'd tongue, a heart of gall,
Is fancy's spring, but sorrow's fall.

Thy gown, thy shoes, thy beds of roses,
Thy cap, thy kirtle, and thy posies;
Soon break, soon wither, soon forgotten,
In folly ripe, in reason rotten.

Thy belt of straw, and ivy buds,
Thy coral clasps, and amber studs,
All these in me no means can move,
To come to thee, and be thy love.

But could youth last, and love still breed,
Had joys no date, and age no need;
Then these delights my mind might move,
To live with thee and be thy love.

SIR WALTER RALEIGH

JOHN MASEFIELD
1878–1967
SEA-CHILL

When Mrs John Masefield and her husband, the author of "I Must Go Down to the Seas Again", arrived here on a liner, she said to a reporter, "It was too uppy-downy and Mr Masefield was ill."

News item

I must go down to the seas again, where the billows romp
and reel,
So all I ask is a large ship that rides on an even keel,
And a mild breeze and a broad deck with a slight list to
leeward,
And a clean chair in a snug nook and a nice, kind steward.

I must go down to the seas again, the sport of wind and
tide,
As the gray wave and the green wave play leapfrog over
the side.
And all I want is a glassy calm with a bone-dry scupper,
A good book and a warm rug and a light, plain supper.

I must go down to the seas again, though there I'm a total
loss,
And can't say which is worst, the pitch, the plunge, the
roll, the toss.
But all I ask is a safe retreat in a bar well tended,
And a soft berth and a smooth course till the long trip's
ended.

ARTHUR GUITERMAN

W. SOMERSET MAUGHAM
1874–1965

from FIRST PERSON CIRCULAR

I do not often care for company on getting back to England from abroad. A slow process of adjustment is both necessary and pleasant, and I find one savours the pleasure a little more sharply if one is alone. On this occasion, however, after attending to arrears of correspondence and putting into order the two or three volumes of notes I had accumulated on my travels, I was finding London, for some reason or other, a trifle flat.

In a longer stay at Kuala than I had foreseen I had contracted the habit of an early Pilsener. How my man Ransom knew this I do not pretend to understand, even though I am, as you might say, a professional observer. It may have been through one of those indefatigable news agencies that collect bits about writers. Certain it was that Pilsener was always waiting for me. I sipped it now wondering whether, after all, London had anything that I could not have got in Tanga Orabiv, or for that matter Claustrophobia, where I had spent an unexpectedly tolerable week as the guest of the local FMG. It may have been due to this slight distaste of mine for London that, when Ransom entered to say that Mrs Waterson was on the telephone, I said at once, "Put her through." Yet if since my return Ransom had answered one call with a polite prevarication he must have answered a dozen.

Mary Waterson, on the telephone at least, has a voice which would move the angels, and I soon discovered that she had an appeal to make.

"Oh!" she said, "so you *are* back! I had so hoped it was true, and that you weren't after all still out in one of those extraordinary places of yours at the ends of the earth—Now, did you get my invitation?"

"I may have," I said. "I haven't opened any."

"That's positively wicked of you. But you will come, won't you?"

"Come? Where? And when?"

"Here, to Felstock. For the week-end."

I thought one moment. Mary Waterson was after all a very friendly person. And they were using a pneumatic drill outside the flat. By comparison her house would be restful. So I said, "Yes, I'll come."

"That's delightful of you! Jack and Gloria will look forward to seeing you as much as myself—If you don't come by road your best train is the two forty-six."

"Good," I said, "I'll do my best to catch it. Tomorrow. Good-bye."

I was roused to look through the two dozen or so invitations I had idly put aside. Among them, though none was very exciting, was one from the Duchess of Glynning. Had I opened it earlier, and Mary had not telephoned, and had I felt more inclined to see the Duchess than to drink two or three afternoon bottles of Pilsener at home I might have accepted it, and this story would not have been written. Though no doubt another one would have been. . . .

L. A. PAVEY

A. A. MILNE
1882–1956

WHEN WE WERE VERY SILLY

There is a great vogue for what is called the Woogie-Poogie-Boo kind of children's book, and I am doing my best to get one ready. I don't know what it will be called, but I rather fancy Songs Through My Hat, *or perhaps* When We Were Very Silly.

Theobald James

I've got a silk-worm,
A teeny-tiny silk-worm;
I call *my* silk-worm
Theobald James.
But nursie says it's cruel,
Nursie says it's wicked
To call a teeny-tiny little
    Silk-
    Worm
    NAMES.

I said to *my* silk-worm
    "Oh, Mr Silk-worm,
I'd rather be a silk-worm
Than anything, far!"
And nursie says he answered,
Nursie says he shouted,
"You wish you were a silk-worm?
You little
    Prig,
    You
    ARE!"

★

"Some one asked the publisher"

Some one asked
The publisher,
Who went and asked
The agent:
"Could we have some writing for
The woolly folk to read?"
The agent asked
His partner,
His partner
Said, "Certainly.
I'll go and tell
The author
Now
The kind of stuff we need."

The partner
He curtsied,
And went and told
The author:
"Don't forget the writing that
The woolly folk need."
The author
Said wearily,
"You'd better tell
The publisher
That many people nowadays
Like hugaboo
To read."

★

Now We Are Sick

Hush, hush,
Nobody cares!
Christopher Robin
Has
   Fallen
      Down-
         Stairs.
J. B. MORTON

JOHN MILTON
1608–74

from THE SPLENDID SHILLING

Thus while my joyless Hours I lingring spend,
With looks demure, and silent pace a *Dunn*,
Horrible Monster! hated by Gods and Men,
To my aerial Citadel ascends;
With Vocal Heel thrice Thund'ring at my Gates,
With hideous Accent thrice he calls; I know
The Voice ill boding, and the solemn Sound;
What should I do, or whither turn? amaz'd
Confounded, to the dark recess I fly
Of Woodhole; streight my bristling Hairs erect
My Tongue forgets her Faculty of Speech,
So horrible he seems; his faded Brow
Entrench'd with many a Frown, and *conic* Beard,
And spreading Band admir'd by Modern Saint
Disastrous acts forebode; in his Right hand

258

Long Scrolls of Paper solemnly he waves,
With Characters and Figures dire inscribed
Grievous to mortal Eye. (Ye Gods avert
Such plagues from righteous men.) Behind him stalks
Another Monster, not unlike himself,
Of Aspect sullen, by the Vulgar called
A *Catchpole*, whose polluted hands the Gods
With Force incredible, and Magic Charms
Erst have indu'd, if he his ample Palm
Should haply on ill-fated Shoulder lay
Of Debtor, streight his Body to the touch
Obsequious (as Whilom Knights were wont)
To some enchanted Castle is convey'd,
Where Gates impregnable, and coercive Charms
In durance vile detain him, till in form
Of Money, *Pallas* set the Captive free.
Beware, ye Debtors, when ye walk, beware,
Be circumspect; oft with insidious Ken,
This Caitiff eyes your steps aloof, and oft
Lies perdue in a Creek or gloomy Cave,
Prompt to enchant some inadvertent wretch
With his unhallow'd Touch. So (Poets sing)
Grimalkin to Domestick Vermin sworn
An everlasting Foe, with watchful eye,
Lyes nightly brooding ore a chinky gap,
Protending her fell claws, to thoughtless Mice
Sure ruin. So her disembowell'd Web
The *Spider* in a Hall or Kitchin spreads,
Obvious to vagrant Flies; the secret stands,
Within her woven Cell; the Humming Prey
Regardless of their Fate, rush on the toils
Inextricable, nor will ought avail
Their Arts nor Arms, nor Shapes of Lovely Hue,
The Wasp insidious, and the buzzing Drone,
And Butterfly proud of expanded wings
Distinct with Gold, entangled in her Snares,

Useless resistance make: with eager strides
She tow'ring flies to her expected Spoils;
Then with envenom'd Jaws the vital Blood
Drinks of reluctant Foes, and to her Cave
Their bulky Carcasses triumphant drags.
So pass my days. . . .

JOHN PHILIPS

THOMAS MOORE
1779–1852

'TWAS EVER THUS

I never rear'd a young gazelle,
    (Because, you see, I never tried);
But had it known and loved me well,
    No doubt the creature would have died.
My rich and aged Uncle John
    Has known me long and loves me well
But still persists in living on—
    I would he were a young gazelle.

I never loved a tree or flower;
    But, if I had, I beg to say,
The blight, the wind, the sun, or shower
    Would soon have withered it away.
I've dearly loved my Uncle John,
    From childhood to the present hour,
And yet he will go living on—
    I would he were a tree or flower!

HENRY S. LEIGH

"I NEVER HAD A PIECE OF TOAST"

I never had a piece of toast,
    Particularly long and wide,
But fell upon the sanded floor,
    And always on the buttered side.

ANON

IRIS MURDOCH
1919–

A JAUNDICED VIEW

Among our leading novelists, some are prolific, some less so. There must be many readers of Miss Iris Murdoch who live in fear of a fallow year, when no more than one novel by the author drops from her pen, leaving them with long empty evenings to waste. The following extract, from a new work called The Sublime and the Ridiculous, *is designed to cater for this eventuality, by having many characters, some of them hardly used at all, who can—under fresh titles like* The Necessary and the Contingent *or* The Many and the Few—*be put through fresh sexual permutations by bereft readers on rainy days.*

"Flavia says that Hugo tells her that Augustina is in love with Fred."

Sir Alex Mountaubon stood with his wife Lavinia in one of the deeply recessed mullion windows of the long gallery at Bishop's Breeches, looking out at the topiary peacocks on the terrace beyond. In front of them the fountain, topped with statuary in which a naked Mars played joyously with a willing Venus, gently coruscated, its tinkle audible through the open windows. The scene before them was of order and peace. They could look down the park at the mile-long drive of lindens, the colour of jaundice; to one side, away from its necessary order, stood one dark and contingent cedar tree. Beneath it their older daughter, Flavia, could be seen from the window, sitting on a white wooden seat, in her unutterable otherness, her pet marmoset on her shoulder, her cap of auburn hair shining like burnished gold on her head. Nearer to the house, in the rose-garden, their younger daughter, seven-year-old Perdita, strange, mysterious and self-absorbed as usual, was beheading a litter of puppies with unexpectedly muscular and adult twists of her slender arms. Her cap of golden hair shone like burnished auburn on her head.

Alex turned, catching sight of himself in the big, gilt, rather battered cupid-encrusted mirror that soared over the mantel. Mortality was there in the darkened eyes, but most of what he saw there, the solid, round face of a man of principle, pleased him excessively. His book, a philosophical study of Niceness, was almost complete; in its writing Lavinia, his second wife, had proved the perfect helpmeet and companion. No one lay dying upstairs. He looked around at the familiar objects, the Titians and Tintorettos, glowing in their serried ranks with jewelled beneficence, the twined, golden forms of bodies twisted together suggesting a radiant vision of another world. In cases stood the Sung cups, the Ting plates, the Tang vases, the Ming statuettes, the Ching saucers; these last must, almost certainly, go.

"Who says whom tells her who is in love with whom?"

Lavinia, her arms full of lilies, did not turn. "Flavia," she said.

"And are they?"

"They didn't think so. I don't think they quite know."

"But at least we know. About us," said Alex lovingly. He looked out of the window and saw Perdita staring strangely up at the house; and suddenly, involuntarily, he recalled again that experience of utter freedom he had known for the first time when he and Moira LeBenedictus had lain naked together in the Reading Room of the British Museum, after hours of course; he, as a senior civil servant, had been entitled to a key. Other moments came back: Moira walking through Harrods without her shoes, Moira on the night they had boxed together on a roof of St Paul's Cathedral, Moira threatening him in the Tottenham Hotspurs football ground at midnight with her whaler's harpoon.

Two miles away, in the bathroom at his house, Buttocks, Sir Hugo Occam laid down his razor. He walked through into the bedroom where Moira LeBenedictus lay. She was his good towards which he magnetically swung. She lay on the bed, gathering her hair together into a cap of black.

"Are we acting rightly?"

"I think we are," she said.

"Oh, Moira."

"Come, come, Hugo," she said. From the alcove, Leo Chatteris, a spoiled priest, long in love with Moira, watched them in protective benediction. Could he surrender her? The pain was so much he knew it was right.

"Do we?" Lavinia had thrown down her lilies and now stood facing Alex. "Alex," she said with sudden passion, "I have resigned from the presidency of the WI." The words struck a sudden chill over him, and he knew that the shapeliness and order about him were about to be violated. "I am in love with Fred."

"You can't be," said Alex, speaking without thought, absorbed in his own misery, "Augustina is in love with Fred. Hugo is in love with Augustina, Flavia is in love with Hugo, Fred is in love with Flavia, Moira is in love with Fred, I am in love with Moira, and you are in love with me."

"No, Fred . . . Hugo . . . Alex rather," said Lavinia, her voice trembling, "I'm afraid you have it *all the wrong way round*. I am in love with Fred, you are in love with me, Moira is in love with you, and you utterly missed out Leo, who is as unutterably particular as anyone else, and who is in love with Moira."

"But how, why?" Alex murmured, his hands over his face.

"It's one of the wonders of the world."

"All right," he said, "Here we go again. Will you call them, or shall I?"

"Do be careful of the Gainsboroughs," said Alex to the men. "And I do think the Renoirs ought to have a van to themselves, and not be put in with the fountain, which is liable to wet them irreparably."

Already seven of the thirteen furniture vans had been filled, and were on their way to Buttocks, where Moira was awaiting him. Bishop's Breeches, descending through the female line, stayed with Lavinia, but most of its exquisite contents, including some singularly heavy statuary, belonged to Alex. He stood in the noble portico, feeling the familiar, loved house around him, so fit for free characters to live in, and knowing he must leave soon, for the last time. The heavy van lumbered away down the drive, beneath the yellow of the lindens, towards the North Lodge. He turned to go back into Bishop's Breeches, and then heard a strange splintering noise. He walked towards the drive, passed under the deep yellow lindens. A very dove-grey Rolls was parked at the side. "I'm afraid there's a rather nasty accident." said Fred Tallin, getting out, "Your first van ran into my first van. There's stuff spilled all over the road. We can't tell whose Titians are whose. As for the Sung and the Ting and the Tang and the Ming and the Ching, I'm afraid all that's gone bang. Awful business, this packing. How the deuce do you pack up a herd of deer? Lav all ready for me?"

"She's in her room, holding daffodils," said Alex.

A flotilla of pantechnicons was turning in by the West Lodge and coming up the other avenue. "I say, that's funny," said Fred, resting his very white hand on the bonnet of the very dove-grey Rolls, "Those vans aren't mine. Mine are from Harrods."

"They're not mine, either," said Alex, "You don't think Moira's got it all wrong? She did know I'm going to Buttocks, not her coming here to me?"

"It rather looks as if not," said Fred, "In any case, I thought Buttocks belonged to Hugo."

"Moira told me it belonged to Leo, who had given it to her," said Alex.

"Very funny girl, Moira," said Fred, "Did she ever show you her sarcophagus?"

A horn blared behind them, and they both turned. There, on the gravel in front of the house, stood another row of pantechnicons, which had evidently come in from the East Lodge, and drawn up unnoticed. "I say," said Fred.

"Now whose . . .?" began Alex, but his question was quickly answered. For now Flavia came running from her white seat by the cedar, the marmoset chattering after her.

"Have these to do with you?" he asked.

"Dear Hugo," said Flavia. She put her arms behind her and suddenly released her hair, which fell across her shoulders and down her back like a shower of gold.

"Flavia," said Alex. Then he stood spellbound. For the unused gate at the South Lodge had been swung open, and up the drive came another line of vans.

"We live in a realm of startling coincidences," said Fred.

They stood and watched as they saw a figure, bounding with joy, running to meet the vans. It was Perdita, strange and mysterious, her puppies forgotten.

Sir Alex Mountaubon stood with his wife Lavinia in one of the deeply recessed mullion windows of the long gallery at Bishop's Breeches, looking down the mile-long drive of lindens to the tightly locked gates at the bottom. The trees, the colour of jaundice, stood in their necessary order; to one side, beneath the dark contingent cedar tree, their daughter

Flavia sat on the white wooden seat, unutterably particular, while in the rose-garden Perdita, still strange and mysterious, was twisting the neck of Flavia's marmoset. "You know, Lavinia, I'm glad matters have reverted to normal," said Alex, "I know it's philosophically wrong, and I'm afraid we've done little for the plot. Am I wicked to say it?"

He leaned forward, and, putting his arms round Lavinia, gently loosened her hair. His book on Niceness was now complete, and Lavinia was proving a perfect proof-reader. Lavinia turned her face and then, her arms full of roses, she smiled at him. "No, it's marvellous," she said, "I love you, you love Moira, Moira loves Fred, Fred loves Flavia, Flavia loves Hugo—"

"You missed out Leo," said Alex.

"To hell with Leo," said Lavinia, "I don't care how unutterably particular he is. There is one thing that worries me, though, Alex. Why is it that, when we sleep with all these people, they're all either titled or in the Civil Service?"

"I don't know. I suppose you might say it's a condition of our world," said Alex, looking around the gallery. Only a few gaps on the wall among the Tintorettos revealed the ravages of the last days. "However," he said, as they both turned and looked out at the Mars and Venus sporting in stone on the fountain, and then, further beyond, the deep yellow light under the lindens, "I do know this. Love is a strange, mysterious and wonderful revelation of others. But, for people in our station in life, it's really far too much of a bother."

MALCOLM BRADBURY

AMBROSE PHILIPS
1675?–1749

NAMBY-PAMBY

*A panegyric on the new versification
addressed to A——P——, Esq*

Naughty Paughty Jack-a-Dandy,
Stole a Piece of Sugar Candy
From the Grocer's Shoppy-Shop,
And away did hoppy-hop.

All ye poets of the age,
All ye witlings of the stage,
Learn your jingles to reform,
Crop your numbers and conform.
Let your little verses flow
Gently, sweetly, row by row;
Let the verse the subject fit,
Little subject, little wit.
Namby-Pamby is your guide,
Albion's joy, Hibernia's pride.
Namby-Pamby, pilly-piss,
Rhimy-pim'd on Missy Miss
Tartaretta Tartaree,
From the navel to the knee;
That her father's gracy grace
Might give him a placy place.

He no longer writes of Mammy
Andromache and her lammy,
Hanging-panging at the breast
Of a matron most distressd.
Now the venal poet sings

Baby clouts and baby things,
Baby dolls and baby houses,
Little misses, little spouses,
Little playthings, little toys,
Little girls and little boys.
As an actor does his part,
So the nurses get by heart
Namby-Pamby's little rhimes,
Little jingle, little chimes,
To repeat to Missy-miss,
Piddling ponds of pissy-piss;
Cracking-packing like a lady,
Or bye-bying in the crady.
Namby-Pamby ne'er will die
While the nurse sings lullaby.
Namby-Pamby's doubly mild,
Once a man, and twice a child;
To his hanging sleeves restor'd,
Now he foots it like a lord;
Now he pumps his little wits,
Shitting writes, and writing shits,
All by little tiny bits,
Now methinks I hear him say,
Boys and girls, come out to play!
Moon do's shine as bright as day.

Now my Namby-Pamby's found
Sitting on the friar's ground,
Picking silver, picking gold;
Namby-Pamby's never old.
Bally-cally, they begin,
Namby-Pamby still keeps in.
Namby-Pamby is no clown.
London Bridge is broken down:
Now he courts the gay ladee,
Dancing o'er the Lady-Lee.

Now he sings of Lick-spit Lyar,
Burning in the brimstone fire;
Lyar, lyar! Lick-pit, Lick,
Turn about the candle stick!
Now he sings of Jacky Horner,
Sitting in the chimney corner,
Eating of a Christmas pye,
Putting in his thumb, O fie!
Putting in, O fie! his thumb,
Pulling out, O strange, a plum.
Now he plays at Stee-Staw-Stud,
Sticking apples in the mud;
When 'tis turn'd to Stee-Staw-Stire,
Then he sticks 'em in the mire.
Now he acts the grenadier,
Calling for a pot of beer.
Where's his money? He's forgot;
Get him gone, a drunken sot.
Now a cock-horse does he ride,
And anon on timber stride.
See and Saw, and Sacch'ry Down,
London is a gallant town!
Now he gathers riches in,
Thicker, faster, pin by pin;
Pins apiece to see his show,
Boys and girls flock row by row;
From their clothes the pins they take,
Risk a whipping for his sake;
From their cloaths the pins they pull
To fill Namby's cushion full.
So much wit at such an age
Does a genius great presage;
Second childhood gone and past,
Should he prove a man at last,
What must second manhood be
In a child so bright as he.

269

Guard him, ye poetic pow'rs,
Watch his minutes, watch his hours;
Let your tuneful nine inspire him.
Let poetic fury fire him;
Let the poets, one and all,
To his genius victims fall.

HENRY CAREY

HAROLD PINTER
1930–

PINTER IN BELGRAVIA

The drawing-room of a palatial house in Belgravia. PINNER, *unshaven and wearing crumpled evening dress, prowls around in the grey morning light. He picks up a vase.*

PINNER:(*Suspiciously*) Ming! (*He looks inside.*) Paperclips. . . .
(*He puts down the vase and moves slowly to a pile of copies of* the Journal of Historical Studies. *Gingerly he prods the pile with the toe of his sandal. It sways precariously.*) Steady!
(*He steadies the pile. Enter* BUTLER. *He looks at* PINNER. (*Long silence.*)

BUTLER: (*Loudly and sharply*) Who are you? What's your name?

PINNER: Pinner.

BUTLER: Pinner. Pin–ner. (*Pause.*) Sleep here last night?

PINNER: Yes, I—

BUTLER: Which bedroom? That one? (*Pause.*) The Louis Quinze. Choosey.

PINNER: The lady said I could. How about it, I said, just 'til I get myself fixed up, I said. She give me a funny look. Sure, she said, just 'til you get yourself . . . fixed up. So I stayed.

BUTLER: What's your name again?

PINNER: Pinner. I told you, Pinner. (*Pause.*) Lord Pinner . . .

BUTLER: *Lord* Pinner? You gentry then? You a member of the, er, aristocracy?

PINNER: No . . . uh, no. Not really. That title . . . it's not real, you see, it's assumed. I'm not actually a peer, not by birth that is. There's this chap, you see, over on the South Bank, he's got my papers. They tell you who I am. Without them, I'm buggered, man. If I can only get over there and get them papers, I can prove who I really am. That . . . Lord, that title, it's not real, you see, it's . . . well, it's *assumed*.

(*Silence.* BUTLER *glares at him.*)

COLIN O'BRIEN

EDGAR ALLAN POE
1809–49

THE GOBLIN GOOSE
A Christmas Nightmare

Once, it happened I'd been dining, on my couch I slept
   reclining,
And awoke with moonlight shining brightly on my bedroom
   floor;
It was in the bleak December, Christmas night as I
   remember,
But I had no dying ember, as POE had; when near the door,

271

Like a gastronomic goblin just beside my chamber door,
                    Stood a bird,—and nothing more.

And I said, for I'm no craven, "Are you EDGAR's famous raven,
Seeking as with him a haven—were you mixed up with LENORE?"
Then the bird uprose and fluttered, and this sentence strange he uttered—
"Hang LENORE," he mildly muttered; "you have seen me once before,
Seen me on this festive Christmas, seen me surely once before.
                    I'm the Goose,"—and nothing more.

Then he murmured, "Are you ready?" and with motion slow and steady,
Straight he leapt upon my bed. I simply gave a stifled roar;
And I cried, "As I'm a sinner, at a Goose Club I was winner,
'Tis a mem'ry of my dinner, which I ate at half-past four;
Goose well stuffed with sage and onions, which I ate at half-past four."
                    Quoth he hoarsely, "Eat no more!"

Said I, "I've enjoyed your juices, breast and back; but tell me, Goose, is
This revenge, and what the use is of your being such a bore?
For goose-flesh I will no more 'ax' if you'll not sit on my thorax.
Go, try honey mixed with borax, for I hear your throat is sore;
You speak gruffly though too plainly, and I'm sure your throat is sore."
                    Quoth the nightmare, "Eat no more!"

"Goose!" I shrieked out, "Leave, oh, leave me! surely you
    don't mean to grieve me?
You are heavy, pray reprieve me, now my penance must be
    o'er;
Though tonight you've brought me sorrow, comfort surely
    comes tomorrow.
Some relief from thee I'd borrow at my doctor's ample store,
There are pills of purest azure in that doctor's ample store."
            Quoth the goblin, "Eat no more!"

And that fat Goose, never flitting, like a nightmare still is
    sitting
With me all the night, emitting words that thrill my bosom's
    core;
Now, throughout the Christmas season, while I lie and gasp
    and wheeze, on
Me he sits, until my reason nothing surely can restore,
I am driven mad, and reason nothing surely can restore;
            While that Goose says, "Eat no more."

ANON

THE REAGAN

Once as Congress sat in session,
    realigned on non-aggression,
Someone used a rude expression,
    someone still outside the door—
What could possibly be ruder
    than a crotchety intruder?
Then, becoming even cruder,
    in he flew and took the floor—
There before them stood the Reagan,
    ghostly on the chamber floor—
        Quoth the Reagan, "Arm for war!"

Congress murmured, "Could we win it?"
    Quoth the Reagan, "Just a minute—
Sure we'd win! Why not begin it?
    We've done worse than that before!"
Was the Reagan simply raving,
    working out some latent craving?
"What a way to start behaving!"
    murmured Congress, "Start a war?"
Surely, sir," they asked the Reagan,
    "You're opposed to nuclear war?"
        Quoth the Reagan, "Nevermore!"

RICHARD QUICK

ALEXANDER POPE
1688–1744

IF POPE HAD WRITTEN "BREAK, BREAK, BREAK"

Fly, Muse, thy wonted themes, nor longer seek
The consolations of a powder'd cheek;
Forsake the busy purlieus of the Court
For calmer meads where finny tribes resort.
So may th' Almighty's natural antidote
Abate the worldly tenor of thy note,
The various beauties of the liquid main
Refine thy reed and elevate thy strain.

See how the labour of the urgent oar
Propels the barks and draws them to the shore.
Hark! from the margin of the azure bay

274

The joyful cries of infants at their play.
(The offspring of a piscatorial swain,
His home the sands, his pasturage the main.)
Yet none of these may soothe the mourning heart,
Nor fond alleviation's sweets impart;
Nor may the pow'rs of infants that rejoice
Restore the accents of a former voice,
Nor the bright smiles of ocean's nymphs command
The pleasing contact of a vanished hand.
So let me still in meditation move,
Muse in the vale and ponder in the grove,
And scan the skies where sinking Phœbus glows
With hues more rubicund than Cibber's nose. . . .

(*After which the poet gets into his proper stride.*)

J. C. SQUIRE

PORTMANTEAU PARODIES

VARIATIONS ON AN AIR COMPOSED ON HAVING TO APPEAR IN A PAGEANT AS OLD KING COLE

Old King Cole was a merry old soul,
And a merry old soul was he;
He called for his pipe,
He called for his bowl,
And he called for his fiddlers three.

★

after *Alfred Lord Tennyson*

Cole, that unwearied prince of Colchester,
Growing more gay with age and with long days
Deeper in laughter and desire of life,
As that Virginian climber on our walls
Flames scarlet with the fading of the year;
Called for his wassail and that other weed
Virginian also, from the western woods
Where English Raleigh checked the boast of Spain,
And lighting joy with joy, and piling up
Pleasure as crown for pleasure, bade men bring
Those three, the minstrels whose emblazoned coats
Shone with the oyster-shells of Colchester;
And these three played, and playing grew more fain
Of mirth and music; till the heathen came,
And the King slept beside the northern sea.

★

after *W. B. Yeats*

Of an old King in a story
    From the grey sea-folk I have heard,
Whose heart was no more broken
    Than the wings of a bird.

As soon as the moon was silver
    And the thin stars began,
He took his pipe and his tankard,
    Like an old peasant man.

And three tall shadows were with him
    And came at his command;
And played before him for ever
    The fiddles of fairyland.

276

And he died in the young summer
    Of the world's desire;
Before our hearts were broken
    Like sticks in a fire.

★

after *Robert Browning*

Who smoke-snorts toasts o' My Lady Nicotine,
Kicks stuffing out of Pussyfoot bids his trio
Stick up their Stradivarii (that's the plural)
Or near enough, my fatheads; *nimium*
Vicina Cremonæ (that's a bit too near).
Is there some stockfish fails to understand?
Catch hold o' the notion, bellow and blurt back "Cole"?
Must I bawl lessons from a horn-book, howl,
Cat-call the cat-gut "fiddles"? Fiddlesticks!

★

after *Walt Whitman*

Me clairvoyant,
Me conscious of you, old camarado,
Needing no telescope, lorgnette, field-glass, opera-glass,
    myopic pince-nez,
Me piercing two thousand years with eye naked and not
    ashamed;
The crown cannot hide you from me;
Musty old feudal-heraldic trappings cannot hide you from
    me,
I perceive that you drink.
(I am drinking with you. I am as drunk as you are.)
I see you are inhaling tobacco, puffing, smoking, spitting
(I do not object to your spitting),

You prophetic of American largeness,
You anticipating the broad masculine manners of these States;
I see in you also there are movements, tremors, tears, desire
    for the melodious,
I salute your three violinists, endlessly making vibrations,
Rigid, relentless, capable of going on for ever;
They play my accompaniment; but I shall take no notice of
    any accompaniment;
I myself am a complete orchestra.
So long.

★

after *Algernon Charles Swinburne*

In the time of old sin without sadness,
    And golden with wastage of gold,
Like the gods that grow old in their gladness
    Was the king that was glad, growing old;
And with sound of loud lyres from his palace
    The voice of his oracles spoke,
And the lips that were red from his chalice
    Were splendid with smoke.

When the weed was as flame for a token
    And the wine was as blood for a sign;
And upheld in his hands and unbroken
    The fountains of fire and of wine.
And a song without speech, without singer,
    Stung the soul of a thousand in three
As the flesh of the earth has to sting her,
    The soul of the sea.

G. K. CHESTERTON

TEATIME VARIATIONS

after *Robert Herrick*

Whenas from cups my Julia sups
And sets her teeth to working
And pouts her lips with pretty sips,
I see old Time a–lurking—
So drain the teapot while ye may,
Too soon it will be cleared away.

*

after *John Keats*

Twilight has fallen and the candled gloom,
Soothing the sober sadness of my soul,
Lights one soft-glowing corner of the room
Where tea is laid in curious cup and bowl.
O for a draught of Soochow that hath been
Brewed just enough in the well-rounded pot,
Tasting of China and the leaf, once green,
Now sable, but when damped with water hot
Exuding amber streams like those that met
The dust-dimmed eyes of Polo when he burst
From out the Gobi desert's sand and sweat
And drank Alph's sacred stream like one athirst.

*

after *Algernon Charles Swinburne*

That tea is not the most benign of latter-day beverages, only
to be matched with the ambrosia consumed upon Olympus,
or with that scarcely less godlike brew wherewith our Viking

forebears braced themselves for battle (or, as Montaigne has it in one of his rather more than wontedly but never unacceptably mellifluous musings, the "mêlée militaire"), that tea, I say again (for fear my penchant for parenthesis may prove perplexing), that tea has not won for itself the peak, nay, proud pinnacle of kinship with both king and commoner, linking in the kindly steam of its infusion the lordly and the lubberly alike, is a profanation only to be looked for from persons of such brutish and unalliterative instincts as would deny the dew at dayspring or recommend the perfume of a pigsty.

★

after *A. E. Housman*

The day had lapsed to twilight
And drowsy was the bee
When you, my lass, and I, your lad,
Sat down to quaff our tea.

We dipped our toast in tannin
And slaked our burning drouth,
Till evening dyed the Wrekin-top
As red as your false mouth:

For false to me were you, lass,
That to your flame was moth—
And had another lad concealed
Beneath the tablecloth.

★

after *Walter de la Mare*

This picnic tea
Beneath the tree
That elves and fairies chanced upon,
This shining pot
No longer hot
They mischievously danced upon—
Lo, it has lain long ages here,
It came from Merlin's scrip
When he escorted Guinevere
Aboard her nuptial ship:
Or can it be an earlier brew,
Primeval herb wet with primeval dew?
P'raps Pan himself has let his tea get cold—
At all events it's very old.

★

after *W. B. Yeats*

I have poured my dreams in the pot's dim womb
And watered them well with the warm, wet rain of
    unreason—
See, I have cloven a cup of tea for you out of the throb of
    things.

Here in the Celtic twilight we will sit and sip and consider
And I will weave words as only a charlatan can—
Drink deep and don't dribble for you are drinking my
    dreams.

★

after *A Thirties Poet*

Left right . . . left right . . .
Thus Compromise, sergeant-majorial, route-marches Man;
Left right . . . left right . . .
God's in his heaven,
All's right with what's left of the world—
That's what they say, the sleep-walkers;
All the fun of the *laissez-faire!*
But *we* say—
Looking at life through our molecules—
We say not left right but only
Left.
The Petition of Lefts.
The Lefts of Man.
Reading, Lefting, and Arithmetic.
Waiting for Mr Left to come along.
Waiting . . .
And in the meantime we have forgotten
That words can be deft
And gracious,
We have forgotten praise—
And above all we have forgotten that this was supposed to
   be
About tea . . .

PETER TITHERADGE

P. G. WODEHOUSE
BY JAMES JOYCE

What ho I said you are doubtless referring to the eminent
French artist of that ilk said Jeeves a Watteau would go nicely
in the drawing-room with your Toulouse-Lautrec artists of
the world unite you have nothing Toulouse but Lautrec he
added misjeevously ah gayparee I said at the stern of the
century with all those cocottes and grisettes la bell epox
Lautrec put it all down on oo–la–la can–canvas ou est la plum
de ma tante vive la tante cordiale are you going to Finnegan's
Wake enquired Jeeves no my head is spinning it's the morning
after precisely so said Jeeves it's the mourning after how long
will it last I asked a wake is a long time. . . .

STANLEY J. SHARPLESS

*

JAMES JOYCE
BY P. G. WODEHOUSE

An affable enough cove Stephen Dedalus, bound to me by
tissues of art and imperishable memory, if that's the phrase
I'm groping for. No doubt Jeeves would know, he still eats
fish regularly, brainy beggar. Years ago the said Dedalus and
I had done a stretch at Clongowes College, then under the
sway of Baldyhead Dolan, master of the pandybat and all
round bad egg. Such sore travails draw striplings together
like hoops of, what is it, steel.

So when I bumped into young Dedalus unexpected outside
Drones one fine summer morning the old ticker leaped.

"Pip pip old horse," I cried. "How are tricks these days?"

"I'm an artist now," he replied modestly.

ROY KELLY

283

NASTY HABITS
EXCERPTS FROM A NOVEL ON
NUN-RUNNING BY A VARIETY OF
SUCCESSFUL WRITERS

after *Mickey Spillane*

"C'mon baby," I said, "you'll just have to kick the habit."

"Keeka de habit? No understan'."

"You can do better than that, sweetheart," I said. "Shed the wrappers, show the goods, peel!"

She still played dumb. But she wasn't fooling me. She wasn't fooling anyone anymore. Not now.

"Okay, baby, if that's how you want to play it." I tore off the starched white headgear and the familiar platinum blonde hair cascaded on to her shoulders. There was fear in her eyes now. She tried to run but I got my fingers in the back of her robe. There was a harsh tearing noise and she spun round, backed up against the door with a pile of black cotton round her ankles. She was still wearing the same gold star transfers. In all the right places.

"Let's go, sister," I said.

M. J. MONK

★

after *Graham Greene*

Foskett locked the nuns in their cabin for the night. He fought down his longing for their young brown bodies by telling himself they belonged to God.

In the tiny saloon aft, the Mauritian steward squashed a fly in the glass before pouring him a Hong Kong whisky. Drinking down the hot sourness, Foskett mused on the whole squalid business.

He no longer asked himself why he got mixed up in it, but

he did wonder how the ascetic Father Ramgoolam would spend the money he received for the air fares.

The Maltese with gold teeth approached. "Mr Foxy, those very fine girls you have. I pay good for them." Foskett said, "They are brides of the Church." "I understand," the Maltese said. "I am good Catholic too."

Dear God, why were they all good Catholics? Downside had been so different.

PETER VEALE

★

after *John Buchan*

Permissive London oppressed me mightily. The long parade of ringleted youth, as unwashed as it was epicene; the sleaziness of Soho oozing out to infect the whole capital; the unmistakable stench of moral *fetor*—all this set me yearning for the cool starlit intoxication of a night on the *veldt*. My unease was compounded by what I read in the *Telegraph* of the latest nun-running mystery. Fifty pure English girls abducted—and still not a trace! I am a peaceable man but I dearly craved five minutes alone with a *sjambok* with the swine responsible.

A nun came and sat at the other end of my park bench. I have always sat lightly to religion—the Church of Rhodesia is an undemanding institution—but there are times when one envies the sweet certainties of Rome.

"Congratulations, Dick, on your peerage."

I gasped. "*Sandy!*"

"Keep your voice down, Dick," she murmured. "This is the tightest spot that even you and I have ever shared."

TIM O'DOWDA

★

after *P. G. Wodehouse*

"O Death, where is thy whatsit?" I moaned, prising my eyes open. It had been a stiff night at the Drones and the top of my head had gone into independent orbit. Jeeves billowed in, bearing, I assumed, a heady beaker of the brew that cheers. No dice. If not distraught, he wasn't exactly traught either.

"A young person, sir, who insists—" Whereupon this young nun broke insistently into my boudoir. Albeit habited *cap-à-pe*, she was obviously a hot tip for the glamour stakes.

"Mr Wooster," gasped this beatific vision, "save me! I have given my kidnappers the slip—" With which she swooned all over me and the counterpane.

"I say, brace up, old thing," I wheedled, easing a finger of brandy into my toothmug and wondering what Aunt Agatha would say if she could see me now—I mean, then.

Jeeves reappeared. "Mrs Gregson," he intoned. . . .

IAN KELSO

DOMESTIC DRAMA

The court case involving John Osborne and the domestic couple he sacked for inefficiency has of course had immense repercussions throughout the sensitive world of the theatre.

Dramatis Personae

SNOUT	Ex-caretaker to Mr Harold Pinter
ANTONIO } IGNACIA	Ex-couple to Mr Tom Stoppard
SADIE	Ex-cook to Mr Arnold Wesker
FIFI	Ex-au pair to Mr Brian Rix
HODGE	Ex-butler to Mr Alan Ayckbourn
MRS GLAND	Ex-governess to Mr Paul Raymond
SPOT DOUGLAS–HOME	A dog

The action takes place in the waiting-room of Madame Parvenu's Domestic Agency, South Kensington.

The curtain rises to reveal SNOUT *sitting in one of a dozen armchairs, examining his boot. To him, enter* ANTONIO *and* IGNACIA.

ANTONIO: Buenos dias!
SNOUT: I come here by boot.
    (*There is a long pause.*)
IGNACIA: Woddy say?
ANTONIO: E say e gum ere by boot.
IGNACIA: O! Wi gum ere by boot, also! Wi gum ere wid S.S. Malateste in 1972!
    (*They perform handsprings.* SNOUT *feels inside his boot.*)
SNOUT: I picked up a stone in Osbaldeston Road. Probably at the junction with Pondicherry Crescent.
IGNACIA: I PICK UP A STONE IN IVER HEATH! I gum to bloody Stoppard ouse, I weigh one hundred pounds, pretty soon I fat like pig.

ANTONIO: She never see bourbon biscuits before. Is ole new world. Is one reason we get bullet. One day, she eat ten packs pinguins.

SNOUT: Or possibly at the point where Mafeking Villas runs parallel with the North Circular. You would not believe the amount of gravel they have put down there. Gravel and loose shale. Loose shale and chippings.

ANTONIO: One day, she eat ten pounds chippings.

SNOUT: Had I come by bus this situation would not have arisen. It would not have come about. Had I taken a Number Fourteen, I could have transferred to a Number Twenty-nine as far as Turnpike Lane. I could then have taken the underground. I could have gone down into the underground. I could have hopped aboard the underground, as it were. My boots would have been completely safe against shale on the underground. Manor House, Finsbury Park, Arsenal. I might have come up at any point.

ANTONIO: Mr Stoppard give us heave-ho.

IGNACIA: E say we no good. E say we bad.

ANTONIO: So I say to im: wod you min, good, wod you min, bad? You min good/bad in metaphysical sense, you blidding ponce? You min good/bad in empirical sense? You min good/bad in comparative descriptive sense?

IGNACIA: You tole im all right! You say: Wod about them situations where it is better to be bad than good? You say: Wod about definin your terms, you iggerant sod?

ANTONIO: E look at me a long time after that. Then e it me wid a double-boiler.

IGNACIA: Then we give notice.

(*They perform double back-somersaults, with half-gainers.*)

SNOUT: Alternatively, I could have called a cab. I could have hailed a cab. It might have set me down on the wrong side of Pontings, of course, if it had come down Kensington Church Street, and I would have been compelled to have crossed the road by the Kentucky Pancake House, walked up as far as the Alpine Restaurant at the bottom of Campden Hill Road, and then taken a Number Nine to Hyde Park Corner. If he wasn't so mean. If Pinter wasn't so bleeding tight. If he wasn't so sodding stingy.

(*He begins to rub his lapel, vigorously.*)

I had no severance pay. I was given no notice. I was offered no compensation in the way of, in lieu of, as an alternative to, I WAS NOT GIVEN TWO HALFPENNIES TO RUB TOGETHER, CONTRARY TO WHAT IS CLEARLY SPECIFIED BY THE LAWS OF THE LAND NOW OBTAINING!

(*Enter Sadie.*)

SADIE: You bring up playwrights, and what do you get? Heartaches you get. Ulcers you get. Possibly a malignant disease. You feed him, he shouldn't get God forbid a chill in the liver, all weathers he goes out in to meet his arty friends, I wouldn't give you a thank you for them, you lay out Sea Island cotton underwear for him. Comfort you already washed it in, it should be nice and soft, it shouldn't give him God forbid a rash on his little pippick. Also it should be nice and clean and a credit to his dear parents, may they rest in peace, they worked, they slaved, in case God forbid he should get knocked down and taken to hospital, you hang garlic flowers round his windows in case God forbid a vampire should get in one night he's not looking, he's lying there, he's drunk from his lousy friends, he's worn out from whatever it is he does all day, such as nothing, which is what he does all day, his poor father should only see him, years he stood in that shop, varicose veins, an enlarged prostate, when they took it out they needed three surgeons, three qualified men, just to carry it out of the operating theatre, but does *he* care? He used his flat like it was a hotel, you use this flat like it was a hotel, I used to tell him, it's *my* flat, he used to say. You're answering

289

back already? I used to enquire, you're already too big to take criticism, Mr Playwright, Mr Big Shot, you're too old to listen to people, Mr Show Business?

SNOUT: Or I could have crossed over when I got to the Alpine Restaurant and gone down the underground next to Derry and Toms.

ANTONIO: I miss Tom and Derry. I say to Mr Stoppard, why wi no got colour tee-vee, you bum, as per Ome Office regulations? E reply television is a bastard word, it not exist, philologically spikkin, as it do not exist, wi do not ave it. I tell im, if it do not exist, wod is all that flickering across the road?

IGNACIA: I say, ow you define exist, wod terms wi dealing wid ere? Then e it me wid a liquidizer.

ANTONIO: Then wi give notice again.

SADIE: Also, Mr Shakespeare, Mr Impresario, while we're on the subject, I said, when was the last time you had a play on in the West End, all of a sudden you're complaining about my works, I haven't got also the right to complain about the work of some people I could mention, they're not standing a million miles away from me, as it happens, God forbid I should mention any names, you think it's nice for *me*, I said, I'm standing in the butcher's you should have a nice piece of calf's liver, a chop, a fresh portion sidebowler, and people say: Well, Sadie, did he write anything new yet, a classic, possibly, a musical, maybe, tunes you can whistle?

SNOUT: I am also prepared to blame *her*. I am also prepared to blame his leman. I am also prepared to lay certain charges at the foot of his paramour.

SADIE: So he sacked me.

SNOUT: Now he is living with me, she said, now he is living with me, she remarked, I should be grateful if you would take yourself in hand. I do not require a caretaker, she expatiated. I require a butler.

(*He begins to pick furiously at a shredding buttonhole.*)

I WAS ENGAGED AS A CARETAKER, I told her, I WAS ENGAGED TO BRING IN THE COKE, TO POLISH FRONT STEP TO REQUIRED STANDARD, TO ENSURE TRADESPEOPLE CAME ROUND TO SIDE DOOR! I AGREED UNDER THE TERMS OF SAID EMPLOYMENT TO WEAR A KHAKI WAREHOUSE COAT, BUT TO PROVIDE OUR OWN STRING FOR KNEEPADS, I informed her, THERE WAS NEVER ANY QUESTION OF BUTTLING, THERE WAS NEVER ANY QUESTION OF THAT AT ALL!

(*Enter Fifi.*)

FIFI: Ooh–la–la! Ma knickers ave disappear! Ah ad zem when ah lef zer ouse! Where can zey bi? Can eet bi e av stuff zem bah mistek in is brifcase for zer umpteence time? Sank God ah ave lef is employ at last! Ah do not ask for much in zis life, only an employer oo does not expeck mi to spen alf zer day in zer wardrobe.

(*Faints. Bra falls off.*)

SNOUT: I WAS NOT ENGAGED TO MINCE ABOUT WITH A SILVER BLEEDING TRAY, I explained to her. IT WAS NOT AN UNDERTAKING WHICH APPEARED ON MY CARDS!

(*Enter* HODGE, *backwards.*)

HODGE: Thank you very much, sir. Will there be anything else?

IGNACIA: Woddy say?

HODGE: I do beg your pardon, madame. I have grown somewhat used to backing into rooms. At Mr Ayckbourn's, do you see, all the rooms were always filled with people, invariably called Ron, Reg, Alf, Sid, Ned, Norman, or Don. There were usually two or three Maureens on the premises, and on one occasion, five Beryls. They were all related to one another, though not always in immediately apparent ways. They tended to drift from one part of the house to the other and carry on extraordinarily confusing conversations under the mistaken assumption that one knew what they were talking about. It was very convenient for Mr Ayckbourn, who used to walk about with two typewriters and a running tape-recorder, thus enabling himself to knock off several tetralogies a week by the simple expedient of over-hearing but it was most confusing for, ahem, a gentle-man's gentleman. It has been said, though not, I hasten to add by me, that these people were not Mr Ayck-bourn's acquaintances at all, but retained by his several agents on a salaried, if tiny, basis. In any event, I have left his service to seek employment elsewhere, despite the fact that I have no references: when I asked for them, my employer began to type on both machines simultan-eously, and by lunchtime they had turned into an eighteen-part sit-com series for ATV.

SNOUT: BUTTLING, I riposted, *Buttling*? I should rather, I should prefer, I should be more willing to take my chances as a conductor of a 737 Greenline bus, commen-cing at Marble Arch, continuing down Edgware Road, along Maida Vale, up Kilburn High Road as far as the point where Cricklewood Lane crosses Cricklewood Broadway, bearing right past the point at which the old Handley Page aeroplane factory used to. . . .

(*The light begins to fade.* SNOUT'S *monologue drones on, counterpointed, after an hour or so, by the sound, from the corridor, of* MRS GLAND *beating* SPOT DOUGLAS-HOME *with a rhinestone-studded riding crop as the curtain falls.*)

ALAN COREN

EZRA POUND
1885–1972

ANOTHER CANTO

Monsieur Ezra Pound croit que
By using foreign words
He will persuade the little freaks
Who call themselves intellectuals
To believe that he is saying
Quelque chose très deep, ma foi!

J. B. MORTON

ANTHONY POWELL
1905–

LITTLE JACK HORNER

Horner had got himself established as far as possible from the centre of the room and I was suddenly made aware, as one often is by actions which are in themselves quite commonplace, that he was about to do something which would give him enormous satisfaction. He had somehow acquired a large seasonal confection which he was beginning to attack with a degree of enthusiasm I had not seen him display since the midnight feasts we had enjoyed at school. Eschewing the normal recourse to eating utensils, he plunged his hand through the pastry and extracted an entire fruit, an achievement which was accompanied by a cry of self-congratulation and a beatific expression reminiscent of some of those on the faces one sees in the more popular of the Pre-Raphaelite portraits.

ALAN ALEXANDER

MARCEL PROUST
1871–1922

from AUBERGINE'S WAY
After reading too much Proust (naturally in translation)

I was particularly pleased at having been asked to dinner at the Enrhumer's, in the first place because I had, in my youth, followed the explorations and excursions of Abbadie with great appreciation and had allowed my mind to become inextricably bound up with the pursuit of adventure in whatever form, a thing we are likely to do whenever we substitute for our own imaginings the imaginings of others, imaginings which we later appropriate as our own, forgetting completely their origin and feeling solely that they are an integral part of our own experience wholly apart from the vicarious nature of their entrance into our consciousness, and, in the second place, I was anxious to learn how Aubergine was faring in her acquaintanceship with Minette.

[*You may take off your coats if you wish.*]

I had left her on the evening of my encounter with the *sommelier* at the hotel which had resulted in so strange an insight into the mysteries and tragedies in the life of M. Odelette, and had heard her say that she was going to sit up with a sick friend, the nature of which illness she had not divulged to me but which I had suspected to be not as serious as she had insisted. I had extracted from her a promise to meet me on the following evening at our rendezvous by the Esplanade and the Café du Doc, but, as she neither appeared herself nor sent word by the young woman who she always maintained was her sister, I was oppressed by the feeling that Aubergine was herself becoming untrustworthy. Although I knew that this uneasiness on my part was in the nature of that indefinable sensitivity which exists in the stamens of certain flowers which imperceptibly sense the presence or absence, or absence-presence, of the insect bearing the fecundating pollen, a sensitivity which, owing to the innumerable subdivisions of the spadix, which, in turn, is connected with the pistil, or, if there be no pistil, then with the nearest group of racemes or small brown people who subsist almost entirely on rice, makes possible the subsequent auto-fecundation, even though the actual agent is not present, I was, nevertheless, worried.

[*Now twice around the track and into the locker-room for a shower.*]

In that great game of hide-and-seek which is played in our consciousness when we first become aware of a suspicion and, at the same time, attempt to elude it, there is no series of gradual approximations. We feel nothing, then suddenly the ugly thought springs full-armed into our mind and very differently accoutred from that which we had imagined in our theorizing over what we should do if it finally did arise. It is not the suspicion which we had suspected. No, I rather believe that, as we go on living, we pass our time in consecutive zones of alternate suspicion and reassurance, the one leading into the other and finally becoming indistinguishable from the other, and it was only by the exercise of my conviction on this point that I was able definitely to come to the conclusion that I suspected Aubergine of duplicity. It was for this reason that I was so anxious to accept the Enrhumer's invitation to dinner.

I had arrived in good time, for parties of this sort are usually without time in themselves. They have little reality until they have become—to the invited guest, at any rate—a figment of an imaginary festivity, a goose, a *garniture*, a *bombe*, or, what is even more difficult to comprehend, a plausible, if unreal, *tour de force* of gastronomy. Mme Vouziers met me in the centre, or so it seemed to me, of the drawing-room, flanked by Baron Geitz, the German ambassador, and Prince d'Egaré. One heard an incessant "Good evening, M. de Huissier, good evening, Mme Grange, good

295

evening, M. Pervers, good evening, my dear Count, is your daughter here? Good evening, Bill! Good evening, Mlle Fichoir, good evening, Duc de Courvoisier, may I introduce you to the Duchesse de Courvoisier? Oh, Marquis d'Arrière, there is someone in the drawing-room who is very anxious to see you! Good evening, Comte and Comtesse de Voyeur, M. le Duc de Polygame, Marquise de Morve *née* du Mesnil, Madame Eléonore-Euphrasie-Humbertine de Croupon, Prince Jarski, George M. Platt, Duc and Duchesse de Créquier, good evening, good evening, good evening!" one heard.

I myself was ushered into the card-room where, much to my delight, I at length had the pleasure of seeing M. de Fréjus leave. My dislike of M. de Fréjus was based on nothing less simple than a certain anaphylaxis, detectable only when the object of my aversion was present, or just leaving, or, as is so often the case with us when our systems have become mithridatized against definite poisons, just coming. I was now able to join the group which M. de Fréjus had just left, and to throw myself, with some degree of vigour, into the conversation. It had been begun by M. de Lentilleux, a distinguished engineer, who was discussing the development of the fan as an instrument of social progress. "For example," he was saying, as I approached the group, "with the ancients the fan (*éventail*) was known as a 'winnower' (*vanneur*) and used as a bellows or fly whisk. Even our modern usage gives us the fan as an instrument for winnowing grain or, to go still further, an appliance in various systems of ventilation. But, with your permission, I shall confine my comments to the fan (*éventail*) as we know it, the screen fan and the folding fan, both excellent appurtenances. In general, the former (or latter) consists of a handle to which is attached a rigid mount—except, of course, I need hardly say, feather fans, which may be included in this class, the usual mount is made of straw, cane, silk, parchment, or and so forth, and is square, circular, pear or leaf-shaped. I mean leaf-shaped. By the eighteenth century it is unquestionable that the fan had become more an item of personal attraction, although I myself could never see it as such, considering it ungainly and slightly dangerous when wielded by a strong woman, as witness the *cabriolet*, a folding fan in vogue during the time of Louis XV. This was named after the light two-wheeled carriage so popular in France at that time, a vehicle which is often represented in the scenes painted, or engraved, on the mounts. This, no doubt, led to the introduction of the Vernis-Martin fan, one of the most rare of collectors' items. The name Vernis-Martin was derived from a certain translucent varnish—

[*This sort of thing is going on for quite a bit longer. I thought you ought to know.*]

a certain translucent varnish accidentally discovered by the brothers Martin when they were trying to imitate Japanese lacquer. It is, of course, with the Japanese that the fan is most closely associated with the lives and customs of the people. Rhead, in his *History of the Fan*, a large but inaccurate book as I shall presently show, says that the Japanese regard the fan as an emblem of life, widening and expanding as the sticks radiate from the rivet. This I cannot agree with, as very often with life the tendency is toward a *con*vergence (from the latin *con* and *vergo*) rather than radiation. However, most interesting of the types of Japanese fans is the *Gumbai Uchuia*, a rigid fan made for use in battle and entirely of iron (eleventh century). The *Akomé Ogi* is the earliest form of court fan, having come into use in the seventh century, or four centuries earlier than the *Gumbai Uchuia*, and was composed of thirty-eight blades (a lot of blades) fastened with a rivet, formed of a bird or butterfly and ornamented at the corners with artificial flowers and twelve streamers of coloured silks."

[*What did I tell you?*]. . . .

ROBERT BENCHLEY

HENRY REED
1914–

NAMING OF PRIVATE PARTS

This perspex model is what you might call a perfect replica
Except of course for the perspex, of a typical shelter,
If such a thing as typical exists. The first thing to notice
Is the door, and this long thing is the radiation reflector,
Which in your case you have not got. This little room here
Is the same as the little room in every house and under it
Is the water re-cycling device, which again you have not
  got.
I see some of you are looking alarmed and a lady in the
  back
Has fainted but there is no need to panic because this is
Only a model and I assure you that in the real thing
That little room I showed you is not made of perspex.

JOHN LLOYD WILLIAMS

DANTE GABRIEL ROSSETTI
1828–82

SOUL-SEVERANCE

Because the cithole hath a thousand tones
    Inwrought with many subtile harmonies
    Of lute and flute wherein sweet music dies,
Yea, all the bitter-sweet that love disowns,
Mournful are they and full of heavy moans
    And tears and interpenetrative sighs,
    Soul-stirred with ultimate immensities,
And incommunicable antiphones!

298

So is the soul fulfilled of saddest things,
  Of multitudinous sighs and more sad than they
  Whereof Earth hears no sound, yet nothing may
Drown the deep murmur of its echoings:
Even so of soul and soul the poet sings
  And what on earth he means can no man say.

ST JOHN HANKIN

DAMON RUNYON
1884–1946

REVIEW OF GUYS AND DOLLS

Guys and Dolls, at which I am privileged to take a peek last evening, is a hundred per-cent American musical caper, cooked up out of a story called "The Idyll of Miss Sarah Brown", by the late Damon Runyon, who is such a scribe as delights to give the English language a nice kick in the pants.

This particular fable takes place in and around Times Square in New York City, where many citizens do nothing but roll dice all night long, which is held by one and all, and especially the gendarmes, to be a great vice. Among the parties hopping around in this neighbourhood is a guy by the name of Nathan Detroit, who operates a floating dice game, and Miss Adelaide, his ever-loving pretty, who is sored up at this Nathan because after fourteen years' engagement, they are still nothing but engaged. Anyway, being short of ready scratch, Nathan lays a bet with a large gambler called Sky Masterton, the subject of the wager being whether The Sky can talk a certain Salvation Army doll into joining him on a trip to Havana. Naturally, Nathan figures that a nice doll such as this will die sooner, but by and by she and The Sky get to looking back and forth at each other, and before you know it she is his sweet-pea. What happens next but The Sky gets bopped by religion and shoots craps with Nathan and the boys for their immortal souls. And where do the sinners wind up, with their chalk-striped suits and busted noses, but at a prayer meeting in the doll's mission house, which hands me a very big laugh indeed. The actors who nab the jobs of playing these apes and essences of 42nd Street have me tuckered out with clapping them.

Nathan Detroit is Sam Levene, who expostulates very good with his arms, which are as long as a monkey'. Stubby Kaye, who plays Nicely-Nicely Johnson, the well-known horse-player, is built on lines which are by no means dinky, for his poundage maybe runs into zillions, but he gives with a voice which is as couth as a choir boy's or maybe couther. He commences the evening by joining in a three-part comedy song about the nags. In fact, it is a fugue, and I will give you plenty of eleven to five that it is the first fugue many patrons of the Coliseum ever hear. Miss Vivian Blaine (Miss Adelaide) is a very choice blonde judy and she gets to sing a song which goes as follows: "Take back your mink to from whence it came" and which hits me slap-dab in the ear as being supernaturally comical. Myself, I prefer her to Miss Lizbeth Webb, who plays the mission doll, but, naturally, I do not mention such an idea out loud.

The Coliseum is no rabbit hutch, and maybe a show as quick and smart as this *Guys and Dolls* will go better in such a sized theatre as the Cambridge Theatre. Personally, I found myself laughing ha-ha last night more often than a guy in the critical dodge has any right to. And I am ready to up and drop on my knees before Frank Loesser, who writes the music and lyrics. In fact, this Loesser is maybe the best light composer in the world. In fact, the chances are that *Guys and Dolls* is not only a young masterpiece, but the *Beggar's Opera* of Broadway.

KENNETH TYNAN

J. D. SALINGER
1919–

ADAM AND EVE AND STUFF LIKE THAT

Boy, when I saw old Eve I thought I was going to flip. I mean it isn't that Eve is good-looking or anything like that, it's just that she's different. I don't know what the hell it is exactly—but you always know when she's around. All of a sudden I knew there was something wrong with old Eve the minute I saw her. She looked nervous as hell. I kinda felt sorry for her—even though she's got one of my goddam ribs, so I went over to talk to old Eve.

"You look very, *very* nice, Adam," she said to me in a funny way, like she was ashamed of something. "Why don't you join me in some apple?"

Goddam, is that all these sophisticated babes think about all the time? It's enough to drive a guy crazy, if you know what I mean. Pretty soon she'll be wearing a goddam fig leaf and dancing around like a big, gigantic horse—but she WAS kinda sexy. She really was. So I talked to her.

We started talking about a few things—nothing much, just some childish stuff, I guess—and I started thinking that, well, maybe I ought to take a little bit of the apple.

Just then old Eve told me that the goddamn viper had told her to eat the goddam apple. Ya know, if she hadn't said that that flitty, perverty punk had told her to eat it, I might have taken a bit—but after thinking it over for a second I just didn't feel like it. You know how it is, don't ya? I just felt kind of perculiar, like I had clothes on and all that crap. Boy, I must be nuts. I swear to God I am. Old Eve just seemed depressing as all hell. In fact, she was sort of a pain in the ass. So I turned around to leave.

"Adam, Adam, please don't go, *pl*ease".

For Chrissake, what a phoney! Boy, if it's one thing I can't stand it's phoneys. I'm not kidding. I didn't feel like eating the goddam apple. I really didn't. So I left.

ED BERMAN

SAPPER (HERMAN CYRIL MCNEILE) 1888–1937 JOHN BUCHAN (1875–1940) and DORNFORD YATES (1885–1960)

THE SCHOOL OF SNOBBERY WITH VIOLENCE

from *Forty Years On*

HANNAY: Ned.

LEITHEN: Yes?

HANNAY: I asked you here for a purpose.

LEITHEN: Yes.

HANNAY: Do you remember the last time I saw you?

LEITHEN: Intimately. It was at a little thing called Mons.

HANNAY: Since then I seem to have lost your spoor.

LEITHEN: I came through the war more or less intact. I lost an arm here, an ear there, but I was all right, a damn sight better off than a few million other poor devils anyway. Then I got back home and there were these Weary Willies and Tired Tims in their hand-woven ties, writing gibberish they called poetry saying we'd all been wasting our time. I couldn't see it myself. If we'd done nothing by 1918 at least we'd saved the follow-on.

SANDY CLANROYDEN: Ned. Did you ever hear of a man called George Ampersand?

LEITHEN: Bostonian philanthropist and friend of kings! Who hasn't?

SANDY: I had some talk with Mr Baldwin this morning. I never saw a man more worried.

HANNAY: Of late, Ned, there have been a succession of small disasters, oh trifling in themselves . . . a Foreign Secretary's sudden attack of dysentery at the funeral of George V, an American ambassador found strangled in his own gym-slip, and in Sudetenland, most mysterious of all, a Laughing Leper who destroys whole villages with his infectious giggles.

SANDY: The tide is flowing fast against monarchy in Europe. Scarcely a week passes but a throne falls. Mr Baldwin thinks it may be our turn next.

LEITHEN: Who is behind it all this time?

HANNAY: Who? That poses something of a problem. To the good people of the neighbourhood he is a white-haired old man with a nervous habit of moving his lips as he talks. To the members of a not unfamiliar London club he is our second most successful theologian. But the world knows him as . . . George Ampersand.

LEITHEN: Ampersand. Good God.

HANNAY: (*Handing him snapshots*) He is surrounded by some of the worst villains in Europe. Irma, his wife. Nature played a cruel trick upon her by giving her a waxed moustache. Sandro, his valet. A cripple of the worst sort, and consumptive into the bargain.

LEITHEN: Is he sane?

SANDY: Sane? He is brilliantly sane. The second sanest in Europe. But like all sane men he has at one time or another crossed that thin bridge that separates lunacy from insanity. And this last week the pace has quickened. Else explain why a highly respected Archbishop of Canterbury, an international hairdresser and a very famous king all decide to take simultaneous holidays on the Black Sea.

HANNAY: Take a look at this snapshot. It's of a simultaneous holiday on the Black Sea.

LEITHEN: But that's . . .

HANNAY: Exactly. A young man not entirely unconnected with the English throne.

LEITHEN: Who is she?

SANDY: She's beautiful, isn't she. An American. Women are queer cattle at the best of times but she's like no other woman I've ever known. She has all the slim grace of a boy and all the delicacy of a young colt.

LEITHEN: It's a rare combination. Who's this?

HANNAY: Completely Unscrupulos, the Greek shipping magnate.

LEITHEN: He's got himself into a pretty rum set. And yet he looks happy.

HANNAY: That's what Mr Baldwin doesn't like about it. During the past few months certain reports have been appearing in what for want of a better word the Americans call their newspapers.

LEITHEN: About her?

HANNAY: Yes.

LEITHEN: And him?

HANNAY: Yes.

LEITHEN: But . . . I don't understand . . . where lies the difficulty? If he loves her. . . .

HANNAY: I don't think you understand. She is what we in the Church of England called a divorced woman.

LEITHEN: God! It's filthy!

HANNAY: A divorced woman on the throne of the house of Windsor would be a pretty big feather in the cap of that bunch of rootless intellectuals, alien Jews and international pederasts who call themselves the Labour Party.

LEITHEN: Your talk is like a fierce cordial.

SANDY: As yet the British public knows nothing. Mr Baldwin is relying on us to see they remain in that blissful state.

LEITHEN: I like the keen thrust of your mind, but where does friend Ampersand fit into all this?

HANNAY: That is what I want you to find out. Sandy will accompany you disguised as a waiter. That should at least secure you the entrée. But be careful. And on no account let His Majesty know that you are meddling in this affair. A sport called Shakespeare summed it up: There's a divinity that doth hedge a King, Rough hew it how you will.

ALAN BENNETT

DOROTHY L. SAYERS
1893–1957

from GREEDY NIGHT

Wimsey sank back with a moan; then rallied himself and swallowed a little tea from the cup which Bunter had filled.

"I don't like this tea," he said peevishly. "I don't believe this is my specially grown Son-of-Heaven china."

"It is, my lord; but in some circumstances the flavour of almost anything is apt to be sensibly impaired. May I urge, my lord, that an effort should be made to eat some breakfast? It is considered to be advisable on the morning after an occasion of festivity, even if the handle of a knife has to be employed to assist the process of deglutition."

"Oh, all right." Wimsey held out his hand for the menu which Bunter produced, like a conjurer, apparently from the air. "Well, I won't eat *avoine secoueur*, anyhow. Give it to the cat."

"The cat has already tried it, my lord, during my momentary absence from the kitchen. The intelligent animal appears to be of your lordship's opinion. I would recommend a little *pâté gonfleur sur canapé*, my lord, for the present emergency."

Wimsey groaned. "I don't believe I could taste even that," he said. "Very well, I'll have a stab at it."

"Thank you, my lord." Bunter laid an armful of newspapers on the bed and withdrew. When he returned with the breakfast tray Wimsey was reading with absorbed interest. "Bunter," he said eagerly, "I see that at Sotheby's on Monday they're auctioning a thing I simply must have—the original manuscript of the Chanson de Roland, with marginal notes by Saint Louis. If I find I can't go myself, I shall want you to pop round and bid for me. That is, of course, if it's the genuine article. You could make sure of that, I suppose?"

"Without difficulty, my lord. I have always taken an interest in the technical study of medieval calligraphy. I should be sceptical, though, about those marginal notes, my lord. It has always been understood, your lordship will recollect, that His Most Christian Majesty was unable to write. However—"

At this point there came a long-continued ringing at the door-bell of the flat; and after a brief interval Bunter, with all the appearance of acting under protest, showed the Bishop of Glastonbury into the bedroom.

"I say, Peter, there's the devil to pay!" exclaimed that prelate. "Topsy's pretty well off her onion, and Bill Mixer's in a frightful dither. Have you heard what's happened? But, of course, you couldn't. They've been trying to get you on the 'phone this morning, but that man of yours kept on saying that he feared his lordship was somewhat closely engaged at the moment. So they rang me up and asked me to tell you."

"Well, why not tell me?" Wimsey snapped. Topsy, the Bishop's favourite sister, was an old friend, and her husband was a man for whom Wimsey had a deep regard that dated from his years at Balliol.

"Dermot's dead."

"I say! What a ghastly thing!" Wimsey scrambled out of bed and into a dressing-gown. "What happened to poor old Dermot?"

"That's just what they don't know. There was absolutely nothing the matter with him, but he was found dead this morning—apparently uninjured, they say. Foul play is suspected, of course."

"Of course," Wimsey agreed, plying his hair-brushes vigorously. . . .

E. C. BENTLEY

WILLIAM SHAKESPEARE
1564–1616

HAMLET'S SOLILOQUY IMITATED

To *print*, or not to *print*—that is the question.
Whether 'tis better in a trunk to bury
The quirks and crotchets of outrageous fancy,
Or send a well-wrote copy to the press,
And by disclosing, end them? To print, no doubt
No more; and by one act to say we end
The head-ache, and a thousand natural shocks
Of scribbling frenzy—'tis a consummation
Devoutly to be wish'd. To print—to beam
From the same shelf with Pope, in calf well bound:

To sleep, perchance, with Quarles—Ay, there's the rub—
For to what class a writer may be doom'd,
When he hath shuffled off some paltry stuff,
Must give us pause.—There's the respect that makes
Th' unwilling poet keep his piece nine years.
For who would bear th' impatient thirst of fame,
The pride of conscious merit, and 'bove all,
The tedious importunity of friends,
When as himself might his *quietus* make
With a bare inkhorn? Who would fardles bear
To groan and sweat under a load of wit?
But that the tread of steep Parnassus' hill,
That undiscover'd country, with whose bays
Few travellers return, puzzles the will,
And makes us rather bear to live unknown,
Than run the hazard to be known and damn'd.
Thus critics do make cowards of us all,
And thus the healthful face of many a poem
Is sickly'd o'er with a pale manuscript;
And enterprise of great fire and spirit,
With this regard from Dodsley turn away,
And lose the name of authors.

RICHARD JAGO

TO BE OR NOT TO BE

Prize-winning parody in the Weekly Dispatch, *1880*

To be, or not to be: that is the question:
Whether 'tis better in this life to suffer
The petty trials of unmarried life
Or add one more unto a list of troubles,
And thus by marriage end them? To wed, to sleep
No more; or, if to sleep, to say we end

The yearnings and the sentimental fudge
Young flesh is heir to—'tis a consummation
Too blessed to be true. To love, to wed—
What then? Perchance repent; ay, there's the rub.
For in the meekest maid what changes come
When we have wriggled on the golden coil,
Must give us pause. There's reason good
That makes so many choose a single life—
For who could bear to give up his quiet pipe,
The close society of bosom friends,
The interchange of bright congenial thoughts,
Which sparkle like the glasses on the board,
For squalling children and a shrewish wife,
While he can cook a herring, or a steak,
And ply a bodkin. None would ever dare
To grunt and growl at lovely maidenhood!
But there's a something after marriage vows—
The trap where foxes lose their tails, and then
Advise their fellows that it's much the best—
Which makes us rather bear the ills we have
Than marry troops of others with a wife—
For woman breeched makes cowards of us all.
And, somehow, all our boasted resolution
Gets sicklied o'er with the pale cast of fear;
And enterprises, which we might have held
In great regard, must then be put aside,
Because, forsooth, "I'm married!"

WILLIAM H. EDMUNDS

MUCH ADO ABOUT NOTHING IN THE CITY

Sigh no more, dealers, sigh no more,
   Shares were unstable ever,
They often have been down before,
   At high rates constant never.
     Then sigh not so,
     Soon up they'll go,
And you'll be blithe and funny,
   Converting all your notes of woe
Into hey money, money.

Write no more letters, write no mo
   On stocks so dull and heavy.
At times on 'Change 'tis always so,
   When bears a tribute levy.
     Then sigh not so,
     And don't be low,
In sunshine you'll make honey,
   Converting all your notes of woe
Into hey money, money.

ANON

"FULL FATHOM FIVE THY FATHER LIES"

Full fathom five thy father lies,
His aqualung was the wrong size.

JUNE MERCER LANGFIELD

NEW IMPROVED SONNET XVIII

Shall I equate thee with a summer's day?
Thou art more valid and more meaningful:
A north-west airstream will devalue May,
And summer's mortgage is foreclosable:
Sometimes the sun is too intensive-phased,
And often is his gold down-marketed,
And every fare by next year's fare's erased,
By an inflation situation fed:
But thy eternal summer's index-linked,
Nor shalt thou thine exclusive image lack,
Nor rate thy life-expectancy extinct,
When hopefully thou'rt out in paperback,
    So long as I'm in print and men are human,
    This is thy life-insurance, I'm thy Pru-man.

PETER TITHERADGE

TWELFTH NIGHT; or, WHAT WILL YOU HAVE?

The other day my wife bought a jar of what were described on the label as "Old English Cocktail Olives". Ah, evocative words! They bring vividly to mind that golden age when England was still covered with primeval olive groves and when the rip-roaring Old English Cocktail Party was in full flower. Like most Old English things, it was at its best in Elizabethan times—to judge, at any rate, from the following fragment, entitled *Ye Cocktayle Partye*, and attributed to Will Shakespeare (by Mike Frayn, at any rate).

Scene: The EARL OF ESSEX's *At Home.*

ESSEX: Ah, good Northumberland! Thou com'st betimes!
    What drink'st? Martini? Champagne cup? or hock?
    Or that wan distillate whose fiery soul
    Is tamed by th' hailstones hurl'd from jealous heaven,
    The draught a breed of men yet unengender'd
    Calls Scotch on th' rocks?
NORTHUMBERLAND: Ay, Scotch, but stint the rocks.
ESSEX: Ah, Gloucester! And your fairest Duchess, too!
    Sweet Leicester! Ah, my Lady Leicester, homage!
    And Worcester, and the Chesters, radiant pair!
    And Ursula, the sister of Lord Bicester!
    Northumberland, methinks thou know'st not
        Gloucester,
    Nor Gloucester Worcester, nor the Leicesters Chesters.
    Lord Worcester, may I introduce Lord Leicester?
    My noblest Gloucester, meet your brother Chester.
    My Lady Chester and my Lady Leicester,
    Meets Ursula, the sister of Lord Bicester.
ALL: Hail!
GLOUCESTER: Well, now, hath Phoebus quit these climes for
                                    ever?

WORCESTER: Ay, are we now delivered quite to gales,
    And spouting hurricanoes' plashy spite?
CHESTER: Sure, 'tis foul weather.
LEICESTER: Why, so 'tis.
NORTHUMBERLAND: 'Tis so.

    (*Another part of the battlefield.*)

ESSEX: What ho, champagne! Crisps, ho! Pass round the
                                 peanuts!

WORCESTER: A peanut, madam? Pardon me, I pray,
    But when we met, the white-hot dazzlement
    Your beauty rains about like thunderbolts

Quite scared my eyes; I did not catch your name.
LADY URSULA: Why, Ursula, and sister to Lord Bicester.
WORCESTER: Not Harry Bicester? Known to th' admiring
world
As Eggy? Wears a red moustache?
URSULA: The same.
WORCESTER: O, Eggy Bicester! and thou, thou art his sister?
Then long-lost cousins must we surely be!
ESSEX: Forgive me, Ursula, if I intrude,
But, Worcester, meet our brother Chester here.
He has the royal birthmark on his arm,
Would know if you had, too.
WORCESTER: Why, so I have.
CHESTER: Why, marry then, you are my brother, stol'n
At birth by she-bears.
WORCESTER: Why then, that I am!
LADY LEICESTER: The truth of th' ancient legend now is clear:
"When Worcester linkt to Chester prove to be,
"Then Gloucester in Northumberland we'll see."
Northumberland is Gloucester, chang'd at birth,
And Gloucester Worcester, while the aged Earl
Of Leicester plainly must be Lady Chester,
All chang'd, and double-chang'd, and chang'd again,
The Chesters Leicesters and the Leicesters Chesters,
Lord Chester, thus, the proof runs clear, is me,
And Ursula, Lord Bicester, his own sister.
NORTHUMBERLAND: Before the discourse turns again to
weigh
Apollo's absence and the pluvious times,
We should acquaint our new selves with each other.
My Lady Chester, once the Earl of Leicester,
Meet Lady Leicester, now the Earl of Chester. . . .
ESSEX: Old friends 'neath curious titles oft are found,
Come, pass th' Old English Cocktail Olives round. . . .

MICHAEL FRAYN

313

SHAKESPEARE EXPLAINED

Carrying on the system of footnotes to a silly extreme

PERICLES

ACT II SCENE III

Enter FIRST LADY-IN-WAITING. *Flourish,[1] Hautboys[2] and[3] torches.[4]*

FIRST LADY-IN-WAITING: What[5] ho![6] Where[7] is[8] the[9] music?[10]

NOTES

[1]*Flourish*: The stage direction here is obscure. Clarke claims it should read "flarish," thus changing the meaning of the passage to "flarish" (that is, the King's), but most authorities have agreed that it should remain "flourish", supplying the predicate which is to be flourished. There was at this time a custom in the countryside of England to flourish a mop as a signal to the passing vendor of berries, signifying that in that particular household there was a consumer-demand for berries, and this may have been meant in this instance. That Shakespeare was cognizant of this custom of flourishing the mop for berries is shown in a similar passage in the second part of King Henry IV, where he has the Third Page enter and say, "Flourish." Cf. also Hamlet, IV, 7:4.

[2]*Hautboys*, from the French *haut*, meaning "high" and the Eng. *boys*, meaning "boys". The word here is doubtless used in the sense of "high boys", indicating either that Shakespeare intended to convey the idea of spiritual distress on the part of the First Lady-in-Waiting, or that he did not. Of this Rolfe says: "Here we have one of the chief indications of Shakespeare's knowledge of human nature, his remarkable insight into the petty foibles of this work-a-day world." Cf. T. N. 4:6. "Mine eye hath play'd the painter, and hath stell'd thy beauty's form in table of my heart."

[3]*and.* A favorite conjunctive of Shakespeare's in referring to the need for a more adequate navy for England. Tauchnitz claims that it should be pronounced "und", stressing the antipenult. This interpretation, however, has found disfavor among most commentators because of its limited significance. We find the same conjunctive in A. W. T. E. W. 6:7. "Steel-boned, unyielding *and* uncomplying virtue", and here there can be no doubt that Shakespeare meant that if the King should consent to the marriage of his daughter the excuse of Stephano, offered in Act II, would carry no weight.

[4]*Torches.* The interpolation of some foolish player and never the work of Shakespeare (Warb.). The critics of the last century have disputed whether or not this has been misspelled in the original, and should read "trochies" or "troches". This might well be since the introduction of tobacco into England at this time had wrought havoc with the speaking voices of the players, and we might well imagine that at the entrance of the First Lady-in-Waiting there might be perhaps one of the hautboys mentioned in the preceding passage bearing a box of "troches" or "trognies" for the actors to suck. Of this entrance Clarke remarks: "The noble mixture of spirited firmness and womanly modesty, fine sense and true humility, clear sagacity and absence of conceit, passionate warmth and sensitive delicacy, generous love and self-diffidence with which Shakespeare has endowed this First Lady-in-Waiting renders her in our eyes one of the most admirable of his female characters." Cf. M. S. N. D. 8:9, "That solder'st close impossibilities and mak'st them kiss."

[5]*What*—What.

[6]*Ho!* In conjunction with the preceding word doubtless means "What ho!" changed by Clarke to "what hoo!" In the original MS. it reads "What hi!" but this has been accredited to the tendency of the time to write "What hi" when "what ho" was meant. Techner alone maintains that it should read "What humpf!" Cf. Ham. 5:0, "High-ho!"

[7]*Where.* The reading of the folio, retained by Johnson,

the Cambridge editors and others, but it is not impossible that Shakespeare wrote "why", as Pope and others give it. This would make the passage read "Why the music?" instead of "Where is the music?" and would be a much more probable interpretation in view of the music of that time. Cf. George Ade. Fable No. 15, "Why the gunny-sack?"

[8]*is*—is not. That is, would not be.

[9]*the*. Cf. Ham. 4:6, M. S. N. D. 3:5, A. W. T. E. W. 2:6, T. N. 1:3 and Macbeth 3:1, "that knits up *the* raveled sleeves of care."

[10]*music*. Explained by Malone as "the art of making music" or "music that is made". If it has but one of these meanings we are inclined to think it is the first; and this seems to be favoured by what precedes, "*the* music!" Cf. M. of V. 4:2, "The man that hath no music in himself."

The meaning of the whole passage seems to be the First Lady-in-Waiting has entered, concomitant with a flourish, hautboys and torches, and says, "What ho! Where is the music?"

ROBERT BENCHLEY

THE SKINHEAD HAMLET

Shakespeare's play translated into modern English

Our hope was to achieve something like the effect of the New English Bible—Eds

ACT I SCENE I

The battlements of Elsinore Castle.
Enter HAMLET, *followed by* GHOST.
GHOST: Oi! Mush!
HAMLET: Yer?
GHOST: I was fucked!
    (*Exit* GHOST.)

HAMLET: O fuck.
  (*Exit* HAMLET.)

SCENE II

The Throneroom.
Enter KING CLAUDIUS, GERTRUDE, HAMLET *and* COURT.
CLAUDIUS: Oi! You, Hamlet, give over!
HAMLET: Fuck off, won't you?
  (*Exit* CLAUDIUS, GERTRUDE, COURT.)
  h(*Alone*) They could have fucking waited.
  (*Enter* HORATIO.)
HORATIO: Oi! Whatcha cock!
HAMLET: Weeeeey!
(*Exeunt.*)

SCENE III

Ophelia's Bedroom.
Enter Ophelia and Laertes.
LAERTES: I'm fucking off now. Watch Hamlet doesn't slip you
  one while I'm gone.
OPHELIA: I'll be fucked if he does.
  (*Exeunt.*)

SCENE IV

The Battlements.
Enter HORATIO, HAMLET *and* GHOST.
GHOST: Oi! Mush, get on with it!
HAMLET: Who did it then?
GHOST: That wanker Claudius. He poured fucking poison in
  my fucking ear!
HAMLET: Fuck me!
  (*Exeunt.*)

A corridor in the castle.
Enter HAMLET *reading. Enter* POLONIUS.
POLON: Oi! You!
HAMLET: Fuck off, grandad!
    (*Exit* POLON. *Enter* ROSENCRANTZ *and* GUILDENSTERN.)
ROS & GU: Oi! Oi! Mucca!
HAMLET: Fuck off, the pair of you!
    (*Exit* ROS *and* GUILD.)
HAMLET: (*Alone*) To fuck or be fucked.
    (*Enter* OPHELIA.)
OPHELIA: My Lord!
HAMLET: Fuck off to a nunnery!
    (*They exit in different directions.*)

ACT III SCENE I

The Throne Room.
Enter PLAYERS *and all* COURT.
I PLAYER: Full thirty times hath Phoebus cart . . .
CLAUDIUS: I'll be fucked if I watch any more of this crap.
    (*Exeunt.*)

SCENE II

Gertrude's Bedchamber.
Enter HAMLET, *to* GERTRUDE.
HAMLET: Oi! Slag!
GERTRUDE: Watch your fucking mouth, kid!
POLON: (*From behind the curtain*) Too right.
HAMLET: Who the fuck was that?
    (*He stabs* POLONIUS *through the arras.*)
POLON: Fuck!
HAMLET: Fuck! I thought it was that other wanker.
    (*Exeunt.*)

A Court Room.

CLAUDIUS: Fuck off to England then!

HAMLET: Delighted, mush.

SCENE II

The Throne Room.

OPHELIA, GERTRUDE *and* CLAUDIUS.

OPHELIA: Here, cop a whack of this.

(*She hands* GERTRUDE *some rosemary and exits.*)

CLAUDIUS: She's fucking round the twist, isn't she?

GERTRUDE: (*Looking out the window*)

There is a willow grows aslant the brook.

CLAUDIUS: Get on with it, slag.

GERTRUDE: Ophelia's gone and fucking drowned!

CLAUDIUS: Fuck! Laertes isn't half going to be browned off.

(*Exeunt.*)

SCENE III

A Corridor.

LAERTES: (*Alone*) I'm going to fucking do this lot.

(*Enter* CLAUDIUS.)

CLAUDIUS: I didn't fucking do it, mate. It was that wanker
Hamlet.

LAERTES: Well, fuck him.

ACT V SCENE I

Hamlet's Bedchamber.

HAMLET *and* HORATIO *seated.*

HAMLET: I got this feeling I'm going to cop it, Horatio, and
you know, I couldn't give a flying fuck.

(*Exeunt.*)

319

Large Hall.

Enter HAMLET, LAERTES, COURT, GERTRUDE, CLAUDIUS.

LAERTES: Oi, wanker: let's get on with it.

HAMLET: Delighted, fuckface.

(*They fight and both are poisoned by the poisoned sword.*)

LAERTES: Fuck!

HAMLET: Fuck!

(*The* QUEEN *drinks.*)

GERTRUDE: Fucking odd wine!

CLAUDIUS: You drunk the wrong fucking cup, you stupid cow!

HAMLET: (*Pouring the poison down* CLAUDIUS' *throat*): Well, fuck you!

CLAUDIUS: I'm fair and squarely fucked.

LAERTES: Oi, mush: no hard feelings, eh?

HAMLET: Yer.

(LAERTES *dies.*)

HAMLET: Oi! Horatio!

HORATIO: Yer?

HAMLET: I'm fucked. The rest is fucking silence.

(HAMLET *dies.*)

HORATIO: Fuck: that was no ordinary wanker, you know.

(*Enter* FORTINBRAS.)

FORTIN: What the fuck's going on here?

HORATIO: A fucking mess, that's for sure.

FORTIN: No kidding. I see Hamlet's fucked.

HORATIO: Yer.

FORTIN: Fucking shame: fucking good bloke.

HORATIO: Too fucking right.

FORTIN: Fuck this for a lark then. Let's piss off.

(*Exeunt with alarums.*)

RICHARD CURTIS

320

PERCY BYSSHE SHELLEY
1792–1822

from THE THIEVES' ANTHOLOGY

I met a cracksman coming down the Strand,
 Who said, "A huge Cathedral, piled of stone,
Stands in a churchyard, near St Martin's Le Grand,
 Where keeps St Paul his sacerdotal throne.
A street runs by it to the northward. There
For cab and bus is writ, 'No Thoroughfare',
 The Mayor and Councilmen do so command,
And in that street a shop, with many a box,
 Upon whose sign these fateful words I scanned:
'My name is Chubb, who makes the Patent Locks;
 Look on my works, ye burglars, and despair!' "
Here made he pause, like one who sees a blight
 Mar all his hopes, and sighed with drooping air,
"Our game is up, my covies, blow me tight!"

THEODORE MARTIN

THE SITWELL FAMILY

THE SWISS FAMILY WHITTLEBOT
In a short exposition of modern art

MISS HERNIA WHITTLEBOT *should be effectively and charmingly
dressed in undraped dyed sacking, a cross between blue and
green, with a necklet of uncut amber beads in unconventional
shapes. She must wear a gold band rather high up on her*

321

forehead from which hang a little clump of Bacchanalian fruit below each ear. Her face is white and weary, with a long chin and nose, and bags under the eyes. Her brothers GOB *and* SAGO WHITTLEBOT *are dressed with self-conscious nonchalance in unusual clothes.* GOB *wears cycling breeches and a bottle-green velvet coat with a big floppy bow, cloth-topped boots and a tweed shooting hat.* SAGO *is faultlessly dressed in a slightly Victorian morning suit. His shirt and boots are not quite right and his silk hat is upside down by his side. Their musical instruments are rather queer in shape.*

(MISS HERNIA WHITTLEBOT *speaks.*) It is difficult for me to explain to you in words that which I have to say regarding Life, and Art, and Rhythm. Words are inadequate at the best of times. To me life is essentially a curve, and Art an oblong within that curve. Rhythm is fundamental in everything. My brothers and I have been brought up on Rhythm as other children are brought up on Glaxo. Always we have tried to create Sound and Reality and Colour. My brothers, on their various instruments (and they have many), and myself, with all the strength and courage I can summon up, will endeavour to prove to you the inevitable Truth in Rhythmic Colour Poetry. People have jeered at us, often when walking in the street they have thrown fruit and vegetables at us, but it is all colour and humour. We see humour in everything, especially the primitive.

My first Poem is an early Peruvian Love Song.

(*Accompanied in fitful gusts by* GOB *and* SAGO *she recites:*)

Beloved, it is Dawn, I rise
　　To smell the roses sweet,
Emphatic are my hips and thighs,
　　Phlegmatic are my feet.
Ten thousand roses have I got

Within a garden small,
God give me strength to sniff the lot,
Oh let me sniff them all.

Beloved, it is Dawn, I rise
To smell the roses sweet,
Emphatic are my hips and thighs
Phlegmatic are my feet.

(*The next poem strikes an exultantly gay note—the colours are vivid and ruthless because they are Life.*)

Rain, Rain, Pebbles and pain,
Trickle and truckle and do it again,
Houpla, Houpla, Dickery Dee,
Trolderol trolderol, fancy me.

(*Musical interlude.*)

Fancy me!
I will now recite my tone poem "Passion" to which special music has been set by my brother Gob on the Cophutican.

Passion's dregs are the salt of life
Spirits trodden beneath the heel of
Ingratitude.
Drains and Sewers support the quest
Of eternal indulgence.
Thank God for the Coldstream Guards.

I will now give you a very long and intensely primitive poem entitled "The Lower Classes". I have endeavoured to portray the bottomless hostility of the Labour Party towards themselves and everybody else—I wrote most of the first part in a Lighthouse.

(At this moment sounds become audible from the Prompt Corner. The STAGE MANAGER is making signs to them that their time is up.)

War and life and the Albert Bridge,
Fade into the mists of Salacious obscurity
Street hawkers cry apathetically
Mothers and children rolling and slapping
Wet on the grass—I wonder why.
Guts and Dahlias and billiard balls
Swirling along with spurious velocity
Ending what and where and when
In the hearts of little birds
But never Tom Tits.
Freedom from all this shrieking vortex
Chimneys and tramcars and the blackened branches
Of superfluous antagonism
Oxford and Cambridge count for naught
Life is ephemeral before the majesty
Of Local Apophlegmatism
Melody semi-spheroidal
In all its innate rotundity
Rhubarb for purposes unknown, etc. etc.

(The STAGE MANAGER, having despaired of making her hear, has signed to the Orchestra to strike up the next number. Unmoved by this, MISS WHITTLEBOT produces a megaphone— at last in desperation the STAGE MANAGER begins to set the next scene and the WHITTLEBOT FAMILY are eventually pushed off the stage still playing and reciting.)

NOËL COWARD

EDITH SITWELL
1887–1964

TO NOËL COWARD

Pale-faced rat!
   Wallowing in the pit of middle-class degeneracy.
Juggling clumsily with the immortal souls
  Of your superiors.
Illogically defying the very canons of beauty.
   Defiling with your touch the plangency of Art,
Restlessly groping with inadequate comprehension
   Among the tinsel stars and tawdry imaginings
Of a squalid mentality.
   Pitifully mean, your very appearance an offence,
Slimy as the ooze of a sluggish river.
   Rough to the insensate touch,
Rough to the insensate fingers.
   Pig-brained, pig-eyed and stupid,
Vulgar, blatant, and self-confident,
   Early beginning of a nauseating manhood,
If such a term can be applied to you.
   Hob-Goblin habits in an ass's skin,
Picking your mental food from garbage heaps
   Rotting in the sun.
Drab—Putrefying—Soul-sickening!
   And anyhow you smell awful.

NOËL COWARD

STEVIE SMITH
1902–71

TO HIS COY MISTRESS

Nobody loves you Chloe, you sly minx,
    Procrastinating:
You'd be much better off now with me
    And not waiting but mating

If we had the time to spare we could
    Just mildly dally
Along the Ganges shore, but let's instead
    Be far more pally.

Oh, no, no, no, no, don't stand here in Hull
    Still hesitating.
Now, now, now, is the day we should be
    Not waiting but mating.

EDWARD BIRD

C. P. SNOW
1905–80

STRANGERS AND MASTERS

Paunceley was regaling us with the clarets of '56.

"This is very civil of you, Senior Tutor," observed Mainwaring.

"Thank you, Professor of Palaeontology and Sometime Fellow of Jesus," replied Paunceley. He seemed nervous, drawn, tense.

It was a languorous February night, heady with the rich evocative reek of sweet-william. The chrysanthemums blazed in the court, a Scotch mist draped the plane-trees and above, in the sky, shimmered the stars—countless, desolate, shining.

I felt increasingly uneasy about my tendency to fire off adjectives in threes. It was compulsive, embarrassing, ineluct-able; but at least it fostered the illusion of a mind that was diamond-sharp, incisive, brilliant.

"I have asked you to come here before breakfast." continued Paunceley, "because I have a most unsavoury revelation to make to you about one of your colleagues."

I glanced at Grimsby-Browne. He seemed suddenly im-mensely old, haggard, shrivelled. Had he committed the unforgivable and falsified a footnote? I studied Basingstoke, the Bursar. He too seemed suddenly bowed, broken, desic-cated. Had he done the unspeakable and embezzled the battels? The scent of Old Man's Beard saturated the combin-ation room.

"It concerns Charles Snow," said Paunceley.

The tension was now unbearably taut, torturing, tense. The plangent aroma of montbretia seemed to pervade every electron of my being.

The Senior Tutor's tone was dry, aloof, Olympian.

"I have discovered that his real name is Godfrey Winn."

MARTIN FAGG

327

ROBERT SOUTHEY
1774–1843

FATHER WILLIAM

"You are old, Father William," the young man said,
  "And your hair has become very white;
And yet you incessantly stand on your head—
  Do you think, at your age, it is right?"

"In my youth," Father William replied to his son,
  "I feared it might injure the brain;
But now that I'm perfectly sure I have none,
  Why, I do it again and again."

"You are old," said the youth, "as I mentioned before,
  And have grown most uncommonly fat;
Yet you turned a back somersault in at the door—
  Pray, what is the reason of that?"

"In my youth," said the sage, as he shook his gray locks,
  "I kept all my limbs very supple
By the use of this ointment—one shilling the box—
  Allow me to sell you a couple."

"You are old," said the youth, "and your jaws are too weak
  For anything tougher than suet;
Yet you finished the goose, with the bones and the beak—
  Pray, how did you manage to do it?"

"In my youth," said his father, "I took to the law,
  And argued each case with my wife;
And the muscular strength, which it gave to my jaw,
  Has lasted the rest of my life."

"You are old," said the youth, "one would hardly suppose
    That your eye was as steady as ever;
Yet you balanced an eel on the end of your nose—
    What made you so awfully clever?"

"I have answered three questions, and that is enough,"
    Said his father; "don't give yourself airs!
Do you think I can listen all day to such stuff?
    Be off, or I'll kick you downstairs!"

LEWIS CARROLL

SAMUEL JOHN STONE
1839–1900

HYMN

The Church's Restoration
    In eighteen-eighty-three
Has left for contemplation
    Not what there used to be.
How well the ancient woodwork
    Looks round the Rect'ry hall,
Memorial of the good work
    Of him who plann'd it all.

He who took down the pew-ends
    And sold them anywhere
But kindly spared a few ends
    Work'd up into a chair.
O worthy persecution
    Of dust! O hue divine!
O cheerful substitution,
    Thou varnishéd pitch-pine!

Church furnishing! Church furnishing!
    Sing art and crafty praise!
He gave the brass for burnishing
    He gave the thick red baize,
He gave the new addition,
    Pull'd down the dull old aisle,
—To pave the sweet transition
    He gave th' encaustic tile.

Of marble brown and veined
    He did the pulpit make;
He order'd windows stained
    Light red and crimson lake.
Sing on, with hymns uproarious,
    Ye humble and aloof,
Look up! and oh how glorious
    He has restored the roof!

SIR JOHN BETJEMAN

ALGERNON CHARLES SWINBURNE
1837–1909

OCTOPUS

Written at the Crystal Palace Aquarium

Strange beauty, eight-limbed and eight-handed,
    Whence camest to dazzle our eyes?
With thy bosom bespangled and banded
    With the hues of the seas and the skies;

Is thy home European or Asian,
　　O mystical monster marine?
Part molluscous and partly crustacean,
　　Betwixt and between.

Wast thou born to the sound of sea-trumpets?
　　Hast thou eaten and drunk to excess
Of the sponges—thy muffins and crumpets,
　　Of the seaweed—thy mustard and cress?
Wast thou nurtured in caverns of coral,
　　Remote from reproof or restraint?
Art thou innocent, art thou immoral,
　　Sinburnian or Saint?

Lithe limbs, curling free, as a creeper
　　That creeps in a desolate place,
To enrol and envelop the sleeper
　　In a silent and stealthy embrace,
Cruel beak craning forward to bite us,
　　Our juices to drain and to drink,
Or to whelm us in waves of Cocytus,
　　Indelible ink!

O breast, that 'twere rapture to writhe on!
　　O arms 'twere delicious to feel
Clinging close with the crush of the Python,
　　When she maketh her murderous meal!
In thy eight-fold embraces enfolden,
　　Let our empty existence escape;
Give us death that is glorious and golden,
　　Crushed all out of shape!

Ah! thy red lips, lascivious and luscious,
　　With death in their amorous kiss!
Cling round us, and clasp us, and crush us,
　　With bitings of agonized bliss;

We are sick with the poison of pleasure,
   Dispense us the potion of pain;
Ope thy mouth to its uttermost measure
   And bite us again!

A. C. HILTON

A MAUDLE-IN BALLAD

Imitation of the School of Swinburne

My lank limp lily, my long lithe lily,
   My languid lily-love, fragile and thin,
With dank leaves dangling and flower-flap chilly,
That shines like the skin of a Highland gilly!
   Mottled and moist as a cold toad's skin!
      Lustrous and leper-white, splendid and splay!
   Art thou not utter? and wholly akin
   To my own wan soul and my own wan chin,
      And my own wan nose-tip, liked to sway
   The peacock's feather, *sweeter than sin*,
      That I bought for a halfpenny, yesterday!

My long lithe lily, my languid lily,
   My lank limp lily-love, how shall I win!—
Woo thee to wink at me? Silver lily,
How shall I sing to thee, softly, or shrilly?
   What shall I weave for thee—which shall I spin—
      Rondel, or rondeau, or virelay?
   Shall I bee-like buzz, with my face thrust in
   Thy choice, chaste chalice, or choose me a tin
         Trumpet, or touchingly, tenderly play
   On the weird bird-whistle, *sweeter than sin*,
      That I bought for a halfpenny, yesterday?

My languid lily, my lank limp lily,
   My long lithe lily-love, men may grin—
Say that I'm soft and supremely silly—
What care I, while you whisper stilly;
   What care I, while you smile? Not a pin!
While you smile, while you whisper—'Tis sweet to
   decay!
   I have watered with chlorodine tears of chagrin,
   The churchyard would I have planted thee in
      Upside down, in an intense way
In a round flowerpot, *sweeter than sin*.
   That I bought for a halfpenny, yesterday.

ANON

NEPHELIDIA

From the depth of the dreamy decline of the dawn through a
   notable nimbus of nebulous moonshine,
   Pallid and pink as the palm of the flag-flower that flickers
      with fear of the flies as they float,
Are they looks of our lovers that lustrously lean from a
   marvel of mystic moonshine,
   These that we feel in the blood of our blushes that thicken
      and threaten with throbs through the throat?
Thicken and thrill as a theatre thronged at appeal of an actor's
   appalled agitation,
   Fainter with fear of the fires of the future than pale with the
      promise of pride in the past;
Flushed with the famishing fullness of fever that reddens with
   radiance of rathe recreation,

Gaunt as the ghastliest of glimpses that gleam through the
gloom of the gloaming when ghosts go aghast?
Nay, for the nick of the trick of the time is a tremulous touch
on the temples of terror,
Strained as the sinews yet strenuous with strife of the dead
who is dumb as the dust-heaps of death;
Surely no soul is it, sweet as the spasm of erotic emotional
exquisite error,
Bathed in the balms of beatified bliss, beatific itself by
beatitude's breath.
Surely no spirit or sense of a soul that was soft to the spirit
and soul of our senses
Sweetens the stress of surprising suspicion that sobs in the
semblance and sound of a sigh;
Only this oracle opens Olympian, in mystical moods and
triangular tenses,—
"Life is the lust of a lamp for the light that is dark till the
dawn of the day when we die."
Mild is the mirk and monotonous music of memory,
melodiously mute as it may be,
While the hope in the heart of a hero is bruised by the
breach of men's rapiers, resigned to the rod;
Made meek as a mother whose bosom-beats bound with the
bliss-bringing bulk of a balm-breathing baby,
As they grope through the grave-yard of creeds, under
skies growing green at a groan for the grimness of God.
Blank is the book of his bounty beholden of old, and its
binding is blacker than bluer:
Out of blue into black is the scheme of the skies, and their
dews are the wine of the bloodshed of things;
Till the darkling desire of delight shall be free as a fawn that is
freed from the fangs that pursue her,
Till the heart-beats of hell shall be hushed by a hymn from
the hunt that has harried the kennel of kings.

ALGERNON CHARLES SWINBURNE

LORD ALFRED TENNYSON
1809–92

THE VILLAGE CHOIR

Half a bar, half a bar,
Half a bar onward!
Into an awful ditch
Choir and precentor hitch,
Into a mess of pitch,
　　They led the Old Hundred.
Trebles to right of them,
Tenors to left of them,
Basses in front of them,
　　Bellowed and thundered.
Oh, that precentor's look,
When the sopranos took
Their own time and hook
　　From the Old Hundred!

Screeched all the trebles here,
Boggled the tenors there,
Raising the parson's hair,
　　While his mind wandered;
Theirs not to reason why
This psalm was pitched too high:
Theirs but to gasp and cry
　　Out the Old Hundred.
Trebles to right of them,
Tenors to left of them,
Basses in front of them,
　　Bellowed and thundered.
Stormed they with shout and yell,
Not wise they sang nor well,
Drowning the sexton's bell,
　　While all the Church wondered.

Dire the precentor's glare,
Flashed his pitchfork in air
Sounding fresh keys to bear
    Out the Old Hundred.
Swiftly he turned his back,
Reached he his hat from rack,
Then from the screaming pack,
    Himself he sundered.
Tenors to right of him,
Tenors to left of him,
Discords behind him,
    Bellowed and thundered.
Oh, the wild howls they wrought:
Right to the end they fought!
Some tune they sang, but not,
    Not the Old Hundred.

ANON

LA MORT d' ARTHUR

Not by Alfred Tennyson

Slowly, as one who bears a mortal hurt,
Through which the fountain of his life runs dry,
Crept good King Arthur down unto the lake.
A roughening wind was bringing in the waves
With cold dull plash and plunging to the shore,
And a great bank of clouds came sailing up
Athwart the aspect of the gibbous moon,
Leaving no glimpse save starlight, as he sank,
With a short stagger, senseless on the stones.

No man yet knows how long he lay in swound;
But long enough it was to let the rust
Lick half the surface of his polished shield;
For it was made by far inferior hands,
Than forged his helm, his breastplate, and his greaves;
Whereon no canker lighted, for they bore
The magic stamp of MECHI'S SILVER STEEL.

WILLIAM AYTOUN

A LAWN-TENNISONIAN IDYLL

I, who a decade past had lived recluse,
Left for a while the dust of books and town
To share the pastimes of a country-house;
And thus it chanced that I beheld a scene
That steeped my rusted soul in wonderment.
The morn was passing fair; no vagrant cloud
Obscured the summer sun, as from the porch
I sallied forth to saunter at my will
Adown the garden path. Anon I came
To where a lawn outspread its verdant robe,
Whose decoration filled me with amaze.
Lawns many I had seen in days gone by,
But never lawn before the like of this;
For o'er its grassy plain a strange device
Of parallelograms rectangular
Was limned in lines of most exceeding whiteness;
Athwart the centre of this strange device
A threaden net was stretched a full yard high,
And clasped in its reticulated arms,
As ivy clasps the oak, two sturdy staves
Upreared on either side. At either end,

Holding opposing corners of the field,
A youth and damsel did disport themselves
In costume airy, mystic, wonderful;
The while in dexter hand each held a quaint
And spoon-shaped instrument of chequered strings,—
Modelled, perchance, upon an ancient lute,—
Whereby they nimbly urged the bounding sphere
Across the meshy bar.

              No space had I
To ponder, ere they spied me and did call
A welcome. "Hast thou come to see us play?"
"What is the game?" I asked. They answered "Love"
"A pretty game," quoth I, "for man and maid,
But one wherein a third is out of place.
Fain would I, therefore, go."

                   "Nay, nay," they cried;
"Prithee remain, and thou shalt stand as umpire."
And so I stayed, and presently besought
To know their prospects. Then the maiden said,
"I'm fifteen now." The gallant, he replied,
"And thirty I." Whereon methought at first
That he did somewhat overstate his case,
Though she seemed rather underneath the mark.
But when they said that she was thirty, too,
And, next, that he was forty, I perceived
They told of other things than length of years;
Since mortals' ages, e'en at census time,
Could scarce be subject to such fluctuations.
Thus did they wage the contest, hither thither,
Running and striking, till, triumphantly,
The damsel shouted "Deuce!" Alas! mused I,
That lips so fair should utter word so base!
Yet would have held my peace, had not the youth
Turned unto me—"How's that? was that a fault?"
"A fault!" I answered; "aye, and worse than that:
Indeed, 'tis nigh a sin." "Go to," he said

"Thou makest merry." So the sport went on.
And then she cried, "Advantage, and I win!"
And then "'Tis deuce again!" And then, "Advantage
To thee!" And then she strove to reach the ball,
And failed; and in despair exclaimed, "Oh, dear,
I'm beaten!" and fell back upon the sward.
"And this," quoth I, "is this your game of love?
Well, I have heard men say that oftentimes
True love, once smooth, is scattered to the deuce!
And she that first advantage hath obtained
Doth lose at last, and suffer sad reverse.
Sweet maid, when thou art wed, the deuce avoid,
And thou shalt ne'er at least deserve a beating!"
She laughed, he frowned; I turned and went my way.

ANON

LITTLE MISS MUFFET

Reset as an Arthurian idyll

Upon a tuffet of most soft and verdant moss,
Beneath the spreading branches of an ancient oak,
Miss Muffet sat, and upward gazed,
To where a linnet perched and sung,
And rocked him gently, to and fro.
Soft blew the breeze
And mildly swayed the bough,
Loud sung the bird,
And sweetly dreamed the maid;
Dreamed brightly of the days to come—
The golden days, with her fair future blent.
When one—some wondrous stately knight—

Of our great Arthur's "Table Round";
One, brave as Launcelot, and
Spotless as the pure Sir Galahad,
Should come, and coming, choose her
For his love, and in her name,
And for the sake of her fair eyes,
Should do most knightly deeds.
And as she dreamed and softly, sighed,
She pensively began to stir,
With a tiny golden spoon
Within an antique dish upon her lap,
Some snow-white milky curds;
Soft were they, full of cream and rich,
And floated in translucent whey;
And as she stirred, she smiled,
Then gently tasted them.
And smiling, ate, nor sighed no more.
Lo! as she ate—nor harboured thought of ill—
Near and nearer yet, there to her crept,
A monster great and terrible,
With huge, misshapen body—leaden eyes—
Full many a long and hairy leg,
And soft and stealthy footstep.
Nearer still he came—Miss Muffet yet,
All unwitting his dread neighbourhood,
Did eat her curds and dream.
Blithe, on the bough, the linnet sung—
All terrestrial natures, sleeping, wrapt
In a most sweet tranquillity.
Closer still the spider drew, and—
Paused beside her—lifted up his head
And gazed into her face.
Miss Muffet then, her consciousness alive
To his dread eyes upon her fixed,
Turned and beheld him.
Loud screamed she, frightened and amazed,

And straightway sprung upon her feet,
And, letting fall her dish and spoon,
She—shrieking—turned and fled.

ANON

DYLAN THOMAS
1914–53

DEAR FATHER CHRISTMAS

Dear Sir, I was born and brought up in one of those steep-sided, smoky little industrial zinc baths. Life was hard then, it smelled of carbolic and clanged when you kicked it. But we were happy, living out our double-breasted days in the hobbledy house full of Olympic mice and gravy-boat-grabbing aunts, and we waited for Christmas, when I would help my mother knead and pummel and funnel and mince my father—oh, and her geological Welsh cakes, her marzipan, green as weeds, and marvellous, confusing, runny sausages. Mam, with her porcelain features, watering eyes and floury arms, sounded like a vase upside down, and looked worse, but to poor, drunken Uncle Ernie she was priest and comforter, bag and baggage, lock, stock and bottle opener. Every time he came into the room, Bass-breathed, beacon-nosed, his eyes like two ballbearings discovered in a pizza, she would stand up, and try to get him to do the same, but Ernie always declined, sometimes quite suddenly, and I would creep away and sit alone, outside in the giant, neighbour-needling hutch Dad had built, needlessly alas, to house the Roget's Thesaurus he had heard of me winning for a prize at school in Cwmclogdans Road.

341

Listen. Listen. Listen, you prodigal old toy-totaller, you whimsical bearded typhoon, I can go on all night like this. The thing is, do you ever call at the University of Texas? If so, will you kindly drop this off, see if they're interested, tell them there's plenty more, and bringing me, say 95 per cent of any fee? Thanks. Also can you lend me three guineas till next Christmas? The doctor has told me the shadow on my lung is caused by an empty wallet. Oh the pain oh

Yours very truly,

DYLAN THOMAS

RUSSELL DAVIES

J. R. R. TOLKEIN
1892–1973

from BORED OF THE RINGS

In the eastern sky, Velveeta, beloved morning star of the elves and handmaid of the dawn, rose and greeted Noxzema, bringer of the flannel tongue, and clanging on her golden garbage pail, bade him make ready the winged rickshaw of Novocaine, herald of the day. Thence came rosy-eyeballed Ovaltine, she of the fluffy mouth, and lightly kissed the land east of the Seas. In other words, it was morning.

The company rose, and after a hurried breakfast of yaws and goiters, Cellophane and Lavalier and their attendants led them through the wood to the banks of the great river Anacin where three small balsa rafts lay.

"It is the sad hour of parting," said Lavalier solemnly. "But I have for each of you a small gift to remind you of your stay in Lornadoon in the dark days to come." So saying, she produced a large chest and drew out a handful of wondrous things.

"For Arrowroot," she said, "crown jewels," and handed the surprised king a diamond-shaped pear and a plover's egg the size of an emerald.

"For Frito, a little magic," and the boggie found in his hand a marvellous crystal globe filled with floating snowflakes.

She then gave each of the other members of the company something rich and strange: to Gimlet, a subscription to *Elf Life*, to Legolam, a Mah-Jong set, to Moxie, a case of Cloverine Brand Salve, to Pepsi, a pair of salad forks, to Bromosel a Schwinn bicycle, and to Spam a can of insect repellent.

The gifts were quickly stowed away in the little boats along with certain other impedimenta needful for a quest, including ropes; tins of Dinty Moore beef stew; a lot of copra; magic cloaks that blended in with any background, either green grass, green trees, green rocks, or green sky; a copy of *Jane's Dragons and Basilisks of the World*; a box of dog yummies, and a case of Poland water.

"Farewell," said Lavalier, as the company crammed themselves into the boats. "A great journey begins with a single step. No man is an island."

"The early bird gets the worm," said Cellophane.

The rafts slipped out into the river, and Cellophane and Lavalier boarded a great boat-shaped swan and drifted a short distance beside them, and Lavalier sat in the prow and sang an ancient elvish lament to the heart-breaking timbre of steel drums:

> Dago, Dago, Lassi Lima rintintin
> Yanqui unicycle ramar rotoroot
> Telstar aloha saarinen cloret
> Stassen camaro impala desoto?
> Gardol oleo telephon lumumba!
> Chappaqua havatampa muriel
> U canleada horsta wata, bwana,
> Butya canna makit drinque!

Comsat melba rubaiyat nirvana
Garcia y vega hiawatha aloo.
O mithra, mithra, I fain wud lie doon!
Valdaree valdera, que sera, sirrah,
Honi soit la vache qui rit.
Honi soit la vache qui rit.

("Oh, the leaves are falling, the flowers are wilting, and the rivers are all going Republican. O Ramar, Ramar, ride quickly on your golden unicycle and warn the nymphs and drag queens! Ah, who now shall gather lichee nuts and make hoopla under the topiaries? Who will trim my unicorns? See, even now the cows laugh, Alas, alas." Chorus: "We are the chorus, and we agree. We agree, we agree, we agree.")

As the tiny boats passed round a bend in the river, Frito looked back in time to see the Lady Lavalier gracefully sticking her finger down her throat in the ancient elvish farewell.

HENRY N. BEARD AND DOUGLAS C. KENNEY

JOHN WAIN
1925–
UNSOLICITED LETTERS TO FIVE ARTISTS

I

Now that I am Oxford Professor of Poetry,
  Django Reinhardt,
I salute your memory with more humility than
  ever.

344

You with crippled hands
Plucked everlasting beauty on that Dicky Wells
Paris Concert LP that I wore out.
You thought that different moons shone over
    France and England
But you played something superlative every
    time. No intellectual,
You were all artist. I wish, increasingly, that I
    were less
Intellectual. I would like to be a gypsy guitarist
With his fingers burned off playing with Dicky
    Wells.
Matching glittering silver guitar-runs to the
    black ripeness
Of his golden horn. I find, myself,
That to be prolific comes easily
But to be memorable takes effort. I wish
I could do what you did on *La Mer*. Wish also,
    Django, *mon cher*,
That I could be more humble.

II

Now that I am Oxford Professor of Poetry,
    Michelangelo Buonarotti,
I revere your achievement and feel increasingly
    less complacent.
The culture which gave rise to you had
    everything you needed
Except the Wolfenden Report. You could design
    buildings,
Write sonnets in Italian, and when you painted a
    ceiling
It stayed painted. But above all, you could
    sculpt.
Michelangelo, *amico*, you once said

That you chipped away the marble until you
    found the statue inside.
As a poet I have been using the same technique
    for years, and wish
That I could be even less complacent than I am
    now. *Capito*?

P.S. Could you use a few bags of marble chips?
    I've
Got a garage full.

III

Now that I am Oxford Professor of Poetry,
    Wolfgang Amadeus Mozart,
The mere mention of your name brings me up
    short, wishing
That I had made better use of my time. At my
    age
You had been dead for years, yet look
At the stuff you turned out. *Figaro*. *Don
    Giovanni*. K488. The Flute.
You never finished your Requiem, of course; and
    I try to take
Comfort from that. As a business brain, you
    were a non-starter
And freemasonry was a blind alley. You would
    never have made it
To the Oxford Chair of Poetry. But taken as a
    whole
Yours was a career that leaves a modern artist
    chastened.
My poem *Wildtrack* was influenced by the slow
    movement of your 4th

Violin Concerto, although comparisons are
    odious. I bow.
Schlaf wohl, Wolfgang—precursor of us all.

IV

Now that I am Oxford Professor of Poetry,
    Rainer Maria Rilke,
I think of your prodigious gift and quell my
    surge of pride.
What was it, three-quarters of the *Duinos* and all
    the *Sonnets*
To Orpheus written in two weeks? Not even
    Wildtrack
Came as such a protean outpouring. And you
    had connections, *Bruder*:
Contacts dwarfing anything of ours. Weekends
In cloud-scraping Bavarian *Schlosses* with
    aristocratic women!
Aus dem besitz der Grafin-Königen Marie von
    Thurn-und-Taxis Hohenlohe
You inscribed, while my lot dedicated stuff to
    Sadie Bloggs.
You make me feel small, Rainer, *mein Freund*,
    Dichter.
As do Wolfgang, Mike and Django.

V

Now that I am Oxford Professor of Poetry,
    Stephen Spender,
I would just like to say Tough Luck, Baby
But that's the way the cookie crumbles.
    Someone has to lose,
So eat my dust.

The Thirties haven't got it in the nuts any more.
    My turn, *padrone*.
But stick around. We haven't forgotten how you
    old guys
Opened up the rackets for the new ideas. Times
    have changed.
But we'll find some action that fits your style.
    Can you drive?

CLIVE JAMES

WALT WHITMAN
1819–92
IMITATION OF WALT WHITMAN

The clear cool note of the cuckoo which has ousted the
    legitimate nest-holder,
The whistle of the railway guard despatching the train to
    the inevitable collision,
The maiden's monosyllabic reply to a polysyllabic
    proposal,
The fundamental note of the last trump, which is
    presumably D natural;
All of these are sounds to rejoice in, yea to let your ribs
    re-echo with.
But better than all of them is the absolutely last chord of
    the apparently inexhaustible pianoforte player.

J. K. STEPHEN

OSCAR WILDE
1854–1900

THE GOURMAND

With profuse and very necessary apologies

He did not wear his swallow tail,
　　But a simple dinner coat;
For once his spirits seemed to fail,
　　And his fund of anecdote.
His brow was drawn and damp and pale,
　　And a lump stood in his throat.

I never saw a person stare,
　　With looks so dour and blue,
Upon the square of bill of fare
　　We waiters call the "M'noo",
And at every dainty mentioned there,
　　From *entrée* to *ragout*.

With head bent low and cheeks aglow,
　　He viewed the groaning board,
For he wondered if the chef would show
　　The treasures of his hoard,
When a voice behind him whispered low,
　　"Sherry or 'ock, m'lord?"

Gods! What a tumult rent the air,
　　As with a frightful oath,
He seized the waiter by the hair,
　　And cursed him for his sloth;
Then, grumbling like some stricken bear
　　Angrily answered, "Both!"

For each man drinks the thing he loves,
    As tonic, dram, or drug;
Some do it standing, in their gloves,
    Some seated, from a jug;
The upper class from thin-stemmed glass,
    The masses from a mug.

The wine was slow to bring him woe,
    But when the meal was through,
His wild remorse at every course
    Each moment wilder grew;
For he who thinks to mix his drinks
    Must mix his symptoms too.

Did he regret that tough *noisette*
    And the tougher *tournedos*,
The oysters dry, and the game so high,
    And the *soufflé* flat and low
Which the *chef* had planned with a heavy hand,
    And the waiters served so slow?

Yet each approves the thing he loves,
    From caviare to pork;
Some guzzle cheese or new-grown peas,
    Like a cormorant or stork;
The poor man's wife employs a knife,
    The rich man's mate a fork.

Some gorge forsooth in early youth,
    Some wait till they are old;
Some take their fare off earthenware,
    And some from polished gold.
The gourmand gnaws in haste because
    The plates so soon grow cold.

Some eat too swiftly, some too long,
    In restaurant or grill;
Some, when their weak insides go wrong,
    Try a post-prandial pill,
For each man eats his fav'rite meats,
    Yet each man is not ill.

He does not sicken in his bed,
    Through a night of wild unrest,
With a snow-white bandage round his head,
    And a poultice on his breast,
'Neath the nightmare weight of the things he ate
    And omitted to digest.

I know not whether meals be short
    Or whether meals be long;
All that I know of this resort,
    Proves that there's something wrong,
And the soup is weak and tastes of port,
    And the fish is far too strong.

The bread they bake is quite opaque,
    The butter full of hair;
Defunct sardines and flaccid "greens"
    Are all they give us there.
Such cooking has been known to make
    A common person swear.

And when misguided people feed,
    At eve or afternoon,
Their harassed ears are never freed
    From the fiddle and bassoon,
Which sow dyspepsia's subtlest seed
    With a most evil spoon.

To dance to flutes, to dance to lutes,
    Is a pastime rare and grand;
But to eat of fish, or fowl, or fruits
    To a Blue Hungarian Band
Is a thing that suits nor men nor brutes,
    As the world should understand.

Such music baffles human talk,
    And gags each genial guest;
A grill–room orchestra can baulk
    All efforts to digest,
Till the chops will not lie still, but walk
    All night upon one's chest.

Six times a table here he booked,
    Six times he sat and scanned
The list of dishes badly cooked
    By the chef's unskilful hand;
And I never saw a man who looked
    So wistfully at the band.

He did not swear or tear his hair,
    But drank up wine galore,
As though it were some vintage rare
    From an old Falernian store;
With open mouth he slaked his drouth,
    And loudly called for more.

He was the type that waiters know,
    Who simply lives to feed,
Who little cares what food we show
    If it be food indeed,
And, when his appetite is low,
    Falls back upon his greed.

For each man eats his fav'rite meats,
    (Provided by his wife);
Or cheese or chalk, or peas or pork,
    (For such, alas! is life!).
The rich man eats them with a fork,
    The poor man with a knife.

HARRY GRAHAM

THE AGE OF OSCAR WILDE

from *Forty Years On*

Enter WITHERS, *the butler, pushing* LADY DUNDOWN, *an Edwardian dowager in a wheel-chair.*

LADY D: Is there anything in the newspaper this morning, Withers?

WITHERS: They have named another battleship after Queen Victoria, ma'am.

LADY D: Another? She must be beginning to think there is some resemblance. I see the Dean of Windsor has been consecrated Bishop of Bombay.

WITHERS: Bombay. Hmm. If I may say so, ma'am, that seems to me to be taking Christianity a little too far.

LADY D: And where is your good lady wife on this bright summer's morning?

WITHERS: Still at death's door, I'm afraid, m'lady.

LADY D: Still? But she has been there now for the last sixteen years.

WITHERS: Yes. And I, m'lady, I have never left her bedside.

LADY D: So I see. A great mistake, if I may say so. You should remember the proverb, a watched pot never boils. Well, Withers, you must not take up any more of my valuable time. And besides, I must speak to my nephew.

WITHERS: But I cannot see him anywhere.

LADY D: A sure sign that he is in the vicinity. Gerald!

(GERALD GROSVENOR *enters in a scarlet military tunic, carrying a pith helmet with plumes.*)

GERALD: Good morning, Aunt Sedilia.

LADY D: The weather is immaterial. Gerald, do I detect a somewhat military note in your appearance? What is the reason for these warlike habiliments?

GERALD: I have been called to the Colours.

LADY D: Indeed? Whereabouts?

GERALD: South Africa.

LADY D: South Africa? I trust that will not interfere with your attendance at my dances?

GERALD: I'm afraid so.

LADY D: Tsk, tsk. How can the Zulu expect to be treated as civilized people when they declare war in the middle of the season!

GERALD: It's not the Zulu, Aunt Sedilia. It's the Boer.

LADY D: It comes to the same thing. I have never understood this liking for war. It panders to instincts already catered for within the scope of any respectable domestic establishment. Which brings me to my point. Your marriage. I have been going through my list and have hit upon the ideal person. Lady Maltby.

GERALD: Lady Maltby!

LADY D: Constance Maltby.

(*She rises from the wheel-chair.*)

I can walk. It's just that I am so rich I don't need to. Consider her advantages. She is in full possession of all her faculties, plus the usual complement of limbs . . . and enough in such matters, I always think, is as good as a feast.

GERALD: I have heard it said that her legs leave something to be desired.

LADY D: All legs leave *something* to be desired, do they not. That is part of their function and all of their charm. But

354

to continue. Like all stout women she is very fat, but then, it would be inconsistent of her to be otherwise, would it not?

GERALD: Is she not connected with Trade?

LADY D: Trade? Nonsense. Her father made a fortune by introducing the corset to the Esquimaux. That is not trade. It is philanthropy.

GERALD: And she is very old-fashioned besides.

LADY D: If by that you mean she dresses like her mother, yes she is. But then all women dress like their mothers, that is their tragedy. No man ever does. That is his. You have something to say?

GERALD: Yes, Aunt Sedilia. You see, I have been engaged before. Several times.

LADY D: I am aware that you have been engaged, though, if I may say so, much after the manner of a public lavatory . . . often and for very short periods. . . . You must be married next week.

GERALD: Impossible!

LADY D: Impossible! There seems to be an element of defeatism in that reply. Why, pray?

GERALD: Lady Dundown, Aunt Sedilia, I cannot marry Lady Maltby next week, because Lady Maltby is my mother.

LADY D: Well, would the week after do? I beg your pardon?

GERALD: Lady Maltby is my mother.

LADY D: For how long has this been the case?

GERALD: Almost as long as I can remember.

LADY D: I see. One question, Mr Grosvenor. Was your mother ever married?

GERALD: No, I must confess it, Lady Dundown, she never was.

LADY D: Splendid. My dear Gerald, wherein lies the difficulty? Your mother is a spinster, albeit not without blot. You, nameless, dishonoured, fatherless creature that you are, are unmarried. Marriage between your mother and yourself would make a decent man of you and an honest woman of her. Indeed the arrangement seems so tidy I am surprised it does not happen more often in society. Dear me. How cold it has turned. I must go in and put on another rope of pearls. The chair, Mr Grosvenor, if you please.

ALAN BENNETT

WILDE'S *ST JOAN*

1956 was the centenary year of both Wilde and Shaw and, to celebrate it, each took a hand at rewriting one of the other's plays.

DAUPHIN: Where do you come from?

JOAN: A little village.

DAUPHIN: All villages are little; that is why they are villages. And as everyone leaves them they can't grow any bigger. Why have you come?

JOAN: To help you.

DAUPHIN: When a woman says that she means that she will help herself.

JOAN: And if a man says it?

DAUPHIN: A man never declares his intentions unless a woman makes him. Are yours honourable?

JOAN: Yes. Will you give me what I ask?

DAUPHIN: That is what they all say.

JOAN: Who?

DAUPHIN: All the women who come to Court. My wife doesn't like it. It takes an exceptional woman to appreciate her husband's generosity to anyone else.

JOAN: Would your wife like to be a queen?

DAUPHIN: Of course. All wives think they should be queens; that is their illusion. Sometimes their husbands encourage it unwisely; that is their collusion.

JOAN: Give me a horse and a suit of armour.
DAUPHIN: The others are more simple. They only want a
carriage and a new dress. But perhaps you are subtler.

VERA TELFER

GODFREY WINN
1908–71

NATURE IS A TERRIBLY
INTERESTING THING
"Lady Chatterley" rewritten

Have you ever wondered, as I do whenever I read of some
little act of unsung sacrifice in places like the Midlands, how
wonderful it is to love *people*—to the *full*, enjoying the simple
things of life even in some honest working man's rude hut?

Ours is really a terribly exciting age, and lots of us refuse to
be *blasé* about the wonderful things of nature, which is full of
great beauty that quite transcends the difference between rich
and poor. I pray with all my heart that nobody would cast the
first stone at a woman just because she liked gamekeepers.

This was more or less Constance Chatterley's position, or
one of them. She had married Sir Clifford, a well-born
marvellous young man with a lovely seat. The seat was called
Wragby Hall, and you have no idea how lovely it was, there
among the sooty, soulless, gruesome workers' cottages,
though they were very sweet inside. How marvellous the
honest working wife is at making the best of her simple
possessions, under such difficulties.

357

Constance Chatterley, although a very different type, had her difficulties too. The war came (the first war, and I cannot tell you how rough it was; I am sure you have read about it in those wonderful stirring books by Philip Gibbs and people) and Sir Clifford was called to a Destiny at the Front, as indeed were high and low, including his late Majesty King George VI, whom I met when I was a *matelot* in that self-same Royal Navy, though indeed that was not the same war.

The brutalities of war caused a scar on Sir Clifford's soul, indeed I am bound to say worse. He had always been a clean-living young fellow. But he was to become even cleaner, *in a certain sense*. For Sir Clifford returned from this man's war *very badly wounded*. To be terribly frank, as sometimes we have to be, he had very little of him left below the waterline, nor had that little long.

I wonder if you can imagine how this distressed Constance Chatterley—so young, so wholesome, so ardent, so full of compassion; and of course such a nature-lover. Seeing Sir Clifford there in his wheel-chair, so patient and undemanding of her, it was as though she, too, sensed the pangs of loss.

After all, she was still so fresh and gay. In the world of imagination she reminds me of my mother, except of course in a way she doesn't. There was this sad thing about Sir Clifford. The sight of his stiff upper lip brought tears to Constance's eyes. She was such a pure girl, it almost drove her insane. What a terrible thing is mental illness; I pray with all my heart we never stoop to mocking it.

So one day Constance was walking through the woods of the estate, admiring the poignant affection of the daffodils and the tender impertinence of the primroses and the gentle laughter of the cowslips, and various other aspects of the sweet challenge of spring. And into the mind of Lady Chatterley came a deep sense of the essential *rightness* of Nature, and of her husband, especially of what he had once used to have been.

She arrived at the clearing flushed and semi-conscious.

There was the shirt-sleeved gamekeeper; his name was Mellors, no more and no less. He was closing up the chickens for the night. But still one trio of tiny things was pattering about on tiny feet, tiny mites, refusing to be called home by the anxious mother.

"I'd love to touch them!" she panted. Before Constance knew it she was touching them. The little tiny chickens ran around "cheeping" at being ignored.

By and by the gamekeeper gazed at her. Compassion flared in his, well, bowels, and the nettles had evoked a strange stirring in his loins.

"Eeh, but thar't winsome, like," he said in the vernacular. "Happen thar'll coom oop to t'oot." His voice had the simple manly honesty so often corrupted by the veneer of education. Education is of course a marvellous thing, but.

A surge of democracy welled up in Lady Chatterley. As they entered t'oot it grew unaccountably stronger, more urgent, more democratic. I often wonder if everyone understands the real affinity between the landed classes and the simple estate-workers—as our Prime Minister does, though of course rather differently.

This is an age of frankness, and my readers know well that there are times when I am forthright. The ensuing hours in the simple woodland home of Mellors was so tender, so simple, so *real*, SO HUMAN, that it has to be described in detail, as tribute to wonderful Mother Nature. These two young people were in *love*. . . . They expressed it in a fashion that I *know* is not customary in the grounds of Buckingham Palace. Nevertheless I am confident that they intended no disrespect to the person of Her Majesty our Queen, whom I had the pleasure of meeting in 1961. This hut was something really quite different. This was direct and *elemental*, and if in retrospect it was a bit sick-making, it was somehow, *right*.

Under his shirt was his slim smooth body, rippling with the play of muscle under the silken skin. His rough manly breeches lay like an offering on the homely floor. Constance's costume was quite pretty, too; she was wearing a cinnamon two-piece by my friend Norman Hartnell, at least to start with. In wonder she confronted the gamekeeper Mellors; he looked so confident, so cocksure. Already she was beginning to forget about wheel-chairs. . . .

For no one knows how long Constance was aware of nothing but a cleaving consciousness, a rhythmic growing motion like the waves of the sea at Antibes, where I had a marvellous holiday two years ago; a convulsion of deepening whirlpools of ecstasy in his man-smell and his man-touch and the quivering maleness of his man-handling. She could have swooned at the carnal rapture of those slender buttocks.

She felt slightly ashamed of enjoying it so much. For of course Lady Constance was aware that *this* is only a part of love, which is really made of companionship, and *understanding*, and common interests. I know a sweet old couple whose marriage was saved time and again by a shared hobby; in this case fretwork. All this Constance knew well; in her heart of hearts she knew full well that the last moments had been just a phallacy. She thought with gratitude of the tiny defenceless chickens that had brought them together.

But then the wondrous magic took possession again, and all this stuff about wispy lingerie and loins and deep breathing, which I assure you is really *nothing*, though it seems important at the time.

Only when it was over did she become aware of the oppressive closeness of the hut, the windows closed, country-style, over the airless heat of passion.

"*What* a fug!" she whispered.

"Tha canst say that agen," he breathed, stretching his great male arms behind his great male head: god-like.

"Tha an' me's a sacred rite," he said. "Sex is nowt wi'out shared faith, companionship, bairns. Tha knows t'body's only part, just a private part."

And for a while Mellors the gamekeeper made with the high philosophical phrases, for we all know, do we not, that the one thing the British working man likes is a bit of cant.

Then they talked about the industrial system for a while, and the need for the workers of the smoking valleys to get a square deal and an eight-hour day.

"Tha mun coom one naight to t'oot," he said. "Shall ter? Slaip wi' me? 'Appen Sat'day?"

"As a matter of fact," said Constance, "I do have a sale of work Sat'day. But next time I'll really try to come."

And as she ran home in the twilight, or gloaming, the trees in the park seemed erect and surging as though they were alive, and who is to say that they were not? Nature is a *terribly* interesting thing.

Next week I am going to continue my series on *Passion Without Pain*, with the Love-Life of Doctor Schweitzer. This is a *terribly* ennobling story, and I really *do* hope that. . . .

JAMES CAMERON

CHARLES WOLFE
1791–1823

THE BURIAL OF THE BACHELOR

Not a laugh was heard, not a frivolous note,
　　As the groom to the wedding we carried;
Not a jester discharged his farewell shot
　　As the bachelor went to be married.

We married him quickly that morning bright,
　　The leaves of our prayer-books turning,
In the chancel's dimly religious light,
　　And tears in our eyelids burning.

No useless nosegay adorned his chest,
    Not in chains but in laws we bound him;
And he looked like a bridegroom trying his best
    To look used to the scene around him.

Few and small were the fees it cost,
    And we spoke not a word of sorrow,
But we silently gazed on the face of the lost
    And we bitterly thought of the morrow.

We thought as we hurried him home to be fed,
    And tried our low spirits to rally,
That the weather looked very like squalls overhead
    For the passage from Dover to Calais.

Lightly they'll talk of the bachelor gone,
    And o'er his frail fondness upbraid him;
But little he'll reck if they let him alone,
    With his wife that the parson hath made him.

But half of our heavy task was done,
    When the clock struck the hour for retiring;
And we judged by the knocks which had now begun
    That their cabby was rapidly tiring.

Slowly and sadly we led them down,
    From the scene of his lame oratory;
We told the four-wheeler to drive them to town,
    And we left them alone in their glory.

ANON

362

A FRAGMENT

Not a drum was heard, not a funeral note,
As his horse on the ramparts we curried. . . .

ANON

WILLIAM WORDSWORTH
1770–1850

ON WORDSWORTH

He lived amidst th' untrodden ways
    To Rydal Lake that lead;
A bard whom there was none to praise
    And very few to read.

Behind a cloud his mystic sense,
    Deep hidden, who can spy?
Bright as the night when not a star
    Is shining in the sky.

Unread his works—his "Milk White Doe"
    With dusk is dark and dim;
It's still in Longmans' shop, and oh!
    The difference to him.

HARTLEY COLERIDGE

FRAGMENT IN IMITATION OF WORDSWORTH

There is a river clear and fair,
'Tis neither broad nor narrow;
It winds a little here and there—
It winds about like any hare;
And then it holds as straight a course
As, on the turnpike road, a horse,
Or, through the air, an arrow.

The trees that grow upon the shore
Have grown a hundred years or more;
So long there is no knowing:
Old Daniel Dobson does not know
When first those trees began to grow;
But still they grew, and grew, and grew,
As if they'd nothing else to do,
But ever must be growing.

The impulses of air and sky
Have reared their stately heads so high,
And clothed their boughs with green;
Their leaves the dews of evening quaff,—
And when the wind blows loud and keen,
I've seen the jolly timbers laugh,
And shake their sides with merry glee—
Wagging their heads in mockery.

Fixed are their feet in solid earth
Where winds can never blow;
But visitings of deeper birth
Have reached their roots below.
For they have gained the river's brink,
And of the living waters drink.

There's little Will, a five years' child—
He is my youngest boy;
To look on eyes so fair and wild,
It is a very joy.
He hath conversed with sun and shower,
And dwelt with every idle flower,
As fresh and gay as them.
He loiters with the briar-rose,—
The blue-bells are his play-fellows,
That dance upon their slender stem.

And I have said, my little Will,
Why should he not continue still
A thing of Nature's rearing?
A thing beyond the world's control—
A living vegetable soul,—
No human sorrow fearing.

It were a blessed sight to see
That child become a willow-tree,
His brother trees among.
He'd be four times as tall as me,
And live three times as long.

CATHERINE M. FANSHAWE

A SONNET

Two voices are there: one is of the deep;
It learns the storm-cloud's thunderous melody,
Now roars, now murmurs with the changing sea,
Now bird-like pipes, now closes soft in sleep:
And one is of an old half-witted sheep

Which bleats articulate monotony,
And indicates that two and one are three,
That grass is green, lakes damp, and mountains steep:
And, Wordsworth, both are thine: at certain times
Forth from the heart of thy melodious rhymes,
The form and pressure of high thoughts will burst:
At other times—good Lord! I'd rather be
Quite unacquainted with the ABC
Than write such hopeless rubbish as thy worst.

J. K. STEPHEN

THE AGED, AGED MAN

I'll tell thee everything I can;
　　There's little to relate.
I saw an aged aged man,
　　A-sitting on a gate.
"Who are you, aged man?" I said.
　　"And how is it you live?"
And his answer trickled through my head
　　Like water through a sieve.

He said, "I look for butterflies
　　That sleep among the wheat:
I make them into mutton-pies,
　　And sell them in the street.
I sell them unto men," he said,
　　"Who sail on stormy seas;
And that's the way I get my bread—
　　A trifle, if you please."

But I was thinking of a plan
   To dye one's whiskers green,
And always use so large a fan
   That they could not be seen.
So, having no reply to give
   To what the old man said,
I cried, "Come, tell me how you live!"
   And thumped him on the head.

His accents mild took up the tale:
   He said, "I go my ways,
And when I find a mountain-rill,
   I set it in a blaze;
And thence they make a stuff they call
   Rowland's Macassar Oil—
Yet twopence-halfpenny is all
   They give me for my toil."

But I was thinking of a way
   To feed oneself on batter,
And so go on from day to day
   Getting a little fatter.
I shook him well from side to side,
   Until his face was blue:
"Come, tell me how you live," I cried,
   "And what it is you do!"

He said, "I hunt for haddocks' eyes
   Among the heather bright,
And work them into waistcoat-buttons
   In the silent night.
And these I do not sell for gold
   Or coin of silvery shine,
But for a copper halfpenny,
   And that will purchase nine.

"I sometimes dig for buttered rolls,
    Or set limed twigs for crabs;
I sometimes search the grassy knolls
    For wheels of hansom-cabs.
And that's the way" (he gave a wink)
    "By which I get my wealth—
And very gladly will I drink
    Your Honour's noble health."

I heard him then, for I had just
    Completed my design
To keep the Menai bridge from rust
    By boiling it in wine.
I thanked him very much for telling me
    The way he got his wealth,
But chiefly for his wish that he
    Might drink my noble health.

And now, if e'er by chance I put
    My fingers into glue,
Or madly squeeze a right-hand foot
    Into a left-hand shoe.
Or if I drop upon my toe
    A very heavy weight,
I weep, for it reminds me so,
Of that man I used to know—
Whose look was mild, whose speech was slow,
Whose hair was whiter than the snow,
Whose face was very like a crow,
With eyes, like cinders, all aglow,
Who seemed distracted with his woe,
Who rocked his body to and fro,
And muttered mumblingly and low,
As if his mouth were full of dough,
Who snorted like a buffalo—

That summer evening, long ago,
A-sitting on a gate.

LEWIS CARROLL

W. B. YEATS
1865–1939

THE HERO

On the Birmingham pub bombings of 21 November 1974

I went out to the city streets,
Because a fire was in my head,
And saw the people passing by,
And wished the youngest of them dead,
And twisted by a bitter past,
And poisoned by a cold despair,
I found at last a resting-place
And left my hatred ticking there.

When I was fleeing from the night
And sweating in my room again,
I heard the old futilities
Exploding like a cry of pain;
But horror, should it touch the heart,
Would freeze my hand upon the fuse,
And I must shed no tears for those
Who merely have a life to lose.

Though I am sick with murdering,
Though killing is my native land,
I will find out where death has gone,
And kiss his lips and take his hand;
And hide among the withered grass,
And pluck, till love and life are done,
The shrivelled apples of the moon,
The cankered apples of the sun.

ROGER WODDIS

THE LAKE ISLE

O God, O Venus, O Mercury, patron of thieves,
Give me in due time, I beseech you, a little tobacco-shop.
With the little bright boxes
    piled up neatly upon the shelves
And the loose fragrant cavendish
    and the shag,
And the bright Virginia
    loose under the bright glass cases,
And a pair of scales not too greasy,
And the whores dropping in for a word or two in passing,
For a flip word, and to tidy their hair a bit.

O God, O Venus, O Mercury, patron of thieves,
Lend me a little tobacco-shop,
    or install me in any profession
Save this damn'd profession of writing,
    where one needs one's brains all the time.

EZRA POUND

INDEX OF PARODISTS AND WORKS

Because so many parodists choose to obscure their identity by pseudonyms, and because some of the parodies listed below were submissions to *New Statesman* competitions and were otherwise undocumented, the birth and death dates in this index are necessarily incomplete.

378

ACKNOWLEDGEMENTS

For permission to reprint copyright material, the following acknowledgements are made.

George Allen & Unwin (Publishers) Limited, for the following items from *Never Rub Bottoms With A Porcupine*, edited by Arthur Marshall: Alan Alexander, "Little Jack Horner"; Maud Gracechurch, "The Archers"; Henry Hetherington, "Jack Sprat"; M. J. Monk, Peter Veale, Tim O'Dowda and Ian Kelso, "Nasty Habits"; Stanley J. Sharpless, "Betjeman at the Post Office" and "The Summonee's Tale".

Max Beerbohm: "Scruts", "The Feast", "The Mote in the Middle Distance" and "P. C., X, 36", from *A Christmas Garland*. Reprinted by permission of Mrs Eva Reichmann.

Robert Benchley: reprinted by permission of Harper & Row, Publishers, Inc., "Aubergine's Way" in *No Poems* by Robert Benchley. Copyright 1932 by Robert C. Benchley, renewed 1960 by Gertrude Benchley. "Shakespeare Explained" in *The Benchley Roundup*, selected by Nathaniel Benchley; Copyright 1921 by Harper & Row, Publishers, Inc., renewed 1949 by Gertrude Benchley.

Alan Bennett: "Place-Names of China". Reprinted by permission of the author. Two extracts from *Forty Years On*. Reprinted by permission of Faber & Faber Limited.

Ed Berman: "Adam and Eve and Stuff Like That". Reprinted by permission of the author.

John Betjeman: "Hymn". Reprinted by permission of John Murray (Publishers) Limited, from *Collected Poems* by John Betjeman.

Malcolm Bradbury: "Voluptia" and "A Jaundiced View". Reprinted by permission of Curtis Brown Group Limited, from *Who Do You Think You Are?*, Copyright Malcolm Bradbury, 1976.

Jon L. Breen: "$106,000 Mud Bunny" and an extract from "The Crowded Hours". Both first printed in *Ellery Queen's Mystery Magazine*, and reprinted by permission of Scarecrow Press, Inc., from *Hair of the Sleuthhound* by Jon L. Breen.

Anthony Brode: "Breakfast with Gerard Manley Hopkins". Reprinted by permission of *Punch*.

Barry Brown: "Funeral Under Water". Reprinted by permission of the author.

James Cameron: "Nature is a Terribly Interesting Thing". Reprinted by permission of *Punch*.

Raymond Chandler: "Beer in the Sergeant-Major's Hat (or The Sun Also Sneezes)". Reprinted by permission of Weidenfeld (Publishers) Limited, from *The Notebooks of Raymond Chandler*, edited by Frank McShane.

G. K. Chesterton: "Variations on an Air Composed on Having to Appear in a Pageant as Old King Cole". Reprinted by permission of Miss D. E. Collins and Dodd, Mead & Company, Inc., from *The Collected Poems of G. K. Chesterton*. Copyright 1932 by Dodd, Mead & Company, Copyright renewed 1959 by Oliver Chesterton.

Cyril Connolly: "Bond Strikes Camp", from *Previous Convictions*, and "Told in Gath", from *The Condemned Playground*. Both reprinted by permission of Deborah Rogers Limited, representing the Estate of Cyril Connolly.

Wendy Cope: "Budgie Finds His Voice" and "Mr Strugnell", from *Poetry Introduction 5*, published by Faber & Faber Limited. Reprinted by permission of the author.

Alan Coren: "Domestic Drama". Reprinted by permission of Robson Books Limited, from *The Rhinestone as Big as the Ritz* by Alan Coren.

Noël Coward: an extract from "The Stately Homes of England". Reprinted by permission of Dr Jan Van Loewen Limited, and of The Overlook Press, Lewis Hollow Road, Woodstock, New York 12498, from *The Lyrics of Noël Coward* by Noël Coward, © 1965 by Noël Coward. "The Swiss Family Whittlebot", from *London Calling*, and "To Noël Coward", from *Poems by Hernia Whittlebot*. Reprinted by permission of Dr Jan Van Loewen Limited.

Frederick C. Crews: an extract from "Another Book to Cross off Your List". Reprinted by permission of Weidenfeld (Publishers) Limited, from *The Pooh Perplex* by Frederick C. Crews.

Richard Curtis: "Sons and Aztecs" and "The Skinhead Hamlet". Both reprinted by permission of Faber & Faber Limited, from *Not 1982*.

Russell Davies: "Dear Father Christmas" (Auden) and "Dear Father Christmas" (Thomas). Both first printed in the *New Statesman*, and reprinted by permission of The Statesman and Nation Publishing Company Limited. "Pleasurebubble Hubbyhouse". Reprinted by permission of Hodder and Stoughton Limited, from *The*

by permission of Faber & Faber Limited.

Peter Titheradge: "Teatime Variations" and "New Improved Sonnet XVIII". Reprinted by permission of the author.

Kenneth Tynan: reviews of Samuel Beckett, Graham Greene and Damon Runyon. Reprinted by permission of the Estate of Kenneth Tynan.

Roger Woddis: "Final Curtain" and "The Hero". Reprinted by permission of the Hutchinson Publishing Group Limited, from *The Woddis Collection* by Roger Woddis, published by Barrie and Jenkins.

While every effort has been made to secure permission, it has in a few cases proved impossible to trace the author or his executor. We apologize for our apparent negligence.